Twayne's English Authors Series

EDITOR OF THIS VOLUME

Kinley Roby

Northeastern University

H.M. Tomlinson

TEAS 308

H.M. Tomlinson

H.M. TOMLINSON

By FRED D. CRAWFORD

TWAYNE PUBLISHERS
A DIVISION OF G.K. HALL & CO., BOSTON

1981

Published in 1981 by Twayne Publishers,
A Division of G.K. Hall & Co.
All Rights Reserved

Printed on permanent/durable acid-free paper and bound
in the United States of America

First Printing

Frontispiece photo of H.M. Tomlinson, 1949, appears with the
permission of his son, H. Charles Tomlinson

Library of Congress Cataloging in Publication Data

Crawford, Fred D
H.M. Tomlinson

(Twayne's English authors series ; TEAS 308)
Bibliography: p. 245–54
Includes index.
1. Tomlinson, Henry Major, 1873–1958—Criticism
and interpretation.
PR6039.035Z6   823′.91209   80-39929
ISBN 0-8057-6800-9

For Janice Schukart, excellent
teacher and valued friend

Contents

About the Author

Fred D. Crawford earned his B.A. from the University of Chicago and his M.A. and Ph.D. from Penn State University. He has taught at the Behrend College of Penn State (Erie) where, in addition to English composition, he taught courses in poetry writing, fiction writing, experimental modern fiction, modern British literature, and technical writing. After three years' full-time teaching, he became Court Liaison for the Abraxas Foundation, Inc., a private, nonprofit organization which serves as an alternative to incarceration for youthful offenders with a history of drug and alcohol abuse. He is currently Education Specialist for the Multnomah/Washington CETA Consortium in Portland, Oregon.

Dr. Crawford's specialty is twentieth-century British literature. He is currently finishing a study of the influence of T. S. Eliot's *The Waste Land* on the modern novel, collaborating on a history of the problems of organizing and promoting a bluegrass band, and writing a study of the World War I poets.

Preface

H. M. Tomlinson is best known, to those few who know him, as a writer of the sea in the tradition of Joseph Conrad. However, his prolific literary career included seven novels, books of travel, antiwar tracts, war propaganda during World War II, literary criticism, reflections on the destructive aspects of progress, bibliography, history, and personal impressions regarding virtually every aspect of British life. Tomlinson, born in 1873, witnessed the modern age from its early harnessing of steam power to the splitting of the atom and the launching of Sputnik. To read Tomlinson's work is to follow the development of modernity from the reign of Queen Victoria through the decline of the British Empire to the British preoccupation with economic and social equality.

Despite the influence that Tomlinson exerted through the 1930s and 1940s, surprisingly little has been written about him. At this time there exists no full-length Tomlinson bibliography, no biography, no comprehensive critical study, no book-length treatment. Except for a few helpful scholarly articles treating specific aspects of his life and art, Tomlinson has been largely ignored. Although part of this neglect might result from regarding Tomlinson as a minor figure, part must surely result from Tomlinson's defiance of a critical label.

During his career Tomlinson developed a style as a journalist which underwent little change during his publication of more than thirty separate books. The changes which one might observe appear in the subjects that he chose to treat and the altered philosophy that became evident in his apparent shift from pacifism to war propaganda. It is the purpose of this study to reveal Tomlinson's achievement in terms of the aspects of life and art that engaged his interest, his well-defined philosophy concerning the problems of writing each of the various types of books that he published, and the diverse roles Tomlinson played in the course of his long career as a free-lance writer. Although Tomlinson constantly shifted from one type of writing to another following the publication of his first novel in 1927, I have tried to discuss Tomlinson's art in terms of each type of writing he produced, his rhetorical stance, and his development.

Following a brief chapter summarizing Tomlinson's life, this study considers Tomlinson as a master of the essay style, a literary critic, a traveler, an historian of British shipping, a polemicist resisting the modern notion of progress, a pacifist, a war propagandist, and a novelist. Although Tomlinson eventually wrote in each of these veins almost concurrently, the foregoing order roughly follows the chronology of his development as a man of letters.

The study concludes with an assessment of Tomlinson's literary career that places him as a significant, if minor, author in the modern literary tradition. The study of Tomlinson has value for an historian of modern Britain, a student of the elusive essay style, and a prospective literary critic. Tomlinson's personal view of the period between 1873 and 1958, and his effectiveness in communicating this view, has lasting value for the student of history and literature alike.

Acknowledgments

I wish to express my gratitude to nine people for their assistance. Stanley Weintraub, Director of the Institute for the Arts and Humanistic Studies of Penn State, offered several helpful suggestions. Charles Mann, Curator of the Rare Books Room of Pattee Library, provided bibliographical information. Professors Judith Caesar and Chet Wolford obtained copies of articles and limited editions I could not otherwise acquire. Russell and Cherie Gula, Gretchen McFarland, and Gerry Alsentzer also eased the process of my research. I am greatly indebted to Richard Winslow for ferreting out obscure sources, providing reprints of material, compiling lists of bibliographical data, and assisting my efforts in many other ways.

In addition, I wish to thank the children of H.M. Tomlinson—H. Charles Tomlinson, Mrs. Florence Dickinson, and Mrs. Dorothy Bailey—for their generous permission to quote from HMT's works.

Excerpts from *All Hands!* and *Gifts of Fortune* are reprinted with permission of The Society of Authors as the literary representatives of H.M. Tomlinson.

Excerpts from "Adelphi Terrace" in *H.W.M.: A Selection from the Writings of H.W. Massingham*, ed. H.J. Massingham, are reprinted with permission of the Executors of the H.J. Massingham Estate.

Excerpts from *The Turn of the Tide* are reprinted with permission of the Macmillan Publishing Co., Inc. Copyright 1942, 1943, 1944, 1945, 1947, by H.M. Tomlinson, renewed 1970, 1971, 1972, 1973, 1975 by Henry Charles Tomlinson, Florence Margery Dickinson, and Dorothy Mary Major Bailey.

Chronology

1873   Henry Major Tomlinson born June 21 in Wanstead, Essex, the eldest of four children.

1886   Taken out of school by an uncle after father's death, he begins work in a shipping office for six shillings per week.

1895   Recommended by Sir Chalmers Mitchell as scientist for the Jackson-Harmsworth Polar Expedition. HMT dissuaded by medical opinion, which he ever regretted.

1898   Marries Florence Hammond. The union results in one son and two daughters (in that order).

1904   Joins the staff of *The Morning Leader*. Meets Ford Madox Ford. In December, takes his first voyage aboard the *Windhover*.

1906   Travels to Algiers aboard the *Celestine*.

1907   Writes "The African Coast," his first travel essay.

1909   First published in Ford's *English Review* in May. Embarks on the *Capella* for a voyage up the Amazon.

1910   Returning from the Brazils, visits New York via Tampa, Florida.

1912   *The Sea and the Jungle.*

1914   In Belfast, receives orders to proceed to Belgium for the London *Daily News* at the outbreak of World War I.

1915   Becomes official correspondent of British armies in France for *Daily News* and *Times*.

1917   In March, encounters George Bernard Shaw at Arras. In November, relieved of correspondent's duties. Accepts H. W. Massingham's invitation to become Associate Editor of the *Nation* at 10 £ per week.

1918   *Old Junk.*

1921   *London River.*

1922   *Waiting for Daylight.*

1923   Leaves the *Nation and Athenaeum*. Travels to Malaysia for *Harper's*.

1924   *Tide Marks.*

1926   *Gifts of Fortune. Under the Red Ensign.*

1927   *Gallions Reach,* HMT's first novel. Takes a lecture tour of the eastern United States.

1928   Wins the Femina-Vie Heureuse Prize for *Gallions Reach. Illusion: 1915.*

1929   *Côte D'Or. Thomas Hardy. War Books.*

1930   *All Our Yesterdays. Between the Lines.*

1931   *Norman Douglas. Out of Soundings.*

1932   Tours United States to lecture against war.

1933   *The Snows of Helicon.*

1934   *Below London Bridge. South to Cadiz.*

1935   *Mars His Idiot.*

1937   *All Hands!*

1939   *The Day Before.* After the invasion of Poland, writes to support the British war effort and publishes several articles in the *Atlantic Monthly* to invite the support of the United States.

1941   *The Wind Is Rising.*

1945   *The Turn of the Tide.*

1946   *Morning Light.*

1950   *The Face of the Earth. Malay Waters.*

1953   *A Mingled Yarn.*

1957   *The Trumpet Shall Sound.*

1958   Dies in London February 5 at the age of 84.

CHAPTER 1

The Man

I *Childhood*

HENRY Major Tomlinson rose to a position of eminence in letters without the assistance of formal education, powerful relatives, or substantial means. Like Charles Dickens and George Bernard Shaw before him, Tomlinson, the eldest of four children, left school early to find employment when his family's financial situation left him no alternative. Unlike Dickens and Shaw, however, Tomlinson bore no grudge against his family for inadvertently bringing him to this pass, nor did he fail to be of genuine assistance.

He was born in Wanstead, Essex, on June 21, 1873. His father, Henry Tomlinson, "had found satisfaction and prosperity in sailing his bark to the corners of the earth. Darkness, however, fell: his father came home for good, and ugly slab-sided steamers elbowed the graceful clippers from East India docks."[1] His mother, Emily Tomlinson, was "the daughter of a master gunner, who as a child had sailed with him in a three-decker, her heritage reached back almost to Nelson's day."[2] Tomlinson described his origins and early connections with the sea in his reminiscent essay, "A Mingled Yarn":

. . . my boyish prospect . . . was of topmasts above a dock wall. I did not think them oppressive. They were attractive topmasts, with their house-flags, and the wall itself was a relic of the East India Company, of which I had heard. My maternal grandmother was a daughter of one of its officers, and she eloped from her father's house in Naval Row, Blackwall, to marry a gunner in the Navy, an act thought to be a distressing fall. The table-talk I overheard was, for the most part, not of the things of the mind, but of sea commerce, its polity, methods, rewards, and accidents.[3]

He also described with tender memory his paternal grandparents. His grandfather on his father's side was a cooper, and his grandmother "filled a cask with the red wine she made each year."[4] When he described the world of his youth, Tomlinson emphasized the Victorian and Dickensian setting of his early years:

> I was a little Londoner when Carlyle was living higher up the river, and I was reading Stevenson when his early tales were appearing serially. It was the day of paraffin lamps, and of the muffin man with a tray covered with green baize balanced on his head, who broke the quiet of Sabbath afternoons with the pealing of a handbell.[5]

When he described his father, Tomlinson revealed the source of many of his economic and political opinions, as well as their intensity:

> He was born in the Hungry Forties, in the period of the Chartists, and in Poplar, and was a radical and nonconformist, even a Brownist. He deferred to authority, but not unless he felt like it, for he was as strict over a matter of principle as another would be over the right inherent in property. This, it could be said, was the easier for him, as he had no property.[6]

Raised himself in Poplar, a London shipping parish, even his earlier memories linked Tomlinson to the "alien sea":

> I remember a tranquil summer afternoon when the portrait of an uncle, who was at sea, fell from its hook on the parlor wall. This portent led to whispered converse between the elders of the family. His ship had been too long on her voyage, and had not been spoken once. There was a secret, and the sea was keeping it. The sea then, to a young listener who had never seen it, became more than ever a mystery, especially when the lamp was lit, and words were passed at table of what had happened far away and long ago.[7]

Tomlinson recalled a brief altercation later between his "Uncle Dave (who once was bo'sun of a China clipper)"[8] and a young man of the steamship tradition when the latter presumed to ask "What's the good of figger-'eds?"[9] Tomlinson took pleasure in recalling the victory of the clipper generation over the steamship tradition in Uncle Dave's final words: "No good in a figger-'ed! Then I'll tell you this, You'll get no good till you learn better, my lad."[10]

After Tomlinson's father "lost his entire savings in a rash stroke of speculation and died soon afterwards"[11] in 1886, an uncle arranged to remove Tomlinson from school and placed him in a shipping office as a clerk. He was thirteen. The shipping firm was Scottish, trading with Bangkok, Brisbane, Shanghai, and Antananarivo, and paid Tomlinson six shillings a week. In 1930 Tomlinson wrote of these years,

What can be made of the fact that my youth was spent among the bills of lading and the cargo manifests of the clippers? It is only of interest to me that, as a lad, I had to make up documents which concerned the *Cutty Sark*—to mention a ship of which everybody has heard. I intensely disliked the exacting routine. Therefore, as a complete change, I gave all the time I could to the Guildhall Library, the British Museum and such odd pursuits as bug hunting (as mockers call it) and attempts at geological surveying.[12]

He also indulged his fascination with ships and travel whenever he "used to pass" Hughes of Fenchurch Street, a shop near the London Docks specializing in shipping and navigational accessories.

And when I say I used to pass it every day, that is not exactly right. I never failed to stop. The windows of that shop would have fascinated any boy, and they did me. I gave much of my employer's time to those windows, time well spent. . . . Sextants, yacht lamps in variety, chronometers, ship logs, charts, compasses and binnacles, foghorns, Morse signaling lamps, marine glasses, protractors and dividers, barometers, and much else was there, and for a lot of it I did not know the use. Books, too . . . .[13]

The day came when Tomlinson "felt awed" to spy one of his books in those windows, "between one on Tubular Boilers, and another on the China Clippers. No best-seller ever did that. How I walked away!"[14] Tomlinson's work among the shipping firm's ledgers and his duties on the docks hardly introduced him to the sea—his origins on both sides were traditionally bound to ships—but they confirmed his desire to be part of this tradition and shaped much of his later writing. When *Atlantic Monthly* Editor Edward Weeks visited England in 1943 as a guest of the British Ministry of Information, he described Tomlinson's tour of the Spice Docks and Ivory Docks. "'Below here,' Tomlinson pointed, 'was where the *Torrens* moored—I have seen her here, when Conrad was her mate. . . . But you can't see it,' he added."[15] Eventually Tomlinson's love for the docks as he saw them and his desire to make others see them resulted in such works as *London River* and *Below London Bridge*.

II *Fleet Street, the Trenches, and Adelphi Terrace*

Tomlinson was dissatisfied with his position as clerk and made one notable attempt to relieve himself of it. In 1895 when he secured the recommendation of Sir Chalmers Mitchell, and others, and "was considered as a possible geologist for the Jackson-Harmsworth ex-

pedition to the Arctic; a way out of commerce appeared to be opening. It was thought, however, that I would prove too frail for the
hardships of it, and I grieved."[16] In 1898 Tomlinson married Florence
Hammond, temporarily reconciled himself to the necessity of sup-
porting a family, and might have remained forever in the employ of
the shipping firm had he been willing to hold his tongue in the
presence of an employer's wrath. He was not.

One day there was trouble in my office. The principal was not angry, but
flushed with fury, and he was wrong. I answered him in his own sort. If you
have never experienced it, then the necessity to explain to your wife, when
you arrive home, and she is preparing for her first child, that she is now
without the full support she needs, is not lightly faced. I did not face it.[17]

Instead, Tomlinson wandered about Fleet Street, "idled round to the
office of that radical halfpenny paper in Stonecutter Street, the
Morning Leader," spoke with the editor Ernest Parke, and found
himself employed as a journalist at thirty-one, marveling at the ease
with which he obtained his freedom. His new career not only removed him from a shipping office, but finally placed him on a ship.
Ashley Gibson, a reviewer for the London *Bookman*, describes this
significant turn of events:

Six months as utility man in the reporters' room gave the new hand a host of
strange and disturbing impressions, some of them worth having, some not.
Came for the editor the task of detailing somebody for duty on the occasion of
the Naval Manoeuvres. Wonderful to relate, the lot fell upon the new hand.
More wonderful still, few were found to question the rightness of the choice.
"What about an evening dress suit out of this so-called salary of mine?" was all
Tomlinson said. "Can it be done? I think not." "Put it down in the expenses,"
said the editor.[18]

In "Off Shore," an essay included in *London River*, Tomlinson described his first voyage, "by steam trawler, the *Windhover*, to the cod
fleet on the Dogger Bank in the days of the Russo-Japanese War."[19]
    Tomlinson's entry into journalism introduced him to several liter-
ary personages. When Ford Madox Ford

began turning up regularly at Edward Garnett's Tuesday luncheons at the
Mont Blanc restaurant in Gerrard Street, . . . he met Thomas Seccombe,
Hilaire Belloc, Chesterton, W. H. Hudson, J. D. Beresford and H. M.
Tomlinson, Conrad and Arthur Marwood.[20]

Ford claimed the honor of discovering Tomlinson, remarking in his autobiography that "I have accepted manuscripts by unknown writers after reading the first three lines. This was the case with D. H. Lawrence, Norman Douglas, (Percy) Wyndham Lewis, and H. M. Tomlinson."[21] In their biographies of Ford, Douglas Goldring and Frank MacShane echo this claim.[22] However, since Tomlinson had been an active journalist five years before appearing in the *English Review*, and by his own report "had been scribbling since I was a child and judicially burning it all, at intervals,"[23] the impression that Ford encouraged Tomlinson to write is an exaggeration of Ford's creation. Writing to Ezra Pound on July 29, 1920, Ford commented "I used to like the prose of a man named [Henry] Tomlinson but I do not know what has become of him,"[24] suggesting that perhaps Ford recalled discovering Tomlinson after Tomlinson's presence became more obvious.

In 1909, "One day, there dropped in, home from the blue, a relative, a sailor, back once more. He casually discussed his next voyage to a place not yet on the map two thousand miles up the Amazon and its main tributary! I pointed out to him that his ship would, in that case, rise to the altitude of about five hundred feet above sea level."[25] The relative maintained that his tale was true and invited Tomlinson to use a spare cabin to see it happen. Tomlinson, never one to waste an idea,

wrote a light-hearted account of this, and the next day, on the editorial stairs, Ernest Parke murmured, "That was an amusing lie of yours today." I assured him that the voyage was to be demonstrated and that I was even invited to go and see it done. "All right," he said, "then go."[26]

That was the genesis of *The Sea and the Jungle*, Tomlinson's account of his voyage to Brazil, his return via Tampa and New York, and his observations and adventures in between. Although the book, published in 1912, did not make Tomlinson instantly famous or wealthy, it established him as an interesting and new voice in English letters.

When World War I broke out in August, 1914, Tomlinson "was in Belfast waiting for civil war."[27] The *Daily News*, which had merged with the *Morning Leader*, dispatched him to Belgium, and in 1915 he became an official correspondent of the British Armies in France for the *Daily News* and the London *Times*. In France, Tomlinson met C. E. Montague, who "was one of our censors, and he showed no hatred for the reading of my manuscripts; never said a word, nor erased a line."[28] Perhaps this was one reason why readers such as Arnold Bennett could say "The best of the correspondents, easily, is Tomlinson."[29] The price of Montague's esteem, however, included accompanying him on harrowing strolls into dangerous territory, sometimes to walk, sometimes to feed gingerbread to neglected hens. Montague's disdain for danger led Tomlinson to admit "I did not go down to the line with Montague if it could be avoided,"[30] and Tomlinson wistfully compared Montague's intrepidity with the attitude of the others who were responsible for conducting correspondents through the lines:

Our other press officers were canny. They were soldiers, and to accompany us down to the certain mud and possible explosions was a sad duty of theirs, and they never pretended to enjoy it. In their hands you were as safe as one can be when nobody knows where the next shell will fall. But not so with Montague. He spurred the flagging spirit. Did the shells appear to be obdurate on that road ahead? Why, that was the road to our objective. We must take it, of course. No detour! One must keep to one's purpose on that line upon which one decided. The shelled road was only another lesson for the shrinking soul. The hairs in one's shirt are all on end this morning, and mighty hard? Good! Courage, brother, do not stumble![31]

According to Frank Swinnerton, whose mother had cut and preserved the early journalism of Tomlinson from the *Morning Leader*, Tomlinson "paid heavily for the experience, being deafened by the din of heavy guns on both sides,"[32] although the deafness has also been attributed to massive doses of quinine Tomlinson took to combat fever. In any case, much of the bitterness toward "progress" and warfare that characterized Tomlinson's between-the-wars writing for many grew from his firsthand experiences of the destruction and horror of war.

One "war experience" which provided a pleasant change of pace was the unexpected appearance of George Bernard Shaw at Arras in March, 1917. Tomlinson encountered Shaw at the right moment—Shaw's car had frozen.[33] Tomlinson offered his car as transport, "becoming in the process 'the chronicler of an historic episode in the war. I was not at Mons; but I was present when Shaw looked first on Armageddon.'"[34] Shaw's *Common Sense About the War* had inflamed many who regarded it as a pro-German document, and Shaw had joked that he had painted the words "HIER WOHNT DER DICHTER SHAW/BITTE/FAHREN SIE WEITER" on his roof so that the German zeppelins would spare the home of their "ally." In like spirit, he disdained the offer of a helmet: "'No,' said he; 'if they do me in, then there is no gratitude in this world.'"[35] Despite the anger Shaw's statements aroused among the civilians, his wit was not lost on the men in the trenches, or the ruins:

> "What the nations of Europe really want," smiled that mocker, whose serious purpose it is not always easy to fathom, putting down his biscuit and cheese to touch off lightly the counter-mine, "what they want is an early and dishonorable peace."
>
> Youth with its military crosses leaned back in its chairs, and its laughter rolled down the ruined corridors of the deserted town.[36]

Despite the relative levity of this dispatch, Tomlinson was in the thick of the fighting and matched the seriousness of the soldiers with his attempts to report the war accurately. Ashley Gibson rated Tomlinson's dispatches highly:

> His dispatches were about the only ones, in my estimation, that told the truth, and I have at least a right to an opinion on that. Not that they found favour among the brass hats. Far from it, I should say. When the tumult and the shouting died and they dished out the K.B.E.'s, there was none for Tomlinson. That was only right. Heaven knows what he would have done with it.[37]

Earlier, in February, 1917, Tomlinson entertained quite a different visitor who was to have a more lasting influence on him.

> One night H. W. Massingham arrived at our château, on a brief visit. He was the editor of the Radical *Nation*, a weekly political and literary review which fought nonsense with such knowledge and persistence that for a time the Authorities declined to allow the soldiers to read it.[38]

Captain Montague was also a radical, and the frail Massingham was left to the tender mercies of Montague as tour-guide. Tomlinson accompanied the pair, and he

> saw Massingham's eyes full of horror as he glanced over the landscape, at the point where Montague judged we had better leave our car. A leg bone with the boot still on it was sticking out of some rubbish beside us. Montague was beginning to look cheerful.[39]

Montague instructed the driver that if the Germans shelled the road, to wait: "don't come to us. We will come to you." Massingham overheard this and was not heartened, although Montague was oblivious to this. Eventually, noting Massingham's civilian clothes, Montague observed that the trio would soon be in sight of the enemy, and that although the Germans would probably ignore three soldiers, they might shoot at an important visiting personage. Montague's solution was to borrow a khaki coat for Massingham, and the latter finally admitted that he had seen all he wished to see.

Montague's disappointment was manifest. He was just beginning to enjoy himself. Could Massingham ever again have such a chance as this to see how very bad the worst could be? Why waste such a day?

Then he got a brief chance, and Montague took me aside. What did I think? Would it do any good to take Massingham on?

I met his look stoutly. No. Evidently, if we were to be shelled there and then, Massingham could learn no more. (I also wanted to go home.)[40]

Tomlinson's argument overcame Montague's disappointment, and the three returned. This encounter with the "pinched figure in a blue-serge suit"[41] was to change Tomlinson's life. Seven months after their meeting Massingham wrote to Tomlinson, "I've pleasure in asking you to take the Assistant Editorship of the *Nation* at a salary of £10 per week."[42] Tomlinson was free to accept the offer. In his words:

When I was recalled from France that spring I ceased to be a war-correspondent because Lord Northcliffe's representative on the Newspaper Proprietors' Association, so I was informed by my own newspaper, had objected to me as a "humanitarian." I don't know what crime that word was intended to imply, but obviously it condemned me, for there can be no answer to it in the nature of things; and as a result I went out of daily journalism to the seclusion of Adelphi Terrace, to sit in an office all day with Massingham.[43]

The signature "H. M. T." appeared at the end of the "World of Books" in the issue of October 13, and Tomlinson continued as Massingham's assistant editor in charge of the literary pages for six years, leaving only when Massingham did.

Tomlinson often recalled these years with affection. "His own fame as a writer was in the making, and he had much to do with the association of the *Nation* with promising young writers—Edmund Blunden, John Middleton Murry, Frank Swinnerton, Aldous Huxley, as well as Sassoon and [Osbert] Sitwell, whose poems continued to appear."[44] When the *Nation* merged with the *Athenaeum* in 1922, a merger which Massingham did not favor, John Middleton Murry took a more prominent role on the staff, and in 1922 Leonard Woolf became the leader-writer on foreign affairs. In addition to these luminaries, Bertrand Russell and Harold Laski became regular contributors, and Tomlinson found himself in the thick of London literary life. Praising Massingham's leadership of the *Nation and Athenaeum*, Tomlinson spoke of "a group of occasional reviewers and writers who appeared to think it was good fun to contribute to the *Nation*—we may name Bernard Shaw, E. M. Forster, Bertrand Russell, and Havelock Ellis—which made my task as literary editor rather like that of a student at his lessons."[45] Near the end of his life, Tomlinson, in 1958, recalled the Adelphi Terrace he had known as gone

to make room for improved rents. In its precincts I used to see J. M. Barrie strolling along, meditative, curved briar pipe pendant from his mouth, both hands behind his back dangling a stick, the little man's visage as worn as age itself, and his eyes upcast in appealing innocence; and young Bernard Shaw, past seventy years, springing blithely upstairs—we shared those stairs—two at a time; and John Galsworthy, his back to an Adam fireplace; and, in the same odd corner of London, Walter de la Mare at tea in a room that was described by Boswell when a former jolly party was in it, Doctor Johnson, Sir Joshua Reynolds, Garrick, Goldsmith, and all. Thomas Hardy, when a young architect, had a room there next to the one in which, in later years, I had to consider the master's poetry for review.[46]

Recalling this time, Tomlinson continued that "The ghosts of this small area of London jostle us. It was ordinary for me in other years to pass, on these pavements, Chesterton, Barrie, Belloc, and Shaw, Bentley of *Trent's Last Case*, Conrad, Muirhead Bone, Max Beerbohm, Dean Inge, Robert Lynd."[47]

For Tomlinson, however, Massingham was the *Nation*, and "When he went, that finished it. There was nothing left."[48] In his tribute to Massingham, Tomlinson described the conditions that prevailed under Massingham's editorship:

Moreover, he expected his staff to be as fearless as he was himself. Just as he had gone for a holiday one year the great railway strike fell across our communications, and he was separated, somewhere in Wales, from his baggage. He telegraphed to me vividly emphatic instructions about the line the *Nation* was to take over this strike; but I guessed what kind of information he had been reading in Cardiff, and did the opposite thing. When he came back to London he thanked me for "putting the telescope to my blind eye." In fact, a chief so inspiring, so quick to appreciate the significant trifle, so sure to understand one's faintest doubt, so well able to guess the unsaid word and to account for it, who could be so frankly abusive over inferior work and cut the heart out of the manuscript of a close friend, and yet never fail to say the just word whenever an obscure contributor pleased him, was not the editor who could be allowed to walk into the street alone.[49]

Massingham resigned on December 10, 1922, after a series of conflicts with the Rowntree Trust which controlled the *Nation*. Although most contemporaries regarded Massingham's resignation as a reflection of questions of policy, Alfred F. Havighurst, Massingham's biographer, has concluded that "In the end it was finance, not policy, which brought a crisis."[50] The fact remains, however, that Massingham virtually created the *Nation*, felt that he was not given adequate opportunity to salvage it, and was reluctant to leave. The reaction of the staff was almost unanimous support of Massingham:

Characteristically, Massingham did not inform his staff of the crisis, but when word reached them they rallied to his support. Nevinson concluded with Tomlinson and Laski that the Rowntree action seemed to have been "underhand and mean." Tomlinson wrote to Murry, "They've done in Massingham" and reported to Blunden that he did not care for "the new colonel and his staff" and had refused the offer to continue with the new group. Hammond (speaking for Tomlinson, Laski and Nevinson) proposed to Hobson that if Massingham left the *Nation*, the chief contributors depart with him. In the end Leonard Woolf was the only regular contributor to remain, and the only one apparently who found the delay in settling the fortunes of the *Nation*, a personal annoyance. "It is unpleasant waiting in a dependent kind of way to know what Massingham will do," Virginia Woolf noted in her diary, 7 February [1923].[51]

Massingham continued to edit the *Nation* until the issue of May 6 and his salary continued through June, but before he completed his stint with the *Nation* Massingham planned to begin a new weekly. He made little progress toward this end, however, and on August 27, 1924, he died suddenly from an attack diagnosed as *angina pectoris*.

III *Development as Man of Letters*

When Tomlinson left the *Nation* in 1923, he was not long finding employment. During his years with Massingham he had published three collections of essays: *Old Junk* (1918), *London River* (1921), and *Waiting for Daylight* (1922). These collections established his reputation as a selling author and introduced him as a master of the essay as a literary form. The subjects of these essays were to become recurrent themes in his later writing: the lure of travel, the glory of British naval and mercantile history, the horrors of war, the value of literature, the mysterious attraction of the sea, and personal musings. Tomlinson characteristically described his published work as the result of accident, mere whims of fate, which he resisted but eventually accepted. Such is his account of his commission by *Harper's Magazine* to tour Malaysia and the Far East.

In fact, I don't think I designed any of my books. They came merely with an unexpected change of wind, as when Mr. T. B. Wells casually one day in Gatti's Restaurant at Charing Cross, told me I'd better go to the Malay Islands for Harpers [sic]. I did not take it seriously. I was unacquainted with the American form of suddenness and merely returned to the books of Massingham's *Nation*. It was only later, to my surprise, that I found that Harpers meant it; and the preliminaries went through with such rapidity that I was at sea again—much better than those channel crossings in the days of submarines!—before I realized that I was outward bound . . . .[52]

The result of this commission, aside from articles published regularly in *Harper's*, was *Tide Marks* (1924), and subsequently Tomlinson traveled often, at the expense of various publications, to write *Côte d'Or* (1929), *South to Cadiz* (1934), and *Malay Waters* (1950). His travels included the Far East, the Mediterranean, and parts of Africa. Closely related to Tomlinson's fascination with travel was his love for the shipping tradition, and he combined his experiences, memories, and research to write such tributes as *Under the Red Ensign* (1926) and *Below London Bridge* (1934).

Despite his close association with the sea, which frequently led to a coupling of his name with Joseph Conrad's, Tomlinson remained active in literary life. In 1927 he toured the United States and delivered his theory of literature, published as *Between the Lines* (published in 1930, and frequently mislabeled by writers of dust jackets as a war book), in lectures at Princeton, Yale, Cornell, Columbia, and Harvard Universities. Tomlinson rarely became involved in literary altercations, partly because he preferred "appreciation" to other forms of criticism and wrote comparatively few critical pieces after leaving the *Nation*. *Thomas Hardy* (1929) and *Norman Douglas* (1931), short pieces which describe Tomlinson's admiration and esteem rather than his perceptions of shortcomings, are characteristic of his critical style.

This did not prevent his involvement in a minor literary skirmish with D. H. Lawrence, whose attitude toward any criticism falling short of the adulatory is widely known. He wrote to John Middleton Murry (January 28, 1925) to make an odd request: "Please don't 'defend' me to H. M. Tomlinson or to anybody else. As for your Tomlinson, I have seen him for about five minutes: can't imagine why you should have to defend me in his precious eyes."[53] Three months later, in a letter dated April 17, 1925, Lawrence perceived the lurking enmity of Murry in the criticism of Tomlinson: "I'm not so very keen on giving those sketches to Murry. It seems to me, it's always his friends who make attacks on me—like Tomlinson: and so often I can acc Murry's words coming out against me, through people who frequent him. I don't like that kind of friendship. But you use your own judgment."[54] In 1926, when Tomlinson's collection of essays *Gifts of Fortune: With Some Hints for Those About to Travel* appeared, Lawrence had an opportunity to review it, and he did not appear happy with it, as he indicated at the outset of his review:

Gifts of Fortune is not a travel-book. It is not even, as the jacket describes it, a book of travel memories. Travel in this case is a stream of reflections, where images intertwine with dark thoughts and obscure emotion, and the whole flows on turbulent and deep and transitory. It is a reflection, throwing back snatches of image.[55]

The chief hint to those about to travel, according to Lawrence, is the "sinister suggestion that they had better stay at home," and he summarizes his objections in no uncertain terms:

There are travellers and travellers, as Mr. Tomlinson himself makes plain. There are scientific ones, game-shooting ones, Thomas Cook ones, thrilled ones, and bored ones. And none of these, as such, will find a single "hint" in all the sixty-six hinting pages, which will be of any use to them.[56]

Apparently satisfied to have exposed Tomlinson's "fraud," however, Lawrence ended his review with a tribute to the book:

Mr. Tomlinson gives us glimpses of a new vision, what we might call the planetary instead of the mundane vision. The glimpses are of extreme beauty, so sensitive to the other life in things. And how grateful we ought to be to a man who sets new visions, new feelings sensitively quivering in us.[57]

Lawrence's exercise of restraint in this review, as well as his praise for the virtues of Tomlinson's collection, is a measure of Tomlinson's relatively inoffensive posture in literary affairs.

By the time Tomlinson left the *Nation*, he had established himself as an essayist, a traveler, an historian of English shipping, a literary critic, and an enemy of the progress that had, as Bernard Shaw often described it, devoted itself to the forces of destruction rather than to the forces of creation. Tomlinson continued in these areas, but he added three dimensions to his literary achievement. The first two grew from his experiences of war. He became known as the strongest pacifist voice following World War I. Unlike Richard Aldington, John Dos Passos, Ernest Hemingway, T. S. Eliot, and others who encountered disillusionment as young men during and after the war, Tomlinson was disillusioned before this particular war began. He found confirmation for his disapproval of man's continuing irrationality, infatuation with "progress," and self-destructive behavior. Before the war, Tomlinson included several wry reflections on earlier conflicts in *The Sea and the Jungle*, and virtually every book he wrote touched on the issue in some way. In 1935 Tomlinson published a long antiwar tract entitled *Mars His Idiot*, although his graphic descriptions of ruin and destruction lacked suggestions of how man was to avoid war. "His writings against war were heavy with a conviction which he never squarely faced: a conviction of futility."[58] Like Swift in his *Conduct of the Allies* (1711) and Shaw in *Common Sense About the War* (1914), Tomlinson could recognize political and economic sources in the conflict but could do little about them.

When Hitler invaded Poland and World War II began, however, Tomlinson performed an apparent shift and decided that this war was different, that Hitler posed a challenge to civilization that England could not ignore. Tomlinson promptly joined the ranks of British war propagandists. From 1939 until 1941, he regularly published articles in the American *Atlantic Monthly*, and while he did not overtly urge America to come directly to England's assistance, that message was implicit in his descriptions of the damage wrought in London by the V-2s, the heroics of common Englishmen, and the significance of this struggle to the future of democracy in the modern age. *The Turn of the Tide*, essays describing the heroic resistance of the English and the subsequent decline of Nazi Germany, appeared in 1945.

A third dimension of Tomlinson's writing began in 1927, when, at the age of fifty-four, he published his first novel, *Gallions Reach*. Ironically, his fiction suffered by comparison with his travelogues and other expository writing, but it attracted more serious attention to his work. In 1928 *Gallions Reach* won the Femina-Vie Heureuse Prize, and his subsequent novels were generally well received. *All Our Yesterdays* (1930) resembled *Gallions Reach* in the extent to which Tomlinson drew from his personal experience to try to chronicle his era. These two novels suffered because Tomlinson ignored the conventions of fiction to intrude autobiography, but they remain pleasurable reading experiences. Perhaps recognizing the shortcomings of these two books, he went to the opposite extreme in *The Snows of Helicon* (1933) and *All Hands!* (1937). The first, departing almost entirely from Tomlinson's personal experiences, is often implausible in the motives and actions of its protagonist, but Tomlinson has better success with the second, which gains from his knowledge of shipping and from his attention to the anecdotes of sailors. Tomlinson's final three novels demonstrate his eventual mastery of the form. *The Day Before* (1939) recalls the years leading to World War I, *Morning Light* (1946) is an historical novel of the clipper era, and *The Trumpet Shall Sound* (1957) is set in London during the Nazi raids. While these three novels rely for their authenticity on Tomlinson's observations and experiences, he has succeeded in writing fiction that focuses on characters and their psychological processes rather than on the personality and interest of the author.

When Tomlinson died on February 5, 1958, at the age of eighty-four, he had long been regarded as something of a legend. As early as 1926, John Gunther wrote that Tomlinson "was a legend in Fleet Street, along the Thames dock roads, at the Savage Club, which is his retreat,"[59] and Gunther proceeded to recall Tomlinson's travels to the Amazon and Malaya, his years on Fleet Street as a journalist, his association with Massingham on the *Nation*, his experiences as a war correspondent, and his Cockney origins. For many men, these adventures would be sufficient for a lifetime, but Tomlinson's future still included a career as a pacifist, war propagandist, novelist, and frequent contributor to numerous periodicals. Gunther added his impressions of a personality that made Tomlinson "the kind of legend which makes friends":

He is shy. His slight quizzical deafness adds charm to the shyness. An incredibly thin man, not so much wiry as leathery. All cartilage, as Miss [Rebecca] West said. A gentle, peering voice; clear, pale blue eyes, with both surface light and depth in them, set in wrinkles against tanned cheeks. Thin blondish hair, spaced over a beautifully molded small forehead. As he himself wrote once, obviously a pure blooded London Saxon. As Mr. Ratcliffe said, no other race could have produced him—the tincture of unaggressive humor in his tremendous seriousness, his inflexible gentleness, his kind, unobtrusive charm. This is a good man. It is only after talking to him half a dozen times that one sees the welling current of irony, even of scorn, under his observations. This is a man with no space in him for anything petty or mean or wooden.[60]

These impressions of Tomlinson's personality—gentleness, charm, seriousness, humor, irony—emerge from his familiar and informal style, even in his more insistent tracts. The tone of Tomlinson's prose forms part of "the kind of legend which makes friends."

CHAPTER 2

The Essayist

I Tomlinson's Essay Voice and Style

ALTHOUGH Tomlinson's writings included books of travel, history, criticism, antiwar rhetoric, and fiction, his earlier readers and critics continued to regard him as primarily an essayist. Almost twenty-five years before his first novel appeared, Tomlinson was writing for the press and for various periodicals, and he established something of a reputation as a stylist. His early critics, even when reviewing his novels, regarded him as a writer of essays, often applying that expectation to their criticism of Tomlinson's travel books and novels.

Robert Lynd, for example, in an article addressing Tomlinson's travel writing and war correspondence, stated that "As a recorder of the things he has seen he has the three great gifts of imagery, style, and humour."[1] Lynd feels that "His writing would be bitter . . . were it not for the strength of his affections. Humanity and irony contend in his work, and humanity is fortunately the winner,"[2] thereby emphasizing the quality of the personality which shines forth more brightly from the work of an essayist than from any other writer of prose. Frederick P. Mayer also stressed the role of Tomlinson in the essay, citing the "youth, or freshness" of Tomlinson's prose as "a quality of good literature," and he summarizes Tomlinson's impact by defining his prose as "a highly personal method of explaining the world.[3] Alva A. Gay, criticizing Tomlinson in 1958, describes him as "essayist and traveller" and finds him similar to Thoreau in his observations of nature, his attitude toward experience, and his resistance to the spirit of his age.[4] Tomlinson often invited this comparison, frequently preferring an identification with Charles Lamb and Thoreau to one with Conrad and Melville.

In an introduction to a collection of essays by Christopher Morley, Tomlinson stated his feeling that the essay has long been unappreciated as a literary form and provided an ironical argument purporting to explain why the essay is not highly regarded.

> The wonders of the universe are inexhaustible.
> Yet everybody writes essays. That may be the reason for our shyness with that form of literature. The child does essays at school, and then, if provoked, for a brief while assaults editors with them just before it writes its first great novel and discards the unprofitable essay for ever. Everybody knows how to manage the essay, that alluring but not too easy form of prose literature; yet, as publishers know, we very rarely read the blessed stuff. We read few essays but our own, perhaps because we see the good intention behind our own work, and therefore know that the virtue which strangers declare harshly is not there happens to be its chief and obvious merit.[5]

Tomlinson also reflects on the nature of the essayist:

> The essay can be as bad as the day of judgment. If he dares to do it, then we shall know the essayist for what he is. The danger is that he doesn't know what he is. You may write objective poetry, or history, or fiction, and need not trouble to smother your cynical amusement behind your hand. Nobody can see you. But when you have set in order the sentences of an essay, they become a number of reflecting mirrors which betray you inside and out from every point of view.[6]

Tomlinson thus links the success of an essay with the personality of the writer, says that Christopher Morley ought to be admired for daring to write in this revealing mode, and concludes:

> This explains why, though it might be anyone's luck to become a popular novelist, yet the right essay is almost as rare as a personality as fine as Lamb's; and to me it has always seemed that the figure of Elia was the wisest and the strongest even in that astonishing group of poets and friends which included Coleridge.[7]

Tomlinson makes a man's style the reflection of the man and argues:

> Only a bad style can come of artful deliberation, as Oscar Wilde and others have shown. Style depends, first and last, on what a writer has to say, and the kind of man he is.[8]

Aware of the role of personality in the essay, Tomlinson carefully developed a persona which became one of the attractions of his essays.

Stuart Hodgson, a critic whose major book consisted of appreciative essays on early twentieth-century contemporaries, described the impressions he derived from Tomlinson's travel essays. He calls the persona

the being whom few who have met will ever forget again: who seems a stranger in all companies and yet in all at home and never out of place. He moves with his "elvyssh countenance" among his fellows like a kind of enchanted child with a child's freshness of mind and keen perception of the immense importance of the tiniest details, and a child's sensitiveness and power of passionate grief and wild delight: but with a power also of conveying them all which no child ever possessed.[9]

Among the impressions that Tomlinson conveys are the freshness of sensory experience, the novelty of the unfamiliar, and the ubiquity of adventure.

His early collections of essays, often generalized as "travel essays," range in their subjects from a visit to a coal mine, to the sighting of a foundered sailing ship from a liner, to impressions of London from the point of view of a soldier on leave from Flanders, to the terrors of public speaking, to an interruption by his three children as he was trying to write an essay. Tomlinson finds everything interesting and conveys his fascination. He also favors anecdotes, either about direct observation (such as his encountering a missionary whose dressing for dinner recalls Conrad and whose wife stares at the Malayan shore, weeping whenever she sees a ship departing for England) or gleaned from varied persons he has met (such as the soldier's explanation of "The Rajah," who has become demented after losing his kingdom to the British). An essay by Tomlinson is as likely to be an appreciation of Herman Melville, a capricious look at civilization from the point of view of the future anthropologists, or a description of a family pet as it is likely to be a piece concerning travel or the sea. Tomlinson's interest in virtually everything is contagious.

Although the style of his essays is personal, remaining at a conversational level and confining itself to his personal view of the world, Tomlinson is curiously reticent about the facts of his own life. For example, at some points he refers to working in a shipping firm when a young lad, but he never names that firm in print. When he describes his three children intruding when he is trying to write, he does not name them beyond calling them "The Boy," "Miss Muffet," and "Curls," and although he refers to having three younger siblings, he never names them. The personality that appears in Tomlinson's essays is one of perspective, not one of detail. Even a late essay describing his Golden Honeymoon fails to name his wife. Although one feels that reading the essays makes one familiar with Tomlinson, giving the impression that one knows him, in fact one learns little about him. Perhaps this is the result of a curiously informal conversational style, complete with such characteristic substitutions in speech as "till" for "until" or "though" for "although" or "however."

II *Immediacy and Description*

The immediacy that Tomlinson's prose communicates appears in the introductory passage to "Shaw at Armageddon," which Tomlinson wrote on the occasion of meeting GBS at the Front:

> When, a day or two since, I saw a tall and alert figure in khaki, with beard and mustache terribly reminiscent, overlooking with disfavor what affairs of war happened to be about him at the moment (to be precise, his army chauffeur was kneeling in the snow trying to persuade a frozen radiator), I wondered whether the war was beginning to affect my mind. You never can tell.[10]

This brief introduction to a dispatch combines several elements characteristic of Tomlinson's style. The description, although brief, is fairly direct: specific visual description of the man soon named in the dispatch but already named in the headline, Shaw's attitude, the chauffeur kneeling in the snow, and the general irrationality of the scene appear in the first sentence. The second sentence is unusual for Tomlinson, since he rarely used literary allusions in his essays, but *You Never Can Tell* was the title of Shaw's play first performed in 1899. Also, Tomlinson included his immediate reaction, whimsically wondering whether his mind was endangered, to establish his perspective and to invite audience identification.

In another essay, describing his first impressions of an ocean liner after acquiring his nautical experience aboard ships which he could measure at a glance, Tomlinson includes his feeling that he is not really on a ship, but in a city.

> A steward appeared at my door, a stranger out of nowhere, and asked whether I had seen a bag not mine in the cabin. He might have been created merely to put that question, for I never saw him again on the voyage. This liner was a large province having irregular and shifting bounds, permitting incontinent entrance and disappearance.[11]

With or without experience of travel, the reader has a sense of being there.

Tomlinson is most often noted for his powers of description. In "The African Coast" he describes the scene vividly enough to allow one to paint it:

Next door . . . was a regular tenant who bred goats, and fed them out of British biscuit-tins. Beyond them the stable was occupied by a party of swarthy ruffians who had arrived with a cargo of esparto grass. In the far corner, a family, crowded out, had been living for weeks under a structure of horrible rags. Smoke, issuing from a dozen seams, gave their home the look of a smouldering haycock. [12]

He renders scenes of a more common nature with equal vividness:

His shop at least had its strange interests in its revelation of the diverse needs of civilised homes, for Mr. Monk sold everything likely to be wanted urgently enough by his neighbours to make a journey to greater Clayton prohibitive. In one corner of his shop a young lady was caged, for it was also the post office. The interior of the store was confused with boxes, barrels, bags, and barricades of smaller tins and jars, with alleys for sidelong progress between them. I do not think any order ever embarrassed Mr. Monk. Without hesitation he would turn, sure of his intricate world, from babies' dummies to kerosene. There were cards hanging from the rafters bearing briar pipes, bottles of lotion for the hair of school-children, samples of sauce, and stationery. [13]

In this passage, true to form, Tomlinson has combined the affected irony of the caged woman, an example of his alliteration in lists, and his personal assessment of Mr. Monk's inventory. He uses a similar technique to describe people:

We met at meals. I think he was a commercial traveller. A tall young fellow, strongly built, a pleasure to look at; carefully dressed, intelligent with hard and clear grey eyes. He had a ruddy but fastidious complexion, though he was, I noticed, a hearty and careless eater. He was energetic and swift in his movements, as though the world were easily read, and he could come to quick decisions and successful executions of his desires. He had no moments of laxity and hesitation, even after a breakfast, on a hot morning, too, of ham and eggs drenched in coffee. He made me feel an ineffective, delicate, and inferior being. [14]

Tomlinson's description consists of a combination of sensory details and his subjective impressions.

Most critics who speak of Tomlinson's powers of description discuss his ability to describe the sea. In his "Initiation," about his son's first voyage, Tomlinson provided this picture of a heavy sea:

As we were about to emerge into the open, the wet, deserted deck fell away, and a grey wave which looked as aged as death, its white hair streaming in the wind, suddenly reared over the ship's side, as though looking for us, and then fled phantom-like, with dire cries. The Boy shrank back for a moment, horrified, but then moved on. I think I heard him sigh. It was no summer sea. The dark bales of rain were speeding up from the south-west, low over waters which looked just what the sea really is.[15]

According to Robert Lynd, Joseph Conrad "may be said to be the first novelist writing in English to have kept his weather-eye open. Mr. Tomlinson shares Mr. Conrad's sensitive care for these things."[16]

Tomlinson consistently does this whenever his essay concerns the sea. He often joked that whenever he stepped aboard a ship, the barometer fell, and he was regarded as something of a Jonah by more than one skipper. He described one adventure aboard a small sailboat piloted by its owner, Yeo:

"Look out!" cried Yeo. I looked. Astern was a grey hill, high over us, fast overtaking us, the white turmoil of its summit already streaming down its long slope. It accelerated, as if it could see it would soon be too late. It nearly was, but not quite. A cataract roared over the poop, and Yeo vanished. The *Judy*, in a panic, made an attempt at a move which would have been fatal then; but she was checked and her head steadied. I could do nothing but hold the lady firm and grasp a pin in its rail. The flood swept us, brawling round the gear, foundering the hatch. For a moment I thought it was a case, and saw nothing but maniacal water. Then the foam subsided to clear torrents which flung about violently with the ship's movement. The men were in the rigging. Yeo was rigid at the wheel, his eyes on the future.[17]

In his descriptions Tomlinson's presence invites the reader to sympathize with his plight. This trait appears in writing which has nothing to do with the sea, as it does in Tomlinson's "Binding A Spell," which concerns Tomlinson's trepidation at an approaching speaking engagement. When he introduces one of the devices by which the novice convinces himself he can speak, he invites the reader to join him: A rustic businessman

has nothing to say, and could not say it if he had; but he can speak in public.

You will observe the inference is obvious. One who is really capable of constructive thought (like you and me); who has a wide range of words to choose from even when running; who is touched, by events, to admiration, to indignation, to alarm, to—to all that sort of thing, he could . . . the plastic audience would be in his skilful hands, there is no doubt. (Hear, hear!)[18]

However, when Tomlinson proceeds to describe discomforts of being behind the podium, he does not invite the audience to share his sense of indignity. He does not have to.

III *Imagery and Irony*

One device that makes Tomlinson's essays readable is his use of metaphor, generally drawn from common experience or current events rather than from the classics. Discussing the role of poetry in the modern state, for example, Tomlinson notes that "To discuss poetry with Mr. Trotsky would be as useful as reciting the *Ancient Mariner* while inside a tank in action. Not only would one's style be somewhat cramped, but one might not be heard."[19] When he uses analogy, he carefully picks examples that are widely recognized:

If the Garden of Eden had been anything like the Amazon jungle, then our first parents would never have been evicted; they would have moved fairly soon on their own account, without giving notice.[20]

The ease with which one can apprehend the meaning of Tomlinson's statements, even when they appear superficially complicated, adds much to his appeal as an essayist.

Tomlinson rarely used aphorisms in his essays, although on occasion one might find "Uniformity is the abortion of creation" or "A Nobody never seems to know anything, but by the grace of God he gets there just the same."[21] Tomlinson's style is more often graced with an irony not intended to be punitive. Writing about Russia, for example, he comments that "I do not know everything of Russia as it is, even though I have not been there."[22] The jibe at most writers of Russia and the diminishing of his stance as the writer combine to lend pleasure to his account of the effect of the Revolution on literature. Sometimes his irony can be more direct, as in his statement "At Bougie, they seemed to have left it all to Allah, with the usual result."[23]

However, Tomlinson's irony is usually gentler, usually an understatement, and usually self-deflating. Frederick P. Mayer, the first scholar to address Tomlinson's style, quoted from a draft of Tomlinson's "Autobiographical Sketch" (1930) which included an example that did not appear in the final version:

My existence has been uneventful and unmarked; except, I fear, by the Recording Angel. And when he publishes it, some day, I do not expect a ripple of excitement to pass round the Judgment hall. It will be heard only in dreary resignation by the few who are still waiting their turn while the T's are being worked through.[24]

Sometimes Tomlinson's irony carries a touch of resignation: "It is probable, we are forced to confess, that a few years of petrol have made a greater difference in the world of men than all the poets since Homer."[25] On occasion Tomlinson's irony finds its target in others, as in his description of the helpfulness of a French captain:

He has an idea I cannot read the menu, so when an omelette is served he informs me, in case I should suppose it is a salad. He makes helpful farmyard noises. There is no mistaking eggs. There is no mistaking pork. But I think he has the wrong pantomime for the ship's beef, unless French horses have the same music as English cows.[26]

One refreshing quality of Tomlinson's prose is that he has no difficulty portraying himself as slightly ridiculous. When Tomlinson and his son toured the Mediterranean on the *Zircon*, they somehow became separated from their ship and boarded the Polish *Kosciuszko*, hoping to meet their ship in the next port. The Polish skipper talks with Tomlinson:

As he talked of the lore and literature of the sea I began to be sure that I had a card to win over this Polish ship's master; so when he mentioned Joseph Conrad I told him casually—playing my ace on the instant—that I had known Conrad. It was no trump. The captain of the *Kosciuszko* brushed Conrad lightly aside. "I speak fourteen languages," was all he said.[27]

Another instance of this occurs in "Interlude," an account of a trip to Switzerland. Tomlinson, temporarily elated, decides to learn to ski. When he has discovered the enormous length of the skis "the right length," his enthusiasm begins to wane.

Then one ski began to move. We will call him Castor. Pollux remained firm for a moment, then saw that Castor was leaving him, and followed in haste. My feet no longer were in my charge. They were controlled by twin spirits,

who were friendly and sportive together, for they had come to a secret and
sinister understanding about me. I could never guess what they had agreed
upon, though sure it was no good to me. Sometimes I divined instantly what
the end of a bit of devilment would be, but while I was frustrating that
manoeuvre they deviated.[28]

Tomlinson frequently encounters temporary reversals in his travels.
During an early voyage to the African Coast, he encounters an elderly
gentleman in Sfax, sits down with him, and finds that he has made a
diplomatic blunder: bystanders "watched him draw his finger across
his throat in serious and energetic pantomime, and saw me nod in
grave appreciation, when he was trying to make me understand what
was his sympathy for the Christian conquerors of Sfax."[29] In the same
town, Tomlinson joins a group listening to a "huckster" and, after a
while, realized that the huckster was pointing fun at Tomlinson, a
trick which "may be seen at work . . . when a curious and innocent
Chinaman joins the group about the fluent quack."[30] Tomlinson's
summary is succinct: "As soon as dignity permitted I passed on, and
my dignity did not keep me waiting for any length of time."[31]

   Although Tomlinson's style naturally varied with different genres,
so that his novels are distinct from his travel books, his essay style
changed surprisingly little during his long literary career. His presentation of an amiable and self-deprecating voice, his preference for an
anecdotal style, his sensory descriptions, his gentle irony, and his
fascination with virtually any topic continued throughout his writing.
Whether he was embroiled in arguments concerning pacifism or
warfare, or writing a novel about the sea, or describing his excursion
into the Brazilian jungle, Tomlinson maintained an easy grace which
was as much the product of his personality as of his efforts to write
elegant prose.

CHAPTER 3

The Literary Critic

I Limitations as a Critic

A LTHOUGH he was the literary editor for the *Nation* for six years and wrote a number of reviews, Tomlinson was never a polished critic. Often subjective, rarely providing useful insight into an author or a work, Tomlinson's reviews and essays remain largely unsatisfying. He favored an eclectic approach to literature which often wandered from the subject. One essay might comment on larger social issues implicit in the works of Conrad, another might focus on the author's personality, a third might comment on the aesthetic or political reasons for an author's acceptance or rejection by his audience. Tomlinson's theory of literature and criticism was often derivative. Much of his understanding of the novel as genre seems to have resulted from his reading E. M. Forster's *Aspects of the Novel*, while many of his comments on style seem to have been inspired by Bernard Shaw's prefaces and Jonathan Swift's essays. Nevertheless, Tomlinson's articles reveal that he had developed a comprehensive theory of literature which included the role of the artist, the purpose of books, the effect of a work on its audience, and the relationship of a work to reality and to the transcendental.

Tomlinson's criticism is deficient, however, in speaking of literary technique. When he praises or blames a work, he often seems subjective because he does not link the final effect of a work with the means the author has used in his attempt to achieve that effect. This deficiency mars Tomlinson's effectiveness when he attempts to apply his theory of criticism to specific authors to appraise their work. Although he wrote scores of articles that might be called criticism, Tomlinson published only three critical works in book form, and, except for the last, these were essentially lengthy essays. *Thomas Hardy*, published in book form in 1929, is a slightly lengthened version of an essay published in *Saturday Review of Literature* in February, 1928. *Between the Lines*, published in 1930, is a lecture on the subject of literature presented to the students of Harvard and is drawn almost entirely from previously published articles. *Norman Douglas*, first published in 1931, was "enlarged and revised" with the addition of an introductory essay in 1952. These three works add little to Tomlinson's stature as a man of letters, and they emphasize the subjective nature of his approach. J. B. Priestley summarized Tomlinson's role as critic when he wrote,

Criticism is not really his business at all, though for some years he was engaged in it. He could probably write about a few books and authors better than any man living, but for the rest, he is no critic. His demands are too narrow and personal, and he would rather explore the world than other men's minds.[1]

Tomlinson himself was aware of his deficiencies in this area, and when he wrote of literary criticism and its relationship to literature, he did not omit to comment humorously on his role as a judge of books.

When he spoke of his role as critic, Tomlinson deprecated his ability to withstand the challenges of his readers. After describing a reader's reaction to his review of a child's diary, he stated:

Let me declare now that I am not a literary critic, though I have been paid to criticize books, and that I could not define the essentials of true literary criticism to save my life. I have never been able to discover what are the standards by which sound opinions are gauged and good taste is measured. Still, I can see that it is natural for those who admire an object to show anger for those who laugh at it.[2]

Although he admits his lack of expertise in judging others' work, Tomlinson relates his lack to a deficiency in criticism itself. Referring to another reviewer's description of the critical process as an "inquest," Tomlinson claims,

But though my own literary criticism is infrequent and amateurish, I think the trouble with criticism in England, of the *intellectual* kind, might have been seen fairly soon by this scholarly critic if he had kept his eye on his own word, inquest, till he saw daylight through it. . . .

There is no joy in an inquest. And there is no understanding of literature which is not won with joy.[3]

He also objects to demands that a critic bring a set of tools to the task of judging literature.

My credentials as a literary critic would not, I fear, bear five minutes' scrutiny; but I never cease to look for that defined and adequate equipment, such as even a carpenter calls his tool-chest, full of cryptic instruments, each designed for some particular task, and every implement named. It is sad to have to admit it, but I know I possess only a home-made gimlet to test for dry-rot, and another implement, a very ancient heirloom, snatched at only on blind instinct, a stone axe. But these are poor tools, and sooner or later I shall be found out.[4]

Despite his description of himself as an inadequate critic, Tomlinson did not entirely dismiss the importance of literary criticism, which he regarded as a useful and important genre.

II *Theory of Literary Criticism*

Tomlinson recognized that "we find it much harder to spot a poet than a good horse, unless someone gives us a knowing hint,"[5] and he felt that good criticism could accomplish at least such a hint. However, as he noted in his introduction to selections of Robert Louis Stevenson, criticism that is too demanding and too far removed from pleasure as a criterion is not useful: "Perhaps it is time we ceased to regard literature as a hardship, and began to enjoy it."[6] However, the enjoyment must not be misplaced. Tomlinson describes an American Army officer who quoted from Dickens to establish that a specific character had come to the same tavern in which he spoke with Tomlinson, but when Tomlinson asked the American about several young American poets,

He had never heard of them. This enthusiast did not even appear to have the beginning of an idea that his was unforgivable ignorance seeing that he knew more than a native ought to know about some of our taverns. Had he been an Englishman and a friend of mine I should have told him that I thought his love of letters was as spurious as the morality of the curate who speaks in a trembling baritone about changes in the divorce laws, but who accepts murder without altering the statutory smile of benediction.[7]

Despite his professed amateurism toward criticism, however, Tomlinson deplored the shortcomings of several reviews. After noting that librarians must trust to the criticism in the press to determine which books to buy, he states that they cannot trust this criticism. Tomlinson provides two reasons for criticism's lapse. First, he points

out that "literary criticism is mainly a matter of opinion, and is no
more absolute than is one's taste in tobacco."[8] This partly explains the
varied opinions which criticism has to offer on such works as *Hamlet*,
so that some explain "that Hamlet was mad, and [others] that he was
wonderfully sane."[9] Second, critics do not always address themselves
to significant issues. After describing the unexpected success of one
novel, which sold exceptionally well while others of its kind lan-
guished, Tomlinson asks,

Now, will some critic explain why? A sufficient explanation would be a
genuine addition to knowledge. The critics who know why Shakspere [*sic*]
did this and that, who can guess the springs of *his* activities, surely ought not
to find the shy little creature who sits in all our tea-shops so utterly beyond
them. But they never so much as glance at such questions.[10]

For Tomlinson, the proper function of criticism is to point us to good
books, to stress the enjoyment of literature, and to add insight into
the particular appeal that a book will have for its readers, not the
evaluation of a book's merits.

Tomlinson sees no validity in literary criteria applied to specific
works.

There may be absolute criteria for the judging of books, but I do not know
them, and cannot submit any. A learned critic may somehow manage to
convey the impression that, like a chemist, he has an array of apparatus of
which every item has its designed purpose, and that his measuring is done by
impersonal scales which never fail to distinguish the just from the unjust. Yet
we need not believe him unless we want to.[11]

He describes "our literary criteria" as "only our personal prejudices
elegantly disguised in reasonable argument,"[12] and he provides an
example of criticism which raises more questions than it answers:

One writer said: "There is but one art of writing, and that is the art of poetry.
The test of poetry is sincerity. The test of sincerity is style; and the test of style
is personality." Excellent, I exclaimed immediately; and then slowly I began
to suspect a trap somewhere in it. Of course, does not the test for sunlight
distinguish it at once from insincere limelight? But what is the test, and
would it be of any use to those likely to mistake limelight for daylight?[13]

Tomlinson's conclusion regarding the inability of critics to report
accurately on literature resembles Henry James's "Figure in the
Carpet":

The means by which we are able to separate what is precious in books from the matrix is not a process, and is nothing measurable. It is instinctive, and not only differs from age to age, but changes in the life of each of us. It is as indefinable as beauty itself. An artist may know how to create a beautiful thing, but he cannot communicate his knowledge except by that creation. That is all he can tell us of beauty, and, indeed, he may be innocent of the measure of his effort. . . .[14]

The inability of a critic to express the truth about a work in terms other than the artist's echoes the artist's inability to express the truth in another way.

Despite his recognition of the problems inherent in the critic's task, Tomlinson recognizes the seriousness of criticism and has no tolerance for the indifferent or misleading critic. Despite the lack of uniform criteria for the judging of books, "one does see errors in criticism which ought not to be made by any one who knows a book from a toast-rack."[15] After commenting on a reviewer who described the prose style of Carlyle as ugly, Tomlinson "gathered that it was the *matter* of a book that was of importance, and not the style."[16] He is intolerant of such statements:

I must say that any press critic who makes such a fundamental mistake as that ought to be dismissed instantly. The style of "Past and Present" ugly, and not beautiful, though it so perfectly embodies its noble purpose! Was there ever a good book with a bad style, or an attractive flower with a disgusting smell, or an honest politician with a dishonest soul?[17]

Tomlinson recognizes the ultimate importance of critical distinctions:

Everything that matters in literature depends on just such distinctions. If we can find no precise rules for the judging of literature, we see, nevertheless, that on our choice a very great deal depends. We may, and without knowing what we do, deny the light. We may hail for our choice, and again without knowing what we do, Barabbas. For let us note carefully that the choice of Barabbas is also a sincere choice, though woeful.[18]

Tomlinson states that,

For my part, I am sure such bad and indifferent criticism of books is just as serious as a city's careless drainage. Of course it is important, for at least frivolity appears unseemly, and carelessness something worse, about the springs of life and death.[19]

It becomes apparent that, despite his avowed lack of credentials as a critic, he took the critical role seriously. For Tomlinson, the importance of just criticism derived from the importance of books themselves, and as he described the purposes of literature, he showed that he felt books were the primary means by which the ills of the world could be cured.

III   Theory of Literature

Although Tomlinson occasionally referred to the common notion that books are quite useless, he often noted specific effects that books have on their readers. These include a source of pleasure that compels a reader to open a book, the opportunity for vicarious experience. Speaking of a popular novel whose unexpected success puzzled many, Tomlinson

ventured to hint that poor folks, whose instinctive desires are like those of the rich, but who are confined to a routine of typewriters and tea and buns, and a train home again, nevertheless must live somehow. Therefore, compelled by our moral conventions, they live also a dream life apart, to which imaginary dark chieftains offer savage but happy release. [20]

Tomlinson finds the extension of a reader's experience a major reason for praising Edmund Blunden's *The Bonaventure: A Random Journal of an Atlantic Holiday*:

Blunden represents here that world where seamen are at home, a world which is full of romantic possibilities to us because we do not know it and cannot enter it. He compels a simple faith in the veracity of his imaginative record. We feel we know the *Bonaventure* and her men and her circumstances. [21]

For Tomlinson, the primary function of a book, whatever its genre, is to increase the pleasure of life.

If we are not happy and enjoying life, then we have missed the only reason for it. If books do not help us to this, if they even devise our thoughts into knots and put straws in our hair, then they ought to be burned. It is true that some of us may get pleasure from searching novels for solecisms and collecting evidence by which shall be guessed the originals of the novelist's characters, just as others extract amusement from puzzle pictures. But book-worming has the same relation to literature, even when it is done by a learned doctor in the Bodleian, as flies in a dairy with our milk supply. [22]

Tomlinson notes that were all the books in the British Museum destroyed, we should still have the simple sensory pleasures of life left to us, and "That is what we look for in books, or something like it, and when it is not there they are not books to us."[23] He insisted that pleasure play a greater role in literary criticism precisely because pleasure is a major justification for the existence of literature.

One effect that literature ought to have on its reader is a heightening of the appreciation of beauty. For Tomlinson,

One of the inexplicable effects of beauty is to inspire us with fear, even with a tremor of terror; we are disturbed, and we find it impossible to say why. Any lover of Beethoven knows this.[24]

An effect of such beauty is to improve the taste of the audience, and Tomlinson, who found literary criticism to be largely a matter of taste, argues that literature is capable of refining the aesthetic perceptions of its readers.

I have noticed that children, by no means clever, who have had easy access to such books as the Bible, the Iliad, and the Odyssey, to Dickens, to Bunyan, Defoe, Shakspere [sic], Milton, Keats, and others that could easily be named, and have not been ordered to read them, but have been casually induced to find treasure there; who have heard read aloud some of the greater passages of the best that man has done—such children, with a free run on all sorts of new volumes in later years, show a native distast for shoddy, and a ready detection of the insincere and pretentious . . . . It is possible to induce in the young the faith that in books they may find happy reflections of truth, which they may know by their beauty.[25]

By improving the taste of its readers, literature serves a useful and satisfying instructive purpose.

Another instructive purpose of literature is to make some sense of life, whose happenings often appear chaotic. The problem is that

Life is more hurried than ever, but has lost its sense of direction and forgotten its traditional values, excepting the certitude of what, without irony, we call progress.[26]

Literature works to solve this problem by, in the American playwright Edward Albee's phrase, twisting "fact into truth":

never before in history have men known so many facts about this mysterious universe as they know now, nor so little what to do with them; never such an unquestioned belief in science, nor so empty a care for the value of life and personality. [27]

Tomlinson introduces poetry as an answer to this modern dilemma:

Poetry, whatever its uselessness, has never caused a war, if it has never brought about a railway track. It has never brought down a city, caused a financial crash, raised the rent, nor the price of the loaf. But its irrelevant value has steadied the soul of many a young soldier when beset by the foulness brought about by calculated folly, and by the instruments of technology so hard to understand that few of us can make head or tail of it; we can but cower underground, as many of us have been doing, and trust this will soon pass. [28]

After noting that "Reason takes us but a short distance, and then leaves us in the air,"[29] Tomlinson compares the despair to which we have been led by reason with the consolation offered by literature. He asks, "Shall we say darkness is the primary principle, uncreate, eternal, and absolute? That truth and beauty are but consoling illusions?"[30] He concludes in the negative and ends his article with the statement that "There are books in nearly every house in America and England which have words in a few verses, a page or two, of more lasting value than is in all the reports that issue from the conferences of the great and important."[31] The role of changing modern man's easy acceptance of the ugliness of a valueless world ultimately becomes the role of the poet:

Is it not true that even gigantic and wealthy New York is but the outer show of its people's commonest opinions and desires? So how if their thoughts should veer? We change our thoughts and change our world. And that is the task of the poet, to persuade his fellows to pause and to look up to the everlasting hills . . . . They could, in the end, give it a spirit which it has not, if perchance they have heard of a better word, and have the courage to let their fellows know it. [32]

The poet, by communicating a higher set of values, can place the traits of the modern world into a perspective of meaning, and thereby impel readers to view modernity in terms of its values.

In addition to providing vicarious experience and pleasure, improving the reader's aesthetic values, and communicating the meaning of life, literature also works toward social and political change. Although he does not mention the effect of Jack London's *John Barleycorn* on the prohibition movement, Harriet Beecher Stowe's *Uncle Tom's Cabin* on the abolitionists, or Upton Sinclair's *The Jungle* on the Pure Food and Drugs Act, Tomlinson speaks of the influence of Robert Blatchford's *Merrie England*,

which sold in such numbers, which was used as a textbook by ardent reformers (nearly all of them young) in every market place and at almost every street corner in Great Britain, [and which] speeded perceptibly the popular impulse which has resulted in a first British Labor Government. Carlyle, Ruskin, and William Morris must not be forgotten. But they were then not greatly read by miners and such.[33]

He cites such writers as viable social and political forces not to be ignored:

Beware of young men when they turn to the poets and seers! People laugh to-day at the idea of faith removing mountains and point out that it took more than faith to cut the Panama Canal. But did it? They don't know what they are talking about. A few words will move the earth, if you give them time.[34]

The first step in the process of moving the earth is increasing people's awareness, similar to increasing their understanding of life in an ethical perspective. Tomlinson cites the effect of Thoreau's work:

You suspect, in sudden alarm, that there is more in life than you had been told; that it may have a nature hitherto unguessed, possibilities unknown; that, in fact, Western civilization may have taken the wrong path and may yet have to turn back—or wish desperately that it could.[35]

To demonstrate the effectiveness of literature on changing political and social awareness, Tomlinson describes the effect John Ruskin had had on him in his youth. "With courage and eloquence he denounced dishonesty in the days when it was not supposed that cheating could be wrong if it were successful."[36]

Ruskin "showed as a social iniquity naked children crawling with chains about them in the galleries of coal-mines" during "the happy years, radiant with the certain knowledge of the British that the Holy Grail would be recognized immediately it was seen, for over it would be proudly floating the confirmatory Union Jack."[37] The immediate effect of Ruskin's writing was minimal:

We had not even begun to suspect that our morals, manners, and laws were fairly poor compared with the standards of the Mohawks and Mohicans whom our settlers had displaced in America a century before. And Ruskin told that Victorian society it had an ugly mind, and did ugly things. When Ruskin said so, with considerable emotion, Thackeray was so hurt that he answered as would any clever editor to-day about a contribution which convinced him that it would make readers angry; he told Ruskin it would never do. Thackeray's readers, of course, were assured they were the best people, and that worldly cynic did well to reject Ruskin, and preserve the *Cornhill Magazine*.[38]

Ruskin has been praised as a great master of English prose, but Tomlinson asks,

or is our tribute to Ruskin only a show of gratitude to one who revealed to us the unpleasant character of our national habits when contrasted with a standard for gentlemen? It ought not to have required much eloquence to convince us that Widnes is unlovely; the smell of it should have been enough. It is curious that we needed festoons of chromatic sentences to warn us that cruelty to children, even when profit can be made of it, is not right.[39]

Writers who instruct in the manner of Ruskin, however, appeal to an aspect of human nature that Tomlinson recognizes but does not define:

it is curious that through all our reading an impression deepens of personal responsibility, and an imperative responsibility. Why? Nobody knows. Perhaps it arises merely in the combativeness and vanity of human nature. I have never seen a satisfactory answer to the riddle, but it is certain that a sense of duty is understood, and that in loneliness it will resist the police of the most unappeasable of dictators.[40]

This moral imperative is an aspect of human nature to which literature unfailingly appeals and which accounts for the power of books. The effects that literature can have on its readers—to provide vicarious experience and pleasure, to increase an appreciation of aesthetics, to explain life in terms of its values, and to change social and political traditions—make the writing of books an extremely powerful means of changing the world.

IV   *The Role of the Reader*

Tomlinson, however, would be the first to admit that the power of literature to change the world has not been entirely successful. He attributes the lack of immediate impact to factors detrimental to the response of the reader. These range in significance from the trivial to the serious. Sometimes a reader will fail to respond to books because of his particular mood. Tomlinson often discussed his lack of interest in reading while on ship, and he explained it in terms of most people's preference for life over reading: "most of us happen to be more or less alive, and therefore feel a keener interest in life than in books."[41] He asks,

What, then, is the reading of books to us? A sort of idleness. But somehow it is not idling to listen passively for hours to those undertones from the outer dark. They are beyond speech. They awaken responses from those secrets in us that are the cause of all great art, and of the love of art, secrets which are never directly revealed. Books, for about the first week at sea, are usually no more than reminders of the distracting affairs about which we want to hear nothing for a while.[42]

A more serious barrier to a reader, however, may be the prevailing spirit of his era. This may be the resistance of the Victorian audience to seers such as Ruskin, but it may also be the inability of the age to harken to a new voice. Tomlinson notes that "We see even in *Moby Dick* what was invisible to the people to whom the book was first given,"[43] and he comments that Whitman's *Leaves of Grass* could not have occurred in England because "Victorian England was simply incapable of it."[44] Addressing the years of neglect of Melville, Tomlinson clarifies his view of the effect of time on a reader:

Now that question is addressed to a mystery of the human mind. There has been such a change, in ten years, in the public consciousness that things in which once only odd men and women delighted have acquired a significance for the general. Where it was all dark, now most people may see something. Melville, in his own day, was addressing an intelligence which was hardly awake. To-day it is apprehensive.[45]

A reader may awaken as time passes, but his ability to apprehend may also suffer from contemporary events. Tomlinson includes among the effects of the Great War a decline in readers' tastes:

But, like it or lump it, the war made a difference. I will speak for a bit of Europe, at least; the war made a revolution. It very definitely displayed in Europe the reality under those polite and smooth appearances of society which till then the young had never questioned. Now they know what is in the family vault. No wonder they cannot sing the old songs! No wonder, as there seems to be no escape, they regard the saxophone an expressive instrument.[46]

Tomlinson suggests that

Very likely we do not understand the poet when we have him, but at least we do not even have him unless ours is an age in which music will make men look up, as though they knew what it was, and were glad.[47]

One reason we do not recognize a poet in his lifetime is our reaction against a new and unique voice. "The original and inventive man is a disconcerting fellow, for he is dissatisfied with us and our ways. He would make our days unquiet with the very kind of activity we most dislike."[48] According to Tomlinson,

The unusual book is read only by unusual people; for all we can tell, only by the high-brows, whose interest may just manage to save it from being stillborn.[49]

This reactionary approach to innovative and unusual works of art often prevents literature from having its full effect.

Tomlinson provides more insidious reasons for literature's lack of effectiveness on some readers. He comments that our prejudice will close our ears to the truth:

For like the people who once stoned the prophets, and killed those who were sent unto them, we are never likely to listen to the words which are strangely not in harmony with the things we want to hear, and a success which cannot be measured by the accepted standard will be failure to us. We want to hear, chiefly, whatever comforts our prejudices, justifies our conventions, and confirms us in the pursuit of the things we desire.[50]

This resistance to discomforting truth finds an ally in contemporary editors, who, according to Tomlinson, are responsible for a general decline in the quality of the mass-circulation periodicals.

The matter is of some importance, because either the producers or the readers are in a bad way; and it would be disheartening to suppose it is the readers, for probably there are more readers than editors, and so less a chance of a cure.[51]

Tomlinson cites the popularity of *La Vie Parisienne* and New York *Life* as evidence that the reading public will select "the gay and frank expression of artists whose humour is too broad for the general; but, as a rule, there is no doubt about the fine quality of their drawings and the deftness of their wit."[52]

The preference of English soldiers for the French and American magazines moves Tomlinson to consider the qualities of *Life* which appeal to the men:

It is not written in a walled enclosure of ideas. It is not darkened and circumscribed by the dusty notions of the clubs. It does not draw poor people as sub-species of the human. It does not recognize class distinctions at all, except for comic purposes. It is brighter, better-informed, bolder, and more humane than anything on this side, and our men in France find its spirit in accord with theirs. One of the results of the War will be that they will want something like it when they come back, though I don't see how they are to get it unless it is imported, or unless they emigrate to a country where to feel that way about things is normal and not peculiar.[53]

If literature encounters impediments to changing the world, these often are the fault of a reader's indifference or prejudice, and of an editor's selection of what the reading public wants.

The reader, however, also has a salutary effect on literature, for he plays an important role in the act of creation itself. Tomlinson states that "Two people . . . go into the making of a poem—the poet and the reader."[54] After commenting that a book can work change as it "conjures up the world we must live in; and we know that words can change that spirit, to give it a new direction," Tomlinson states,

The reader of a book may further the creation of its writer. Whatever fame may be a poet's, his part is to serve, out of a faith in a light that is not, but may come. Without his reader he would be in the dark. There is no light, it cannot be seen, unless it falls on an object. It takes two to make a book, the poet and whoever responds in a like way. The power of art, as of religion, is to bring communion of the spirit.[55]

This spirit of communion is not the prerogative of an elite, as Tomlinson points out in no uncertain terms:

For even if we know of no absolute criteria for the judging of literature, or of any art apart from its technicalities, we need make no mistake about one thing. Art certainly is not, as some commentators would have us believe, a choice and decorative thing set apart for the privileged who have been initiated into its mysteries, as though it were like the cunning collecting of old French clocks or Chinese snuff-bottles. For my part, if literature is not a flowering of life, just as is any rose, then it is no better than any other indoor game.[56]

Tomlinson has assigned to literature the role of changing the world by enhancing readers' perceptions of reality and beauty, and he has demanded that the reader contribute to the act of creation. Although Tomlinson enumerates such barriers to readers' responses as prejudice and the spirit of an age, he implicitly demands that the reader, with the help of a more judicious editor, work to overcome these barriers.

V   The Role of the Author

Tomlinson is less explicit concerning the role of the author in the literary process, but he does require that the writer fulfill specific obligations. In his praise of C. E. Montague, he notes that Montague's "position as a witness is . . . unassailable,"[57] implying that a writer must be able to establish his veracity as an accurate reporter. His criticism of Ruskin's ennobling of warfare implies that an author is responsible for the values he communicates to his readers, and Tomlinson attributes a base motive to Ruskin's success in his argument:

He anticipated those who have been most popular because they made our War entrancing and endurable. He went to the heart of the matter. He knew that the audience which would the more readily agree with him when he made an emotional case for the ennobling nature of war would be mainly of reclused women. He addressed them. So did, of late, some of our most successful writers on war. They, like Ruskin, made their appeal to that type of mind which obtains a real satisfaction, a sensuous pleasure, from contemplating the unseen sufferings of the young and vicarious victim, sobbing, and feeling noble and enduring.[58]

For Tomlinson, Ruskin had betrayed his responsibility by appealing to the prejudices of his audience, and in doing so had acted for no other reason than to have a favorable reception from his readers.

Tomlinson, however, was willing to relieve an author of total responsibility for the way his work might be interpreted, "For that is the way of a word—it grows—and its author is not altogether responsible."[59] However, an author could not evade his responsibility to

communicate truth. Tomlinson demanded that "a writer should be
. . . moved to a controlled passion by the conviction that there is
something new and important to be said to his drifting and casual
fellow men."[60] He criticizes James Joyce's *Ulysses* because, for Tomlinson, the book only says "that there is nothing in it all; that it is not
worth while, and that one may as well be ribald and stick out his
tongue in a noteworthy manner as do anything else. Not so, we sadly
see, did the masterpieces arise."[61] Tomlinson states that "You cannot
do polemical prose like Swift's, let it be hinted, nor like Shaw's,
without positive conviction moved by passion."[62] He refers to "the
deadly wit of Mr. T. S. Eliot's hopeless *Hollow Men* and *Waste
Land*"[63] as evidence that "we have lost our positive convictions, and
so feel no passion."[64]

Tomlinson, unlike Henry James, who demanded that art separate
itself from morality, insists that morality must prevail in art. He
relates an artist's ethical perspective to the artist's veracity and declares that

> Literature and religion have so much in common that, for my part, I find it
> impossible to separate the works of Isaiah and Swift. There is a passion for
> truth in these religious and writing fanatics, a terrible zeal, which puts upon
> what they do the sign of beauty. Some prefer to call it the love of God.[65]

The author who would betray his trust, "The writer who would give
his public what it wants, with his tongue in his cheek, is in the same
class exactly as the other fellow who once took pieces of silver in
payment for treachery. He denies the light."[66] Tomlinson relates
such treachery to the problems of modern civilization:

> We have to remember, for instance, that art and letters, once of first conse-
> quence in a civilized community, have sunk to the level of intricate plays for
> intellectual circles. We might have expected that lapse. When religion goes,
> out goes art. When there is no faith except in material power, how raise a
> joyous song about it?[67]

Elsewhere, he commented that a novelist was born, not made,[68] and
he extends his preference for inspiration over craftsmanship by stating that "the highest things in Art are outside common experience,
and perhaps, as in the case of religion and great music, outside
experience altogether."[69] For Tomlinson, the writer represents more
than a filter of experience or perception:

Literature is different. It is not a profession, if we mean by that a means to food and shelter. It is, in a vital sense, a profession of faith; and it is well known that a man's faith evades every new concrete image to which he would reduce it. The most we can say of his faith is that it is expressed in his work, if his work so interests us that we attach importance to its implications.[70]

In view of the importance of the effects of literature on its readers, Tomlinson could not state the responsibility of the author in less insistent terms than those of a religious profession.

When Tomlinson approaches the relationships between literature and reality, he maintains the necessity of the artist to communicate the truth. His praise of Montague's *Disenchantment* emphasizes the importance of an accurate representation of life.

There was no doubt about its quality as prose. There was no doubt about the truth of it. It was the first real book given to England out of the experience of one of its sons in the war. It will remain where Montague placed it. It is indisputable testimony; it is indisputable, because Montague more than fulfilled the conditions which the implacable bigots set down as tests of patriotism in wartime: much over age, engaged in an "indispensable" industry, he left his family, dyed his hair, persuaded the recruiting officer that he was a game chicken, and went to the trenches in France.[71]

This establishes Montague as a reliable witness to the events he describes.

Tomlinson emphasizes that while many regard books of escape as "a form of cowardice,"[72] they actually increase one's perceptions of reality rather than providing an escape from it:

For all novels, at least, are means by which we can escape from the insistent present, perhaps only to meet worse trouble. If those novels truly are books, and give the mind a sense of precipitancy and danger, then they must have been done by poets who had freed themselves from whatever has us in bond; books, not so much of escape, as of release. When Melville went to sea in a whaler, to get marooned in the South Seas, he did that, he confesses, as a way of escape from a reality he found irksome, and so enlarged his apprehension of Reality, the bounds of which are lost in mystery, as we see in *Moby Dick*.[73]

Tomlinson wishes this enlarged reality to appear in prose style which avoids abstractions in favor of such images as the smell of "unescapable new paint,"[74] and he also prefers to find characters in books who seem, like Conrad's Singleton, immediately recognizable from one's own experience.[75] He argues that "There is a need in literature, as in politics, to clear the mind of cant,"[76] and an author has the responsibility to perform this feat by maintaining the highest quality of veracity in his writing.

VI   *Literary Technique*

Although Tomlinson was explicit regarding the limitations of criticism, the effects of literature, the nature of modern readers, and the requirement that an author bring an ethical perspective to his work, he was less revealing of his expectations of a work in terms of literary technique. He enumerated requirements of a work as a whole without specifying particulars which would fulfill those requirements, partly due to his professed inability to respond to beauty and to analyze it simultaneously. His comments on works of literature in relationship to the requirements of art remain general, which may account in part for the failure of his criticism when applied to specific authors. According to Tomlinson,

literature is an expression of fundamental life, and won't be denied; at its lowest it is an indication of the health of a nation no less certain than a battle fleet and the statistics that prove increasing trade; at its highest it may put us beyond time and chance.[77]

Even when he defines literature, he prefers to remain in the general realm of the whole rather than in the more specific techniques which contribute to an effect. He has defined literature in terms of its content, and he also defines it in terms of the artist: "I suppose a book—what all good people would agree to call a book—is sublimated personality."[78] For Tomlinson, "Style is good or bad according to the spirit which forms it,"[79] and he rarely goes beyond such general criteria when speaking of style.

However, he does indicate some ways by which one can recognize superior style. He describes having heard a "clever young English critic" comment that "to read Whitman aloud was as bad as chewing glass," but another immediately rose to read aloud "Out of the Cradle Endlessly Rocking," and the young critic was refuted:

Nobody spoke after that. There was nothing to be said. Beauty silences us; but we are not the same after we have seen it revealed. The change is incalculable; it is not to be estimated in confessions or set words, but afterwards life is seen differently.[80]

Tomlinson does make one explicit demand of a work, however, when he states: "That is our first demand of prose: that it should know where it is going and how to get there."[81] Beyond this, however, he has little to say of the requirements of style except that even an author does not consciously form it:

Only a bad style can come of artful deliberation, as Oscar Wilde and others have shown. Style depends, first and last, on what a writer has to say, and the kind of man he is. It is not his dress, but the essential man, the man even his friends may not know.[82]

Tomlinson is insistent that a worthy writer does not trouble himself about style except in one sense:

It is certain that a great writer never worries about his style, that ticklish subject in a course of English for aspirants to journalism, and we see the reason for it. Something else possesses the man. The importance of what he has to say controls him, and his chief anxiety is that we should clearly understand it. . . . If this seems a hard saying, then let an unbeliever try to write like Swift.[83]

For Tomlinson, "the problem of style may be left to whoever has something to say."[84]

The problem of interpretation also remains vague in Tomlinson's critical construct. When one asked him the meaning of Walter de la Mare's "Listeners," Tomlinson responded:

What a question to ask a poet or a poet's reader. Who knows? It means nothing, if it means nothing to us. It is like listening to the surge at night. What does that mean? Nothing, perhaps, except to the listeners. What does music ever mean? But what chiefly sounded in that book from our modern poets, I thought, was a melancholy plaint, something far, thin, and weak, that fell into the mysterious silence enveloping life's thickets, and died.[85]

Although Tomlinson is willing to advance an opinion based on his own impressions, he shrinks from making a concrete statement of interpretation or significance. In one instance, after he stated that "there is nothing more important than human relations,"[86] he appeared to judge the effectiveness of Conrad's *Nigger of the Narcissus* on a failure of Conrad's technique.

Conrad should never have shipped that man Donkin. He is not a man, but an unresolved dislike, a blot on a good book. Donkin does a little to spoil the voyage of the *Narcissus*, for Conrad imagined that he had shipped a Cockney; yet Donkin, whenever he speaks, distresses the ear of a Londoner. We do not know his dialect.[87]

This is unusually precise criticism for Tomlinson. More typical is his assessment of Kipling's drawing of character:

If he had watched the Crucifixion, and had been its sole recorder, we should have had a perfect representation of the soldiers, the crowds, the weather, the smells, the colours, and the three uplifted figures; so lively a record that it would be immortal for the fidelity and commonness of its physical experience. But we should never have known more about the central figure than that He was a cool and courageous rebel.[88]

Tomlinson's theory of literature is consistent in his various critical pieces, but his application leaves something to be desired.

VII *Approach to Specific Authors*

Most of his shorter essays on literary figures focused on one or two characteristics of the featured author, or commented on the relation between a writer and his time, or a writer and his reputation, or a writer and his early influence. While such information can be valuable, one expects more than partial glimpses from a literary critic. When Tomlinson wrote about Joseph Conrad, for example, he commented that "I cannot pretend to intimacy with him, nor to complete absorption in his work. There was something in him not to be clearly discerned."[89] Tomlinson knew Conrad, and Frank Swinnerton wrote that Conrad "once walked across a room to H.M. Tomlinson, and abruptly said: '*You* don't think I'm a fraud, do you?'"[90] When Tomlinson wrote about Conrad, he concentrated on the sense of alienation Conrad felt among the English and Conrad's desire "to be taken as English."[91] Most of his comments relate directly to Conrad's almost unique position as an English writer entering the English tradition: "The trouble with almost any foreigner who would serve another tradition is that he treats that tradition with greater reverence than they who were born in it."[92] Even when Tomlinson praises Conrad's achievement, he does so in terms of Conrad's displacement in England.

Again, he had done what no other Englishman had done, and, as it happened, what no other Englishman could do, because the time for it was past; for Conrad contributed to the body of English literature authentic and noble testimony to a phase of British ships and British seamen which had gone and was all but forgotten. Not an inconsiderable achievement. All the same, if another Englishman acknowledged him in gratitude for that, why then it was surprisingly discovered that Conrad was a novelist to whom the sea was no more than a background for a study in psychology. The Englishman ought to have known better than to mention ships and seamen, when paying him a tribute.[93]

One wonders what Tomlinson would have found to say about Conrad had he not known Conrad and the sea personally.

Tomlinson also wrote a short tribute to Robert Louis Stevenson, whose works he admired despite Stevenson's waning reputation among critics. Tomlinson focuses on Stevenson's values as a reason for taking him seriously as a writer.

Stevenson had a literary conscience. He really thought that a writer should never give the public anything less than the best he had. He gave more thought and work to mere expression than some of his latter-day critics give to the matter.[94]

Tomlinson argues that Stevenson had more to him than many are willing to acknowledge.

Stevenson is accused of being without depth, and of not having a philosophic background, and of other defects of that kind, which, of course, make it absurd to name him with Sir Walter Scott. Those critics never give themselves time to remember that Dickens and Thackeray are in the same boat. They, too, were merely generous and compassionate men, who were unusually concerned with the moral problem of conduct. That interest is desirable in a novelist. It is a fair substitute for a coherent and profound philosophy of life.[95]

He proceeds to justify reading Stevenson on the grounds that he is a pleasant author to read, and he argues that Stevenson should be allowed his niche in the temple of literature. Like his essay on Conrad, his essay on Stevenson chooses to follow one line of argument rather than to present a more comprehensive assessment.

Literary influence was also a favored springboard for Tomlinson's critical arguments, and he even applied the approach to his own work. He felt it was important for others to realize that "an early reading of Stevenson's essay on Thoreau . . . disclosed to me not

Thoreau's deficiencies but Stevenson's own,"[96] and that

There have been reviewers who have hinted at origins for my books, but not one of them has ever noticed that I must have brooded long on Walden Pond, in apparition, as a youth. I well remember my schoolmaster rebuking me for frequenting "that moonshine."[97]

He mentioned in his lecture at Harvard that

before I was twenty I was familiar with all Emerson's work. I felt his nudge. And that gave me a further thought. There was a greater teacher than Emerson, and to him I came but a little later. There was a man named Thoreau. I put him with Melville and Whitman, and I could hardly say more than that, except that, when young, I carried his *Walden* about in my pocket, as did many young Englishmen then. . . .[98]

When he wrote a short article dated July 6, 1918, considering Conrad Aiken's *The Jig of Forslin*, Tomlinson attributed shortcomings of the work to another influence.

One cannot help feeling while reading this product of the modern mind that we are all a little mad, and that the cleverest of us know it, and indulge the vagaries and instability of insanity. In an advertisement to Mr. Aiken's poetry we are told that it is based on the Freudian psychology. We are not seldom reminded today of that base to the New Art. We are even beginning to look on each other's simplest acts with a new and grave suspicion. . . . Instead of the truth making us free, its dread countenance, when we glimpse it, only startles us into a pallid mimicry of its sinister aspect.[99]

Tomlinson proceeds to apply this insight to the view of postwar modern man:

Soldiers . . . do not want the truth. Without knowing anything of Freud, they can add to their new and dreadful knowledge of this world all they want of the subconscious by reading the warlike speeches of the aged, one of the most obscene and shocking features of the War. The soldiers who are home on leave turn in revolt from that to hop-scotch. Yes, the truth about our own day will hardly bear looking at, whether it is reflected from common speech, or from the minds of artists like Mr. Conrad Aiken.[100]

One might argue that such restrictions as Tomlinson's focusing on a single characteristic of an author or his work might result from the brevity of his reviews and essays, but his longer critical works are equally unsatisfying, for similar reasons.

VIII   Thomas Hardy *and* Norman Douglas

Tomlinson's acquaintance with Thomas Hardy was less formal than his relationship with Conrad, and his essays include several anecdotes of Hardy. On one occasion Hardy visited Tomlinson and engaged in a battle of wills with Joey, a pet owl. The two tried to stare each other down.

They did not speak; they regarded each other intently, but I do not know what passed between them. Presently the poet turned sadly away; and the owl directed his gaze elsewhere as though entirely satisfied.[101]

In a short article entitled "The England of Hardy," published in 1921, Tomlinson argued that Hardy's reputation would rest on his ability to capture the essential spirit of England in his novels, so that even the scholarly would agree that the opening pages of *The Return of the Native* provided "an Englishman with the thought that there was the origin of his bones, and his nurture, and his destiny."[102] Tomlinson states that "Hardy's sanction to represent us does not come from the critics and readers who are what is called 'literary,'"[103] but from an entire generation which "has grown up accepting the Wessex Novels as a natural feature of its circumstance."[104] The article ends with Tomlinson's claim that

There is a finer and deeper significance, more of our gist, a tonic and native vitality, in Thomas Hardy's works, which will be young and fertile when the work our great statesmen are now doing, a mere apparition of towering importance, is lost with the bones of the young men they sent to the war.[105]

Seven years later Tomlinson, after Hardy's death, published an article on Hardy's latter years and his contribution to letters. He expanded the article slightly for publication in book form as *Thomas Hardy* (1929). Early in the work, Tomlinson provides a disclaimer to the effect that "We cannot stand apart from our personal feelings, and so we cannot be critics, for . . . we ought to consider the work of a poet apart from changeable human opinions, and see it simply as an isolated work of art, bereaved of kinship."[106] After claiming that this is impossible for Hardy's contemporaries, Tomlinson comments on English newspapers' apparent indifference to Hardy's death and the attacks made on Hardy after *Tess of the D'Urbervilles* and *Jude the Obscure* appeared. He then discusses how "A meeting with Hardy was comforting to self-esteem" (*TH*, xiii) and that he appeared "a simple man" whose manner led others to underestimate him (*TH*, xiii-xiv).

Tomlinson comments that Hardy never fully understood how much his characters were part of the English world and then moves to defend Hardy from charges that his characterization might be inferior to that of the Russian novelists.

So what of it? Modern novels are full of characterisation, and, good and bad together, they all soon die. Their candid revelations of character do not save them. So there is a chance, as the story called *MacBeth* still lives on, that we are deceived by what the fashion of the hour declares to be chiefly good in a story. We may as well be called provincial for it as anything else if we decline to displace the author of the Wessex novels. (*TH*, xxi)

After remarking that "the creator of beauty is unaware of what he does" (*TH*, xxii), Tomlinson proceeds to praise Hardy for the immortality of Hardy's characters. He criticizes a "damaging critic" who doubted whether Hardy "wrote more than thirty good poems" and asks, "When is a poet not a poet?" (*TH*, xxvii). Tomlinson ends his tribute by claiming that "Hardy the poet is ourselves, at our best. If there is a God to be known, it is by looking to such a man" (*TH*, xxix).

For Tomlinson,

The poet is not a man apart, without aid for us in the manifold affairs of this busy world, an ineffective dreamer whose vision is unrelated to the things about us, and whose music is but Aeolian and of the empty air. He is the best that the crude realities have created. He is the outcome of all our doubts and strivings. He, if we but knew it, is the true culture and the crowning flower of the mud and compost out of which he and all of us came. He, more than any other man, expresses what is the essential nature of the clay, and what it could be, and perhaps shall be. (*TH*, xxix-xxx)

There is no mistaking Tomlinson's admiration for Hardy and his attempts to identify the sources of Hardy's appeal, but his book as a whole seems discursive and vague. His reliance on personal impressions of Hardy enlivens his narrative, but it did not endear him to Mrs. Hardy, who "wrote some violent and terrible letters, notably to H.M. Tomlinson and to other people who, she thought, belittled life at Max Gate in the last years."[107] Perhaps Mrs. Hardy's unfavorable reception explains why Tomlinson never expanded his book on Hardy and refrained from writing directly about Hardy in "Thomas Hardy Country," published over twenty years later. Even as late as 1953, Tomlinson spent only a few words to describe the company of Hardy, Mrs. Hardy, Siegfried Sassoon, and T.E. Lawrence before shifting emphasis to the modern English countryside accessible in Hardy's work.

Tomlinson's *Norman Douglas*, published in 1931, was more a statement of appreciation than a biographical or critical work. The book rarely alludes directly to Douglas's work, but Tomlinson comments often on the superiority of Douglas's style and the character which that style represents. However, Tomlinson addresses literary issues more directly in *Norman Douglas* than he did in his work on Hardy. He begins by disparaging the critical necessity of dividing books and their authors into genres and attributes Douglas's neglect by critics to Douglas's resistance to categorization.

He has no label, not one that stays on. He has had several, but he has lost them. He wrote books of travel, and essays, and was a critic, and then a novelist; there are plentiful signs in his books that he is also a biologist, a musician, an archaeologist, a linguist, and knows more than a novelist needs to know about trees and herbs; several other things, too. What name can we give to all that?[108]

Tomlinson argues that critics' inability to label Douglas has resulted in their avoiding him entirely, and he proceeds to rectify that lapse. While Tomlinson appreciates Douglas, he dislikes what he considers to be serious flaws. He views *South Wind* as Douglas's deliberate attempt to give the public what the public wants, and he dislikes the amorality implicit in Douglas's monograph on aphrodisiacs.

However, he frequently praises the quality of Douglas's prose style and the inventive freshness of Douglas's mind.

Douglas is of that tribe of nomads, small and select, who find their native English the right rich and various expanse, never to be fully explored, with unexpected but risky pleasances, heights and deeps, where their versatility may wander for a lifetime, and never find tedium for us. (*ND*, 20)

Frequently Tomlinson compares Douglas favorably with D.H. Lawrence, making his most telling point by contrasting Lawrence's "maligning an unknown young man, Maurice Magnus, who wrote a book called *Memoirs of the Foreign Legion* and then committed suicide," and a rebuttal by Douglas entitled "Plea for Better Manners" (*ND*, 34). Characteristically, Tomlinson speaks at length of the contrast between Douglas and Lawrence without providing samples for the reader to compare, but makes the desired result of such comparison clear:

Now as to character, compare the strident dishonouring voice in that introduction to the *Memoirs*, by Lawrence, with the defence of Magnus, by Douglas. Whose opinion would we prefer to seek? Personality, the sum of a man, is clearly of importance in both art and conduct. (*ND*, 35)

Tomlinson indicates his disapproval of *South Wind*, not on aesthetic grounds but on the basis of moral principle. He then returns to the subject of Douglas's neglect by the critics as the result of Douglas's versatility and resistance to classification.

When Tomlinson praises Douglas's style, he becomes more specific than in his other statements:

There are no stylistic flourishes in his prose. It is almost entirely colloquial, the communication of a narrator who is familiar with your capacity and his own; he keeps tactfully within measure. He enjoys telling you this; he never doubts your intelligence, but tries it; he is sure you will be risable, and that you will know what value to give to his extravagance when he is denouncing picturesquely a fond faith you hold. He has no tricks but only the idiosyncrasies of an original man, good-natured and humorous, of whom you will learn nothing but what he chooses to disclose. (*ND*, 59)

After continuing to praise Douglas's style, Tomlinson concludes his book with a statement describing Douglas's attitude:

He is a sad and lonely man, confined to his Chott country, all that is left to him, because that sterile salt depression alone is exempt from potato-planters, military parades, and improvements by politicians. Only in Ultima Thule is there escape for one who can see no health in us, and nothing to be done for us that we would not reject, yet who would still cherish, his only solace, an old memory of fellowship and goodwill, and the thought of the Grecian Urn. (*ND*, 63)

Although Tomlinson's *Norman Douglas* is more than twice the length of his book on Hardy, it seems to have made little difference in terms of what Tomlinson could communicate about his subject. The sincerity of his appreciation is unquestioned in both cases, but except for being slightly more explicit in comparing Douglas with contemporaries and specifying aspects of his work that Tomlinson did not appreciate, Tomlinson did comparatively little with the added space. He digressed more often on Douglas's reputation and participation in the literary arena with contemporaries, but he did not approach literary techniques as such.

In 1952, Tomlinson presented an "enlarged and revised" edition of *Norman Douglas*, but the revision consisted of an introduction entitled "The Man I Knew." Tomlinson described how reading an excerpt of *Siren Land* first drew him to Douglas's work, alluded to Douglas's subsequent withdrawal from the world, and added biographical details such as date and place of birth, schooling, and subsequent career in the Foreign Office before Douglas took up his pen. Tomlinson also described the circumstances under which he wrote *Norman Douglas*—he was approached by a publisher to help "attract the attention of a public which somehow had missed his quality."[109] Tomlinson reports that the book helped neither himself nor Douglas and proceeds to blame this entirely on his mentioning D. H. Lawrence in a tone less that submisive.

According to Tomlinson, his earlier comments on Lawrence had pushed Douglas from mention in the reviews.

To my astonishment and confusion I discovered that I had idled into a sacred place instead, and there had behaved most unseemly. The name of D. H. Lawrence had been written into my secular pages, and his devotees were outraged. Not knowing where I was, so to speak, my careless elbow had upset the candles upon an altar.[110]

He reports that

I have learned since that, long before this, Lawrence had counted me as one of his enemies, I don't know why, except that I kept my head when reading him. What a host of enemies any writer could damn, if he brooded over the multitude which did not rise in reverence before his books![111]

On this note, Tomlinson closes the introduction with a plea:

I have not deleted the offending words in this re-issue of my tribute to Douglas. They must stand. Their old power to offend may have faded from them. I hope so. Salute to Lawrence, who should be saluted. Salute to all the Lawrences. But may Douglas now be allowed his rightful place?[112]

Ironically, Tomlinson's subjective statements met with a purely subjective response that frustrated his purpose in writing his study.

Tomlinson's theory of the shortcomings of literary criticism, the effectiveness of literature, the response of the audience, the role of the author, and the relationship between art and reality were sound enough, but he failed to refine his critical theory so that it would serve him in application to specific authors or works. The recognition that there are no absolute literary criteria should not prevent one from trying to find a relationship between literary technique and final effect, nor should it serve as a rationalization for remaining entirely subjective in one's evaluations of others' work. If Tomlinson's criticism remains unsatisfying to us, I think this results from his too easy surrender to the complexity of the critical task. Had he taken more effort to demonstrate Douglas's virtues objectively and focused on more specific aspects of Douglas's style to argue his merits, Tomlinson might have found his critical appreciation much better received.

CHAPTER 4

The Traveler

I   *Essays of Travel*

ALTHOUGH Tomlinson's reputation as a man of letters is largely that of a writer of travel books, surprisingly few of his full-length works were sustained narratives of travel. For all practical purposes, Tomlinson's full-length travel books number three: *The Sea and the Jungle* (1912), *Tide Marks: Being Some Records of a Journey to the Beaches of the Moluccas and the Forest of Malaya in 1923* (1924), and *South to Cadiz* (1934). He also wrote lengthy essays of travel, notably "Log of a Voyage, 1935" (taken with his grown son) and "After Fifty Years" (a description of his golden honeymoon in the Mediterranean with his wife), but most of his travel essays were comparatively short. This was not entirely his decision, since he wrote most of his travel pieces on commission for such periodicals as *Century*, *Harper's*, and *Holiday*. *Tide Marks*, based on a voyage undertaken for *Harper's*, is a series of chapters which were published separately in article form.

The bulk of collections of essays, widely touted as travel books by reviewers and dust-jackets, consists of essays on other subjects. *Gifts of Fortune: With Some Hints for Those About to Travel* (1926), as D.H. Lawrence pointed out in his review, is not a travel book as such. It begins with a lengthy essay discussing travel in general and contains some anecdotal material derived from previous voyages. "Out of Touch," for example, tells of Tomlinson's meeting a youth during his Amazon voyage. The young man had crossed the Andes to meet a ship, marveled at finding books in Tomlinson's cabin, and admitted that his father was indeed an eminent English judge. The youth comments, "Fancy your knowing my dad. I thought I was quite out of touch here." Another essay derives from Tomlinson's travels to Malaya. "Elysium" describes his meeting with a missionary who dresses for dinner despite his distance from London. Tomlinson notices the missionary's wife, sitting by the shore, staring at the ocean, and the missionary tells him, "She sits there, and when she sees a ship going home, she weeps." (This story also seems to have a literary source. Somerset Maugham's "The Outstation" is also set in Malaya and features a Mr. Warburton who dresses for dinner. Each morning at breakfast his special pleasure is to open a fresh number of the *Times* from its mailing wrapper to read the issue in its entirety. However, by the time Warburton receives his monthly packet of mail, each number is weeks behind date.) Tomlinson also included "The Rajah," a description of a native in outmoded uniform wearing useless spangled decorations, and Tomlinson's fellow countryman tells him that the rajah is "Quite mad, you know. Used to be a rajah until we turned him out, and thinks he's one still. Just as well to humour the poor old thing."

While these essays contribute a flavor of travel, they do not make *Gifts of Fortune* a travel book, and the collection also includes essays commenting on Melville and Conrad, traveling widely about one's own suburb in the manner of Thoreau, riding in a motor car, visiting the zoo at Regent's Park, and speculating that when archeologists investigate the remnants of civilization, they will discover only "corks and bottles." *Gifts of Fortune* is not solely about travel, but other works labeled "travel books" are even less so: *Old Junk, London River, Waiting for Daylight, Under the Red Ensign, Out of Soundings,* and *The Face of the Earth*. This is not to detract from Tomlinson's reputation, but to point out that his well-deserved fame as a master of prose style has not resulted entirely from travel essays.

•When his contemporaries regarded Tomlinson as a travel writer, they were quick to focus on his communication of an attitude. Frederick P. Mayer, in his pioneer analysis of Tomlinson's style, noted that

Tomlinson . . . gives his readers enthusiasm. For him the world is born new every morning. He has never lost a boy's pleasure in a new sight or sound or smell. That, in an old world, ought to assure him of fame. Tomlinson has never sought eternal youth—he is the eternal youth. Men who grow old lose the capacity for enjoying things . . . .

This youth, or freshness, is a quality of good literature. We must grant Tomlinson much for it. Many wise men regret its passing.[1]

Mayer also notes that this freshness does not detract from the maturity of Tomlinson's approach, and J.B. Priestley tries to identify the source of that maturity. After commenting that Tomlinson looks like a "hard-bitten city clerk" and "a gnome, who has come up from some elfin solitude to observe the stir of things on the bright surface of the world," Priestley suggests that

These two contradictory appearances bring us close to the secret of his unique power as an essayist of travel. His work would not have the force it has unless he were at once the city clerk, that is, the man who knows the life of the dark streets, and knows what it is to escape, and the elfin recorder, with such a wealth of exact yet luminous imagery, who travels here, there, and everywhere in search of strangely significant facts.[2]

While "strangely significant facts" were always of interest to Tomlinson, he did not see the purpose of travel essays as arming his readers with arcane dialect or descriptions of the outlandish. He described *The Sea and the Jungle* as an "honest" book of travel, and he tried to present in his prose as realistic an impression as the traveler who followed him would receive.

Tomlinson thought, and wrote, often of the requirements of travel narrative. After arguing that Thoreau should be among those respected for writing excellent travel books, he asks,

What is the test for such a book? I should ask it to be a trustworthy confidence of a kingdom where the marches may be foreign to our cheap and usual experience, though familiar enough to our dreams. It may not offer, but it must promise that Golden City which drew Raleigh to the Orinoco, Thoreau to Walden Pond, Doughty to Arabia, Livingstone to Tanganyika, and Hudson to the Arctic. The fountain of life is there. We hope to come to our own.[3]

Tomlinson preferred to emphasize the "trustworthy" nature of the travel essay. On board, Tomlinson "had the saloon to myself, and tried to read from a magazine I extracted from my pillow. The first story was rollicking of the sea, and I have never seen more silly or such dreary lies in print."[4] When he criticized the Reverend Frank Tatchell's *The Happy Traveller*, he indicated what he wished to see in travel writing:

But what I sought in his volume was not the Malay for Thank you, which he gave me, but what set him going. Why did he do it? There is a word frequently seen in glossy narrative, "wanderlust." The very lemmings must know it. It excuses almost anything in the way of travel lunacy, even to herding with Russian emigrants for fun. It is used as a flourish by those who hope we will fail to notice that they are uncertain what to do with themselves. Mr. Tatchell, however, does not use it once.[5]

Tomlinson does not dismiss Tatchell's book, but indicates what he feels is wrong with it:

Mr. Tatchell himself was decidedly a happy traveller, and the cause of happiness in others—his book can be commended in confidence—for he admits that his method of enjoying himself in a strange bed is to sing aloud the aria, "Why do the Nations?" But he does not tell us what sent him roving, nor does he produce any collection of treasures, except oddities such as the warning to white men about approaching the behinds of elephants, and Vinakka vinakka! (Fijian for Bravo).[6]

He is appreciative of the obscure, but prefers to see it in the context of the voyager's personality, ideals, and ambitions.

Tomlinson, commenting on the nature of travel books, reveals one reason why he traveled so widely during his lifetime:

My journeys have all been the fault of books, though Lamb would never have called them that. They were volumes which were a substitute for literature when the season was dry. A reader once complained to me, and with justice, that as a literary feuilletonist I betrayed no pure literary predilections. "You never devote your page," he said fretfully, "to the influence of the Pleiades. You never refer to eighteenth-century literature. You never look back on the names familiar to all who read Latin. What is interesting to truly curious and bookish people might not exist for you. I wonder, for example, if Nahum Tate were mentioned in a conversation, whether you would be able to say what it meant?"[7]

After stating that "Our literary predilections were cast at our birth,"[8] Tomlinson reports that with a pile of books for review beside him, he remains

Sitting in the shade, looking absently at a dazzling summer afternoon just beyond the chair, for I had just read with close attention this fragment of English prose:
"From three to nine miles north-eastward of the northern part of Sangi is a group of islets named Nipa, Bukit, Poa, and Liang, respectively, and about nine miles farther eastward is a chain of six islets and two detached reefs, which extend about nine miles in a north-north-east and opposite directions . . . ."
Then there followed, for over 300 closely printed pages, references to many outlandish names, probably occult, such as Busu Busu ("good drinking water may be obtained from a spring at the foot of the hill behind the missionary's house"), ...[9]

Tomlinson justifies his preference on the basis of realism:

I would sooner read any volume of directions for Pilots than the Latin poets. (And I should like to ask whether Ceram Laut has not been sighted since 1898). On the whole, I would much rather sit in a cabin of a ship which had just made fast again, and listen to the men who had brought her home, than read the best modern fiction. I should feel nearer to the centre of life.[10]

He recalls, in another essay,

How different was the day when Stanley's *Through the Dark Continent* was published! That caused enough excitement. Africa then was really dark, and he had traversed it by taking one step after another. . . . His book is almost forgotten now—nobody, as far as I know, ever called it a good book of travel—but on the day of its publication the brown stacks of it at Mudie's were besieged. I could not get near it for a week.
No book of travel will ever again rouse that interest.[11]

After discussing other examples, including a modern description of a dramatic jaunt in an airplane, Tomlinson provides a succinct criterion for travel literature: "Prose is good which gives no more than that vivacity; and perhaps that is the most we should expect from a narrative of travel; it is enough to prompt us to make the journey with the writer."[12] All his travel essays so prompt his reader.

Unlike Tatchell and other travelers whom he criticized, Tomlinson provides specific reasons for his jaunts, although the reasons do not always reflect the pleasure that Tomlinson evidently took in the experience of travel itself. In "Exploration," published in *Out of Soundings* in 1931, Tomlinson suggests escape as a motive for wandering:

But we are not satisfied. A vague desperation is suggested in our tours round the world. Something is missing from our civilization. Perhaps we think that the farther we go the more likely we are to recover whatever it is we have lost. It is possible that the Communist risings in the Garden of the East come of the same disquiet which sends rich Westerners circling the globe.[13]

Five years later he noted that "A deal of the attraction of that almost inaccessible spot by the shore of the frozen sea was the long and difficult journey thither, by canoe and dog-sledge,"[14] adding to the dimension of escape a distinction noted a decade earlier by Priestley, who called it "hard escape."

Priestley notes that the task of a reporter "is to be an onlooker, an eager spectator, an epicure of vivid pages, and nothing more. . . .

But such a one as H.M. Tomlinson revolts against being a mere spectator, against his task of finding new adjectives with which to conjure up the vision of death and disaster."[15] Although this could refer to Tomlinson as a writer against war, Priestley carefully specifies the "hardness" of Tomlinson's travel writing:

And even where the War was not in question, the position of such a writer as Tomlinson would still not be easy. If he goes to sea, it is not as a seaman, who can lie back and think no more about things once his watch is done, nor yet as a mere passenger, who knows nothing, who is all innocence, merely so much superior freight. Thus he is condemned never to take things easily, and has more responsibility, in the honest depths of his mind, than the skipper himself, for the skipper has only the ship and the crew and the freight on his back, but this brooding spectator of heroic routine has skipper, ship, crew, freight, the wide sea itself, on his back. Naturally despising the rôle of mere idle spectator, delicate and heartless collector of sensations, he has no alternative but to feel passionately about the life he has escaped into, to share—as it were—every watch, climb to every mast-head, to go down with every doomed ship.[16]

Although Tomlinson's travels may have provided escape from the mundane scenes of landbound drudgery, they were never an evasion of his ethical responsibility.

II *Stylistic Devices of Travel Writing*

In a revealing comment, Tomlinson wrote that "I have never made a voyage for pleasure."[17] At the time the statement was published, 1934, it was true in at least one sense. His early excursions, including his voyage up the Amazon which resulted in *The Sea and the Jungle*, were journalistic assignments for the *Morning Leader*. His subsequent journey to Malaya resulted from commission by *Harper's* after Tomlinson severed his connection with the *Nation*, and virtually every travel essay he wrote was on assignment. Tomlinson often assumed the pose of a reluctant traveler who could not evade the demands of his editors and who, perforce, only left his wife and family under protest. An early essay, "The African Coast," which Tomlinson originally published in 1907, began in this fashion:

I shall not forget the silliness which gave me my first sight of Africa. The office telephone bell rang. "Oh, is that you? Well, we want you to go to Algeria at once." I went downstairs hurriedly to disperse this absurdity. But it was no

good. I had to go. And because I was argumentative about it they added
Tripoli and Sicily, which served me right. After all, while in Africa one is
necessarily absent from Fleet Street. I should have remembered that.[18]

Two years later, after a meeting with his brother-in-law resulted in an
invitation to travel in an ocean-going steamer up the Amazon and into
the South American interior, Tomlinson attributed his subsequent
voyage to editorial caprice:

I never gave that preposterous suggestion a second thought, but I did write,
for a lively morning newspaper, my sailor's mocking summary of what that
strange voyage might have in store. The editor, a day later, met me on the
office stairs. "That was an amusing lie of yours this morning," he said. I
answered him that it was written solely in the cause of science and navigation;
and what was more, I assured him earnestly, I had been offered a berth on the
ship for the proof of doubters. "Well," said the editor, "you shall go and prove
it." He meant that. I could see by the challenging look in his eye that nothing
much was left about which to argue. He prided himself on his swift and
unreasonable decisions.[19]

The characteristic reluctance of Tomlinson to voyage became part of a
persona he was to develop in the course of writing travel narrative.
    His voyage to Switzerland followed the same pattern, if more
playfully.

This time I must go to Switzerland. There was no escape, I was assured. The
command to go—it amounted to that—had that note of imbecile frivolity
known to every man who is advised by an editor to depart; for it was assumed
that I should enjoy the experience, but preferred to pretend, such was my
obstinate humour, that I should hate it. What was the reason for the journey?
Winter sports. And the Olympic games would not draw me across the road,
even for the minute when the international quarter-mile race is being run;
though it is true a sprint across a field, without a stop-watch, in an effort to get
to a gate before a bull, is well worth watching.[20]

The implied, if tongue-in-cheek, resentment against such editorial
demands explains much of Hankey Todd in *The Day Before*, Tomlinson's 1939 novel. Tomlinson does not use this device at the beginning
of *Tide Marks*, probably in the interest of trustworthiness since he
accepted the assignment from *Harper's* when it became clear that
Massingham would leave the *Nation*, but he reported his resistance
to the assignment that resulted in *South to Cadiz*.

There was also, that morning, a voice at the telephone, an authoritative voice, yet reproachful, as though sadly expecting only the accustomed answer to its bright suggestion of good; it was the voice of a busy editor.

"No," I answered it. "I can't. I won't."

What! The far voice at once enlarged close and loud with indignation. It was as though the editor had burst into the room to sack me.[21]

Like editors before him, this one approached Tomlinson with the argument of obligation:

This, I heard most distinctly, was the limit. Here was a matter of public duty. It could not be refused. Did I know what I was talking about? This Economic Conference was our Last Chance, as near as he could see it. And how did I like the look of that? I murmured that I liked it no better than the Thin Edge of the Wedge; for what I really lacked was the courage to hang up the receiver and go away. The editor then tried persuasion. I wouldn't have to go far to this conference he assured me; only to the Geological Museum.[22]

Tomlinson rang off, and when the telephone began again, "I knew what that ring meant. He was pursuing me, and I was sure to be caught. Editors never give up."[23] Tomlinson's young daughter comes into the room, and ignoring the ringing telephone, Tomlinson walks with her into the garden where the bell cannot be heard. After a few minutes, however, he is summoned to return to the house and

had to carry my guest indoors. The telephone receiver was handed to me gravely; it could not be avoided, this. At first, though intent, I did not understand. I fancied the voice at the other end was mistaken. It supposed it was addressing another man; that man, too, was to go to Spain, at once, whoever he was. Wrong number?[24]

This reluctant traveler, subject to the whims of unreasonable editors, was a suitable persona for Tomlinson's purposes. It enabled him to assume the stance of a traveler who does not like his assignment and therefore, whether the reader likes it or not, will only report reluctantly. This enhances the reader's credence since the traveler is not trying to impress an audience with his spirit of adventure or his marvelous observations. He is merely trying to finish an unsought task. This attitude changes as Tomlinson, in spite of himself, becomes enthusiastic, but by then he has established his trustworthiness and can convey his sense of wonder to his audience. The persona has become an important part of the flavor of Tomlinson's travel essays.

Another distinguishing trait of his travel writing is his use of anecdotal material. Not only can he use the device to comment on the marvelous or unusual, but he can maintain his stance of objective reporting by confining the fabulous to hearsay. In *The Sea and the Jungle*, for example, Tomlinson meets an English shipping clerk who tells him about Captain Davis, of Barry. Davis, in the course of drinking with the clerk, admits that he has become tired of boat-running jobs and wishes to return home, where a friend owns a pub. The clerk notes of Davis that "Over his left eye he had a funny hairy wart, a sort of knob, and whenever he got excited it turned red."[25] Davis begins to inquire of the clerk where he can obtain a shrunken head for his friend's pub and the clerk tries to persuade Davis to abandon the notion. Shortly afterwards business takes the clerk away for a year, and when he returns he learns that Davis has disappeared. The clerk dismisses thoughts of Davis and then tells Tomlinson that "A month ago an American civil engineer touched here, and had to wait for a boat for New York." The American had been in the jungle, surveying, and had acquired a number of souvenirs which he no longer desired, including a collection of butterflies. Something wrapped in a ball of newspaper, however, the American planned to keep.

"Then the Yankee picked up a ball of newspaper off the floor, and began to peel it. 'This goes home,' he said. 'Have you seen anything like that? I bet you haven't.' He held out the opened packet in his hand, and there was a brown core to it. 'I reckon that is thousands of years old,' said the American.

"It was a little dried head, no bigger than a cricket ball, and about the same colour. Very like an Indian's too. The features were quite plain, and there was a tiny wart over the left eyebrow. 'I bet you that's thousands of years old,' said the American. 'I bet you it isn't two,' I said."[26]

Tomlinson frequently includes such tales in his works, but he carefully excludes them from direct observation and allows the reader the option of believing or disbelieving the English shipping clerk who told the tale.

Another device which Tomlinson employed frequently was the authorial intrusion. Tomlinson often reminded the reader that he was subject to the limitations of travel narrative, that several conventions of travel books governed his writing, and that he was trying to maintain scrupulous honesty. In *London River* Tomlinson pointed out the limit placed on unrestricted veracity:

I got to the ship's side in time to see a liner's bulk glide by. She would have been invisible but for her strata of lights. She was just beyond our touch. A figure on her, high over us, came to her rail, distinct in the blur of the light of a cabin behind him, and shouted at us. I remember very well what he said, but it is forbidden to put down such words here.[27]

Frequently in *The Sea and the Jungle* Tomlinson reminds the reader that this is a travel narrative:

Christmas Day. In case it has become necessary for me to show again the symbols of verity, as this is a book of travel, here they are: "Lat. 37.2 N., long. 14.14 W. Light wind and moderate swell from S.W. Vessel rolling heavily at intervals. 961 miles out. Miles by engines 226. Actual distance travelled (because of the swell on our starboard bow) 197 miles." I cannot see that these particulars do more than help me out with the book, but as they have been considered essential in narratives of voyaging, here they are, and much good may they do anybody.[28]

He often asserted his trustworthiness, as in his statement early in *The Sea and the Jungle*: "This is a travel book for honest men."[29] While such interjections are not so common as to distract a reader, Tomlinson never allows his reader to forget who is writing the book.

A fourth trait of Tomlinson's travel narratives is his vivid description of his observations, including a realistic presentation of the hardships of voyaging, often presented with sardonic wit.

If the Garden of Eden had been anything like the Amazon jungle, then our first parents would never have been evicted; they would have moved fairly soon on their own account, without giving notice. . . . Tigers, snakes, lovely but malignant nymphs, and head-hunters are not the dangers. What kills men in the wilderness is anxiety, under-nourishment, and mosquitoes.[30]

On occasion, Tomlinson presents paragraphs of pure sensory description without philosophical embellishment, as in this passage from *The Sea and the Jungle*:

Your glance caught a wave passing amidships as a heaped mass of polished obsidian, having minor hollows and ridges on its slopes, conchoidal fractures in its glass. It rose directly and acutely from your feet to a summit that was awesome because the eye travelled to it over a long and broken up-slope; this hill had intervened suddenly to obscure thirty degrees of light; and the imagination shrank from contemplating water which overshadowed your foothold with such high dark bulk toppling in collapse. The steamer leaning that side, your face was quite close to the beginning of the bare mobile down, where it swirled past in a vitreous flux, tortured lines of green foam buried far but plain in its translucent deeps. It passed; and the light released from the sky streamed over the "Capella" again as your side of her lifted in the roll, the sea falling down her iron wall as far as the bilge. The steamer spouted violently from her choked valve, as it cleared the sea, like a swimmer who battles, and then gets his mouth free from a smother.[31]

He devotes the same care for descriptive language to his rendering of people, jungle scenes, unusual smells, and even the taste of new foods.

Another trait of Tomlinson's travel style is his sense of irony, frequently heavy-handed. He mentions his reading

a recent narrative by an American writer, who had been collecting in Africa for a museum. He confessed that if he had not been a scientist he would have felt some remorse when he saw the infant still clinging to the breast of its mother, a gorilla, whom he had just murdered; so he shot the infant without remorse, because he was acting scientifically. As a corpse, the child added to the value of its dead mother; a nice group. That tableau, at that moment when the job was neatly finished, must have looked rather like good luck when collecting types in a foreign slum. He must have felt happy when skinning the child.[32]

After this expression of almost Shavian disgust with the scientific attitude toward animals, Tomlinson follows with another instance, Shavian in its pointedness:

Some years ago, on the arrival of fresh news at headquarters in France of another most ingenious and successful atrocity, I remarked to a Staff officer of the Intelligence Department that if this sort of thing developed progressively it would end in the enforced recruitment of orang-utans. "No good," he replied. "They wouldn't do these things."[33]

In another passage he regrets the encroachment of civilization on the remote places of the earth.

We find satisfaction, which need not be altogether misanthropic lunacy, in the thought of unprofitable deserts and waste lands. Some parts of earth, we may be assured, will remain exempt from the effects of our appalling activities. Let us pray for more power to the mosquito's elbow on the Amazon and such places.[34]

Many of Tomlinson's ironic expressions are lower keyed and more succinctly put, however, as his comment on finding a concrete quay in Casablanca reveals: "Then we might have been in France; and the French, as civil engineers, could improve Utopia into Detroit."[35] Of the devices enumerated—persona, reported anecdote, authorial intrusion, sensory description, and irony—the last reveals a source of weakness in Tomlinson's sustained travel narratives. In the process of reporting his travels, Tomlinson increasingly yielded to a desire to polemicize on the state of the world, the folly of progress, the destructive impulses of man, and the pessimistic outlook for the future of modernity. In the case of his later travel narratives, such a focus detracted from the appeal of his style.

III *"The African Coast"*

In 1907 Tomlinson completed "The African Coast," a piece of approximately eight thousand words describing his journey to Algeria, Tripoli, and Sicily. His resistance to his editor unavailing, Tomlinson dutifully takes his journey but hardly mentions Algiers. After noting pessimistically that "the barometer, wherever I am, seems to know when I embark,"[36] he devotes few words to Algiers, boards the French ship *Celestine*, and bids Algiers farewell. Unlike most writers of travelogue, Tomlinson devotes a few lines to the dreariness of tourism:

I had travelled from Morocco to Algiers, and was tired of tourist trains, historic ruins, hotels, Arabs selling picture-postcards and worse, and girls dancing the dance of the Ouled-Nails to the privileged who had paid a few francs to see them do it.[37]

Tomlinson turns his attention to the characters aboard the ship, including the solicitous skipper whose efforts to improve Tomlinson's enjoyment of the menu do not assuage his petulance:

He has an idea I cannot read the menu, so when an omelette is served he informs me, in case I should suppose it is a salad. He makes helpful farmyard noises. There is no mistaking eggs. There is no mistaking pork. But I think he has the wrong pantomime for the ship's beef, unless French horses have the same music as English cows.[38]

Tomlinson describes the "black Mediterranean," which can be "as

ugly as the Dogger Bank" in December, and he turns his attention to
the suffering deck passengers: "What those Arabs suffered on deck I
cannot tell you. I never went up to find out. At Bougie they seemed to
have left it all to Allah, with the usual result."[39] The irony of the
persona who travels to Algiers but has nothing to say about it and who
reports sufferings that he refused to observe is an agreeable change
from many travel essays.

His first view of Africa is also unusual:

Now you understood why it was called the Dark Continent. It looked the
home of slavery, murder, rhinoceroses, the Congo, war, human sacrifices,
and gorillas. It had the forefront of the world of skulls and horrors, ul-
timatums, mining concessions, chains, and development. Its rulers would be
throned on bone-heaps. You will say (of course you will say) that I saw Africa
like that because I was weary of the place. Not at all. I was merely looking at
it. The feeling had been growing on me since first I saw Africa at Oran, where
I landed. The longer I stay, the more depressed I get.[40]

However, Tomlinson brings himself to disembark at Sfax, where his
narrative picks up a bit. He sees a "venerable fellow with an important beard, with a look of wisdom and experience,"[41] and even as he
regrets his lack of Arabic, the fellow addresses Tomlinson in English.
Tomlinson sits down to engage in conversation which rapidly exhausts
the Arab's vocabulary, but others gather to watch the Moslem "draw
his finger across his throat in serious and energetic pantomime, and
saw me nod in grave appreciation, when he was trying to make me
understand what was his sympathy for the Christian conquerors of
Sfax."[42] After removing himself from this encounter, Tomlinson
quickly finds himself involved in another with an Arabic huckster.
Joining his "outrageous tourist tweeds with the graceful folds of the
robes" in the crowd about the huckster, he has a sudden revelation:

The huckster kept glancing at me, and from grave side-long glances that
crowd of men went to the extraordinary length of grim smiles. Suddenly I
recognised the trick of that Arab cheapjack. It may be seen at work in Crisp
St. Poplar, when a curious and innocent Chinaman joins the group about the
fluent quack.
    As soon as dignity permitted I passed on, and my dignity did not keep me
waiting for any length of time.[43]

Tomlinson, jarred into involvement, begins observing the sights and sounds around him, and the reader, like Tomlinson, finds himself intrigued by the sights and sounds of a strange marketplace.

He begins the final section of his essay with a personal description of the appeal of foreign places, and it is the more convincing after he has described his temporary funk.

You probably know there are place-names which, when whispered privately, have the unreasonable power of translating the spirit east of the sun and west of the moon. They cannot be seen in print without a thrill. The names in the atlas which do that for me are a motley lot, and you, who see no magic in them, but have your own lunacy in another phase, would laugh at mine. Celebes, Acapulco, Para, Port Royal, Cartagena, the Marquesas, Panama, the Mackenzie River, Tripoli of Barbary. They are some of mine. Rome should be there, I know, and Athens, and Byzantium. But they are not, and that is all I can say about it.[44]

This passage, characteristic of Tomlinson, invites immediate identification with the reader by free use of the second-person pronoun. Tomlinson even draws the reader into his descriptive passages in this manner, as he did in the description from *The Sea and the Jungle* of the *Capella* weathering a rough sea. When Tomlinson reaches Tripoli, one of the names that has aroused his imagination, his description becomes vivid:

Tripoli, like other towns on these shores, looks as though it were sloughing away. Where stones fall, there they lie. In the centre of the town is a marble triumphal arch in honour of Marcus Aurelius. Age would account for much of its ruin, but not all; yet it still stands cold, haughty, austere, though decrepit, in Tripolitan mud, with mean stucco and plaster buildings about it. The arch itself is filled in, and is used as a dwelling. Its tenant is a greengrocer, and the monument to Marcus Aurelius has an odour of garlic; but it need not be supposed that that was specially repugnant to me. How could the white marble of Marcus, to say nothing of a warmer philosophy no less austere, be acceptable to our senses unless translated, with a familiar odour of garlic, by modern greengrocers?[45]

"The African Coast," short though it be, gives some indication of the direction his longer travel narratives will take: a highly personalized view of the world, an almost intimate accord between writer and reader, and an apparent disregard for reporting places or events except as they involve Tomlinson's interest or his mood.

IV   The Sea and the Jungle

Alva Gay's assessment of Tomlinson as a travel writer, which she wrote for a 1958 festschrift, results from her reading of *The Sea and the Jungle* and concludes with a quotation from it:

Without question, it seems to me, he belongs to that noble fraternity of travellers among whom are found the James Boswell of *A Journal of a Tour to the Hebrides*, the Thoreau of *A Week on the Concord and the Merrimack Rivers*, the George Borrow of *The Bible in Spain*, the Charles Doughty of *Arabia Deserta*, the George Gissing of *By the Ionian Sea*, the Henry James of *The American Scene*, the Norman Douglas of *Old Calabria*, the D.H. Lawrence of *Sea and Sardinia*, the E.E. Cummings of *Eimi*. Of such as these Tomlinson may be said to write, and it can be written of him as well: "We borrow the light of an observant and imaginative traveller, and see the foreign land bright with his aura; and we think it is the country which shines."[46]

Since Tomlinson often invited identification with Thoreau, Doughty, and others on the list, it seems a fair assessment. However, in *The Sea and the Jungle*, Tomlinson revealed some difficulties in unifying a narrative of substantial length and left some pertinent questions unanswered. This is relatively harmless to the work's effect, primarily because of the strong appeal of characteristics named by Christopher Morley in his 1928 introduction to the Modern Library edition. First, "Although it is a book of escape, it is not a book of flight from reality. Heavens, no! There is not a page in it that does not exhale the strangest flavour of veracity. . . ."[47] Second, the book contains "a tapestry of pictures and episodes" which one could discuss "indefinitely. For here is richness, here is the scrutiny of a wise and grave and tender mind, swift to every movement of pity and loveliness."[48] Third, there are

the three or four interpolated yarns, plummed in with such startling effect—yarns brilliant enough to make the reputation of any fictioneer. Each has its own co-efficient of truth, which you can gauge for yourself, and you'll come upon them unexpectedly and thereafter read them aloud when fit company is gathered. Sandy's tale of Handsome Jack, for instance; the story of the Steam Shovel; the fable of the Tiger in Hampshire; Captain Davis's Head.[49]

In a later introduction, V.S. Pritchett found that

Tomlinson's manner is a mixture of the poetic, the Biblical and the scientific; he is all metaphor, yet he is all event and fact. The combination is novel and powerful, and, from a literary critic's point of view, Tomlinson's prose has to be seen as the last fling of that style which runs from Meredith to Stevenson, Belloc and C.E. Montague.[50]

The devices that add appeal to Tomlinson's travel writing, mentioned above, receive full play in *The Sea and the Jungle*, but occasionally his discursive style, which tends to favor the part more than the whole, disrupts the organization of his book as sustained narrative.

Tomlinson begins *The Sea and the Jungle* with a comment warning the reader implicitly that this is not going to be a book conforming in all particulars to the usual travel narrative.

Though it is easier, and perhaps far better, not to begin at all, yet if a beginning is made it is there that most care is needed. Everything is inherent in the genesis. So I have to record the simple genesis of this affair as a winter morning after rain. There was more rain to come. The sky was waterlogged and the grey ceiling, overstrained, had sagged and dropped to the level of the chimneys. If one of them had pierced it! The danger was imminent.[51]

He proceeds to describe his unexpected meeting with the skipper, not specifically identified as his brother-in-law, and the skipper's subsequent persuasion that Tomlinson accompany the *Capella* as ship's purser. Tomlinson, in the role of the city's prisoner, asks,

"What . . . shall I do about all this?" I waved my arm round Fleet Street, source of all the light I know, giver of my gift of income tax, limit of my perspective. How should I live when withdrawn from the smell of its ink, the urge of its machinery?

"*That*," he [the skipper] said. "Oh, damn that!" (*S&J*, 7–8)

After the skipper extends his invitation, Tomlinson finds himself committed to the voyage, but he spends a few pages talking of his feelings, warning the reader that his travelogue will leave land when he does, and preparing to embark. On the *Capella* Tomlinson acquaints himself with the ship's officers and men, discovers in his conversations with sailors about the Plimsoll Line that he has not left politics at home, weathers a storm, and begins to understand the mystic identification of a sailor with his ship. He also meets the ship's doctor, who

tried me with such things as fevers, Shaw, Brazilian entomology, the evolution of sex, the medical profession under socialism, the sea and the poets. But
my thoughts were in retreat, with the black dog in full cry. It was too cold and
damp to talk even of sex. (S&J, 33)

Tomlinson's duties as a purser were comparatively light, judging from
how seldom he spoke of them, but he found several subjects to
occupy the reader while he waited for the ship's arrival in Para.
    In addition to discussing the superstitions and loyalties of sailors,
their activities battening down hatches and resisting an angry sea,
and their conversations, Tomlinson described their foibles. One
sailor, named Chips, becomes upset when he cannot find his Victoria
Cross, and Tomlinson helps in the search. The object was discovered
in Chip's sea chest, and as Chips was securing it,

a low foreign sailor snatched it from him. The Cross fell to the deck. I
recovered it from the feet instantly in a white passion, and chanced to look at
it. It confirmed that one, named Chips here, was something in the Royal and
Ancient Order of Buffaloes. (S&J, 51)

After one sailor has related the tale of Handsome Jack, a fable recalling Rip Van Winkle, and Tomlinson has heard the English shipping
clerk's tale of Captain Davis's head, the *Capella* prepares to sail from
Para to the interior. The ship takes aboard sixty head of cattle,
including an extremely rebellious heifer, and proceeds upriver, combining river travel with the irritants of the jungle. Tomlinson inter-
jects to speak directly to his reader:

If you find any pleasure in maps, flying in shoes of that kind when affairs
pursue you too urgently (and I suppose you do, or you would not be so far into
this narrative), you will hardly thank me when I tell you it is possible for an
ocean steamer exceeding 23 feet in draught to make such a journey, and so
break the romance of the obscure place at the end of it. (S&J, 160)

Tomlinson proceeds to discuss the efforts of American engineers and
other invaders of the jungle to bring civilization to the interior and
then confides, halfway through his narrative, that

The Madeira-Mamoré Railway has been recommenced, and our steamer, the
"Capella," is taking up supplies for the establishment at Porto Velho, from
which the new railway begins, three miles this side of San Antonio. (S&J, 165)

Since the ship was literally in the jungle, Tomlinson had ample opportunity to describe flora and fauna, usually in connection with anecdote.

Then there are the other things which, so far as most of us know, have no names, though a sailor, wringing his hands in anguish, is usually ready with a name. Today we had such a visitor. He looked a fellow the Doctor might require, so I marked him down when he settled near a hatch on the after-deck. He was a bee the size of a walnut, and habited in dark blue velvet. In this land it is wise to assume that everything bites or stings, and that when a creature looks dead it is only carefully watching you. I clapped the net over that fellow and instantly he appeared most dead. Knowing he was but shamming, and that he would give me no assistance, I stood wondering what I could do next; and the cook came along. The cook saw the situation, laughed at my timidity with tropical forms, went down on his knees, and caught my prisoner. The cook raised a piercing cry. (*S&J*, 187)

Tomlinson saw enough of insect life to conclude "I do not wonder Bates remained in this land so long; it is Elysium for the entomologist" (*S&J*, 190). For a time, Tomlinson speculates on the absurdity of regarding the richness of Brazil merely as a source of rubber, and eventually the *Capella* arrives at Porto Velho. The contrast between the efforts of the ship to arrive and the "bland indifference of Porto Velho to the 'Capella', which had done so much to get there" (*S&J*, 211) amuses Tomlinson. He meets several interesting people, including Neil O'Brien, whose rumored "dangerously inflammable nature" prevented Tomlinson from finding "common footing with him for some time" (*S&J*, 215). He also meets others who have tales to tell, including the story of the Steam Shovel.

Tomlinson, becoming restless, failed to convince others to accompany him into the jungle beyond Porto Velho, but providentially an American, "Marion Hill, of Texas," invites Tomlinson to take a holiday in the jungle, and although the captain of the *Capella* warns Tomlinson that "if I returned too late I should have to walk home" (*S&J*, 263), he accepts the offer. After some exploration, fearing that he will be too late to sail home with the *Capella*, Tomlinson participates in a madcap dash back to Porto Velho by way of railroad handcar. At one point Hill and Tomlinson fear that they will collide with a locomotive, only to discover that what they had mistaken for a headlamp was a firefly. They return the night before the *Capella* sails homeward, and Tomlinson plans to accompany her until he learns that the *Capella's* return journey will be leisurely. When the ship docks at Tampa, Tomlinson takes the train to New York and then returns to England on a Cunard liner. When he arrives at Paddington Station and is met by his son, Tomlinson ends his book.

The Sea and the Jungle provides fascinating reading, although it raises some questions of plausibility which Tomlinson did not resolve. For example, his taking a chance of missing his return trip home, thereby risking a lifelong sojourn at Porto Velho, requires more explanation than Tomlinson's boredom. Years later, in an interview with John Gunther, Tomlinson indicated other areas where he might have been more complete in his rendition.

And what happened to O'Brien, the adventurer in "The Sea and the Jungle"?
  "O'Brien," commented his discoverer, "was hanged."
  Did Mr. Tomlinson see again the Doctor in "The Sea and the Jungle," whom he left behind precipitously in Para? He did. Doctor James is one of his best friends.[52]

Gunther's questions reveal a curious lack in Tomlinson's travel book. Very few individuals, including his brother-in-law and the people he met on his journey, are named. One man is merely the skipper, another Chips, another the Chief. Those few who are identified, such as O'Brien, are almost inaccessible should one wish to verify the travelogue, while others, such as Marion Hill of Texas, would be extremely hard to locate. There is no reason to doubt Tomlinson's veracity, but despite the charm of his anecdotes, the authenticity of his descriptions, the playfulness of his irony, and the force of his personality, a reader sometimes receives the impression that some episodes are imperfectly unified with the basic narrative, while some details remain unnecessarily vague.

V Tide Marks

Tide Marks (1923) presents different problems than does *The Sea and the Jungle*. In his earlier work Tomlinson could draw not only from his own inexperience with a long ocean voyage and the nature of the Amazon jungle, but also from the drama inherent in an ocean-going vessel's journey more than two thousand miles inland. *Tide Marks* begins with less drama, but in one sense Tomlinson more than compensates for the lack of ready-made adventure. Frederick P. Mayer comments,

To read "Tide Marks" and see how surprising it is to Tomlinson to set sail on a ship; to see how splendid all the sailors are and how glorious every prospect (nor is man vile), is to be convinced that Tomlinson never rode a ship before. You believe he is young, inexperienced. You become startled to learn that although he may be easy to surprise, he is not young in years or in experience. You wonder at his fifty or more years.[53]

The quality of enthusiasm, of freshness, tends to overcompensate for the lack of spontaneity in Tomlinson's movements.

In "Tide Marks," Mr. Tomlinson describes a splash bath, one of those tropical inconveniences by which many Europeans on tour have kept themselves clean. Now, a splash bath, I am told, is a novelty, rudimentary, honest, but nevertheless a very ordinary and sometimes messy substitute for the delights of sanitary bathing. To the traveler weary of civilization, it may seem refreshing in its Biblical simplicity, but it is, after all, a splash bath.

But to Mr. Tomlinson there never was such a thing as a splash bath! There never will be again so splendid, so delightful, so humorous, so insinuating a diversion as a splash bath! It pleases him in the same unmeasured way as a tin toy gratifies a youngster. He will not eat, he will not sleep, he will not work while he has a splash bath.[54]

Mayer qualifies his description of Tomlinson's enthusiasm, however, by noting that "Tomlinson plays with his delight in a thoroughly knowing and sophisticated way"; he realizes "his own extravagance and sometimes plays on it. That takes some of the sting away."[55] In *Tide Marks* this exaggerated extravagance mitigates the absence of a structured plot of circumstance which helped *The Sea and the Jungle* to grip its reader.

Tide Marks has several traits in common with *The Sea and the Jungle*, however. Tomlinson embellishes his account with anecdotes, descriptions of interesting characters, tongue-in-cheek comments on other travelogues, and powerful description of natural and man-made phenomena. However, he frequently comments negatively on the nature of man's progress and also, every time he meets a fellow European, introduces the subject of the Great War. Like his other books of travel, *Tide Marks* begins with a view of Tomlinson's life in London. His editor, Massingham, "was on a journey to interview the proprietor, to learn whether he should continue to hold up a lamp in a dark and naughty world, or blow it out. Oil costs money."[56] Tomlinson, at this point, has been visited by a one-armed man selling Christmas cards, and he inquires how the man lost his arm. The veteran replies that "if you were a nice lady, I'd say it was cut off by a

German on the Somme" (Tide, 4), but actually he was bitten by an
Army mule.

Although he does not specify this in Tide Marks, Tomlinson agreed
to travel and write for Harper's after Massingham severed his connection with the Nation. Then Tomlinson began his voyage. While
crossing the Red Sea, he converses with his skipper about the hazards
of sailing, and the captain tells him a story of a ship striking an
uncharted rock in the Red Sea which eventually becomes an important part of the plot of Tomlinson's novel All Hands!

When Tomlinson enters new realms, however, the quality of his
description reveals several changes. Instead of trying to describe in
wholly sensory language, he constantly comments on the significance
of what he sees and its relationship to civilization.

I regretted I could not seek his opinion about Java, a land that was a serious
disappointment to me some time before I reached it. The gorgeous East
obviously could not be, and ought not to be, so gorgeous as Java's holiday
posters, which are in the style of the loudest Swiss art. "Come to Java!" Well,
perhaps not. Not while the East Indies are so spacious and have so many
other islands; not if Java is like its posters. Why should the East call itself
mysterious when it advertises itself with the particularity of a Special Motor
Supplement? (Tide, 89–90)

Tomlinson's stop at his first Javan port, Tanjong Priok, results in his
abandoning ship in the face of mosquitos' onslaught, and he decides
to take the railway from Tanjong Priok to Batavia. According to the
guidebook and to actual observation, black monkeys remain on one
side of this track while gray monkeys remain on the other. Tomlinson
is weary of hearing about this fact from fellow voyagers.

By the time you have persuaded the customs officer that you have no
explosives in your luggage, that your face and its photograph in the passport
really do approximate, and have got the man from the hotel at Weltevreden to
understand that you intend to go by train and not in an automobile already
wrecked, the monkeys are forgotten. (Tide, 91)

Soon after the train begins to move, however, a friendly Dutch
traveler points out this over-reiterated fact to Tomlinson. "I was going
to ask him whether they would forfeit the government subsidy if they
broke the contract and spoiled the story" (Tide, 91), but Tomlinson's
peevishness passes and he "nodded, and looked first at the black

tribe, and then at the gray, to show him that his good nature was not wasted on me."

Tomlinson's observations of Java confirm a pessimism which had begun to grow before World War I.

The Javanese agriculturists, ever since they had a civilised government—and that was early in the Christian era—have had to make their fields meet the extortions of so many conquerors before they dared to call any rice their own that now they deserve the glowing testimonial of all directors of empire and great business affairs. Their training has been long and thorough. Hindu, Mohammedan, and European each has taught them the full penalty for Adam's fall; and so the habit of very early rising, and of a long day in the sun, with but a meager expectation of any reward, give them the right aspect of sound and reliable workers. (*Tide*, 100–101)

As the work proceeds, however, Tomlinson's funk declines, as it did in "The African Coast." When a diminutive native lady tries to sell him works by Ethel M. Dell, his irony is more gentle, and he moves to a characteristic source of amusement in his travels—his refusal to follow guidebooks or to view such wonders as the "ancient Buddhist tope at Borobudor." An eminent archeologist informs Tomlinson that "It is probably the only chance in your life to see one of the most remarkable temples in the world" (*Tide*, 108), and after Tomlinson has resisted the notion ("Why, if Buddha were to come to Java, Borobudor is probably the one place he would be careful to avoid!"), he concludes that there is no escape from the Borobudors of the world. However, as he wanders about the marketplace and muses on the sights and sounds and smells, he successfully forgets Borobudor until he is on a train, departing for Sourabaya,

when an official from my hotel, whose anxious face was peering into every coach, presently found me. There had been a mistake. I had not paid for my motor-car to Borobudor. It had waited for me all day. Borobudor? (*Tide*, 115)

This is a more amiable Tomlinson who continues to surface in various comments. He notes at one point that Celebes "has received less critical attention than Laputa" (*Tide*, 139) and proceeds to rectify that lamentable oversight, meets an adventurer named Maguire with whom he explores part of the jungle, suffers himself to taste durian (which he finds horrible) at the behest of a missionary who finds the fruit as tempting as the mythical lotus, scales the walls of Ternate, a volcano, and generally becomes a more active participant in his travels. However, despite the growing enthusiasm that Tomlinson feels as a result of splash baths and his scaling of Ternate, he cannot forget bitter memories of the war. "But for the durian, the spell of Ternate might not have been broken," but when he returns to his rest-house, he encounters a strange smell.

What was that? I forgot the crimson lories. My memory had gone straight back to an old German dugout with its decaying horrors. I thought I must have been mistaken, but advanced cautiously. Nothing could be there, I told myself, that was like the trenches of the Flers line. Confidence returned; the suggestion had gone. Then the ghost passed me again, invisible, dreadful, and I clutched the table, looking round. (*Tide*, 193)

The smell comes from the durian, which Tomlinson can barely abide but which he samples rather than hurt the feelings of the well-meaning missionary.

He continues his narrative in better spirits, but he restricts himself to recounting a series of episodes (often using the form of diary entries) to describe his progress. This book becomes a pleasing mixture of history, misadventure, suspense, and humor. At one point he states:

In 1906 the Dutch were at war with a rajah of the island, who came out with all his court in a sortie, not with the intention of fighting, but of dying to escape dishonor. Brahma does not seem to encourage Falstaffs. (*Tide*, 210)

On ship, Tomlinson views the perplexity of the mate, who has discovered women in the crew's quarters, ostensibly selling matches. When the mate appeals to Tomlinson for advice, fearing to lose his crew,

I assured him that certainly this was a matter which only our captain could decide. The captain would know what ought to be done, for not only is he an experienced navigator, but a member of the Dutch Reformed Church. I am neither. (*Tide*, 212)

Tomlinson and another Englishman, Smith, decide to take a trek through part of the jungle, and shortly after Tomlinson has defied the laws of probability by successfully using a slippery log as a bridge over a river, his companion Smith lay down on the trail, too fatigued to move.

Poor Smith was indeed on his back. He had propped his head on his helmet, and he confessed that this heat and fatigue were outside his specification. He was finished. He could not go another step. While kneeling beside him, pointing out that he was yet too young to give himself as food for ants, I noticed that my breeches were bloody and had to touch the leeches off my legs with my pipe. This was our introduction to those indefatigable creatures. The revulsion was mental, not physical. It is a shock to see the worms feeding on you before their time. Such haste is unseemly and not by the rules. I glanced at Smith, and then saw a group of them attached to his belly. He had not noticed them. How soon he was up! How well he stepped out! Even leeches can have their good points. (*Tide*, 241)

The prevailing tone of *Tide Marks*, despite such diversions, remains somewhat pessimistic. Even on Tomlinson's return home, when he inquires of a sailor about a rumored SOS call, he learns that the ship had put about because a young hand had gone overboard. "The passengers complain of a draught" (*Tide*, 289), the sailor reports before returning to his business. However, on his return, sighting at night the formless shadow that was England, Tomlinson muses that perhaps the presence of England

may have been retired within the night, dominant on its seas, making no sign, knowing the supreme test of all its labors was at hand, vigilant but composed, waiting for another morning to dawn in the hearts of men, when there should be light to build the City of God. (*Tide*, 295)

The ending of the travel book holds some promise of hope, but as a whole *Tide Marks* suffers from Tomlinson's increased pessimism following World War I. Rarely does his narrative proceed more than a page without a reflection, a grim reminder, of the nature of the civilization which a traveler is escaping. Tomlinson, carrying his taboos with him, has no escape, nor does his reader. John Gunther, in his interview with Tomlinson, raised questions about omissions in *Tide Marks*.

And what happened to McGuire [*sic*], the Irish adventurer who was turned by war to the East, and who had a better time among tigers in Borneo than with corpses in France? Mr. Tomlinson, after an expedition with him to the jungle, leaves McGuire in a very precarious situation indeed. What happened to him?

"Oh," said Mr. Tomlinson, "he got out, of course. Only fever could kill him."[57]

Gunther also notes that Tomlinson abandoned his boat to scale Ternate and wonders why, as well as how he managed to return.

"I was tired of knocking about," Mr. Tomlinson told me, "and I wanted to see
something of the life of those islands. I just got off the boat. I knew another
one would come along—some day. One did."[58]

These answers may seem somewhat flippant, but I think they reveal
something about Tomlinson's attitude toward the purpose of his travel
writing, both a justification and a source for such conflicts between his
record of his experience and its plausibility. For Tomlinson, such
details were trivial compared with his feelings at the time, the immediacy of his experience, and the significance of his observations.
His attempt to render his travels vivid, partly aided by the exaggerated enthusiasm Mayer has noted, also accounts for the lack of
attention he has paid to transitions between episodes. For Tomlinson,
his journey was not a unified whole so much as a string of unpredicted
adventures occurring *seriatim*. Perhaps his desire to maintain his
veracity prevented his embellishing to provide more plausible expla-
nations or transitions. In his final sustained travel narrative Tomlinson demonstrated that his alternative was to present a unified work at
the expense of the appeal of his style.

VI   South to Cadiz

South to Cadiz (1934) is the least satisfying of his travel books,
although it employs the same devices that had worked previously. It
is less a travelogue, however, than a commentary on such aspects of
modern life as the role of culture, the revolution that resulted in the
Spanish Republic, the role of machinery in modern life, and the
prospects of war. Included are digressions concerning the successes
and failures of democracy and the sad state of world economics during
the Great Depression. The book begins with Tomlinson's characteristic attempt to evade the demand of his editor that he cover the
Economic Conference in Spain. However, he makes his journey with
three other journalists—James Bone, Robert Lynd, and Horace
Horsnell, to whom he extends apologies in his dedication of the
book—and Tomlinson spends almost all his time in their company.
When the four cross the Channel to Calais, one recalls that "on the
last occasion, . . . he stumped ashore there with a gun."[59] Tomlinson
describes passing scenery and such occurrences as himself and a

railway porter's referring to each other as *caballeros*, but the focus of
the beginning chapters is on the discussion of such literary matters as
Ruskin's never having seen the French abandon Amiens and
Hemingway's *Death in the Afternoon* presenting a better picture of
Spanish countryside than their view can offer. The four discuss
Lawrence as a novelist, the detrimental impact of nationalism, and
related topics. The discussion is entertaining, but not what a reader of
travel books expected.

When the four arrive in Madrid, Tomlinson begins to explain why
this book is different.

We found ourselves in the Plaza de las Cortes. That this was Madrid was fairly
certain, but we saw at once that if there is an old Madrid it is only a fable to
furnish songs for guitars and gramophones. The city looked what it is, the
outcome of a political need for a central place where the government could
reach out more easily all round. (*South*, 35)

When the four, after a brief separation, convene at a *taberna* called *El
Cocodrilo*, Tomlinson describes the works of a caricaturist, Bagaria,
on the tavern's walls.

Their line was simple but extravagant, their colours surprising, and their
subject preposterous. It is doubtful if even Mr. Grock, whose adventures
seemed to be the story these walls serialized, could have won that coy and
languishing expression into the face of a lady crocodile, but there it was.
(*South*, 45)

At the insistence of Robin, the group's art critic, the four seek more of
Bagaria's work in a newspaper office in Madrid. They work their way
into the office of *El Sol*, where they view Bagaria's caricature of
"about sixty of the world's famous men, ancient and modern, each
holding a refreshing cup. His selection from our English notabilities
is curious. I found only Shakespeare, Dickens, Darwin, Herbert
Spencer, and Oscar Wilde" (*South*, 47). Tomlinson's description of
the work's effect recalls his earlier ironies:

About all this representation of the men the world reveres plays a merry
hooting so cruel in its uncanny divination into frailty that it would keep
Jupiter indoors, if he thought Bagaria was looking up to the clouds; though I
do not think that Spaniard wastes much time gazing heavenward. Shakespeare and Dickens have slightly intimidated the artist, and his effort to show
respect for them must have given him a dreadful internal spasm; and he

appears to have gone through the same agony of composure for the sake of El
Greco. (*South*, 47)

In Toledo Tomlinson also devotes some time to overt description,
mixed with history.

Nor does it matter which way you turn, for you are sure to get lost. Confused
by the romantic signs at every corner of the long, mixed, and sombre glory of
this occult city, getting lost is quite right. This was a capital of the Goths,
portentous early with the row over Arius, for Protestantism began reasonably
soon after the Apostles left it to us to do our best. Then the emirs and caliphs
came, and protestants of all kinds, for four centuries, had to be tactful. The
Christians returned to Toledo a few years after William the Norman landed at
Hastings, and the Cid became its alcaide. Its archbishops began their empire
of souls and bodies with an authority few emperors have possessed, or even
desired, and ruled for ages with a magnificence which lingers. You enter the
remaining glow and shadow of it. The glory of confident power subdues
doubt, but its very brightness is the cause of the dread which lives dumbly
within the cold gloom it casts. (*South*, 57)

The emphasis has shifted from a description of sensory impressions to
one overshadowed by historical and political significance. The same
trait occurs in a description of Cordova, which, according to a
guidebook, had become

a hot and dreary barren.
    Very likely it is that, when compared with what it was when the Arabs
ruled it, for Cordova under its Califate in the tenth century was the most
civilized city in Europe. The Moors left this region a garden, but the
reforming swords of the Christians were not the proper tools for irrigation
works, which therefore lapsed. . . . The same religious severity destroyed
the public baths in Cordova, and abolished the libraries and the learning with
the trees. (*South*, 88)

However, the description, even with its moral point, is less severe
than the above introduction would suggest:

As we saw the valley, its corn, olives, vineyards, oranges, and pomegranates
were sufficient to lessen the threat of stony barrens, should our morality ever
cease to be eager for the punishment of tolerance, and should we lose our fear
when faced by knowledge which is strange. As a barren, it is doing as well as is
asked of it. (*South*, 88)

The pattern continues throughout. Tomlinson asks, "Is the generous

spirit gone which shaped the cathedrals?" (*South*, 116) and sees the
mean spirit of civilization lurking in barrens and ruins.

In Cadiz he returns to the spirit of anecdote that pervaded his
earlier works, but the nature of Spanish anecdotes is political. He
reports the conversation of Mr. Pablo, who

gossiped quietly of the revolution. You could see it gave him pleasure to have
a journalist listening to him. That revolution was nothing. It was not bloody.
It was only like an orange, which falls when it is very ripe. No trouble, no
trouble at all. The people of Cadiz, sir, are always reformers. They had been
waiting for it how long? and then the day came. Then they went into the
streets. People must go into the streets when there is a revolution, a fiesta.
Certainly there was a little burning, but the people were polite. He himself
saw that. There was no cruelty. He himself watched, and the reformers went
into a church, and came out holding pictures, and other things which are in
churches, in their arms, to burn them. But they were not angry. There were
many people in the square, and a man who was carrying a picture of the Holy
Family to burn pushed it into Mr. Pablo, but he was not rude. He said,
"Excuse me. I am truly sorry to crush you." (*South*, 129)

Shortly afterwards the four journalists encounter a Briton, and
Tomlinson has an opportunity to report an anecdote more to his style.
This man and his friend Bill had been on the *Serpent*, and Bill had
taken photographs as the German *Potsdam* sank. Bill had not realized
how important such an exclusive photograph would be to Fleet Street
journalists, but he soon discovered its value as he was besieged with
offers for the photograph. Befuddled by so many willing to pay
unheard of sums for the photograph, Bill sold it to a man who
promised to have the balance of the payment for him on Monday. Bill
returned to his ship a day late as a result, and since this occurred in
wartime, he was sentenced to five years' imprisonment. Malaga also
provides an opportunity for an anecdote, this time concerning the
confusion of the Spanish workmen when they learned that their king
had fled the revolution. They wanted to burn a church, but they were
advised not to burn something that was their own. Instead, they were
advised, since they insisted on burning something, to kindle the
house of the priest after warning that unfortunate cleric.

Tomlinson ponders the meaning of this and related adventures
hoping to discover something of value. During his reflections he
realizes that "I had found Granada, but felt I had lost it as soon as I had
found it. Its savour had gone" (*South*, 156). However, he ends the
book on a hopeful note by noticing that after sundown,

at last I saw Granada. It was no more than one bracket-lamp showing the
bluish walls of a street corner at a great depth, a street either in this age, or
that of the Moors. Anything might have entered that limited nimbus. It was
ready. I watched for the spirit to move whatever was to come, though nothing
came while I looked down. Yet you would see that a significant drama was
possible; and what a drama it could be! Beyond that lamp, and the black
ravines about it, the spread of Granada was the inversion of the lighted
heavens. It was a lower density of stars, unwinking and glacial. The universe
was a hollow sphere, and the constellations continued below me uninter-
rupted. Granada was part of the Galaxy. (*South*, 157)

Tomlinson seems to find meaning in his final view of Granada, but
South to Cadiz, more reflective and less optimistic than his previous
travel books, brightens and fades like a spirit fighting depression. The
remembered pleasures of the earlier style occasionally surface, but
submerge under the weight of various philosophical and political
reflections. It becomes lighter at the end, but for how long?

Tomlinson's three major travel books—*The Sea and the Jungle*,
Tide Marks, and *South to Cadiz*—demonstrate the impact which
World War I and the postwar years had on Tomlinson's ability to put a
cheerful face on the world. The techniques of the travel books do not
change, but their proportions do. The three works reveal a marked
decline in the entertainment of Tomlinson's enthusiasm and irony,
and a corresponding increase in the philosophical seriousness with
which he viewed even the commonplace. I do not feel that his later
writing uniformly reveals a growing pessimism, but it became more
difficult to maintain the light touch in longer narratives as Tomlinson
became more assured in his perceptions of impending disaster.
Perhaps this is why, after 1935, he changed his approach to the
literary marketplace. Except for *Mars His Idiot* (1935), Tomlinson's
publications consisted of essays printed in periodicals or gathered in
collections. His only attempts at longer sustained narratives were his
novels.

CHAPTER 5

The Chronicler of London and the Sea

I The Shipping Tradition

BECAUSE he was born in a shipping parish in the days of oak and hemp, Tomlinson was witness to several changes in the shipping trade. He saw the emerging dominance of the steamship over sailing craft during his young manhood, and he was also able to see the effects that such change wrought on the men who sailed. His awareness of the significance of what he had seen resulted in his resolve to make others aware. In 1944 he wrote:

My days of the sailing-ship, though fairly recent, are with Columbus.

I resolved in the first shock of this surprise that some day, and the sooner the better, landsmen, who are most of us, must be told of it.[1]

Tomlinson, in several articles and three books, often told of it. He was ever sensitive to the significance that the shipping trade has had on all aspects of British life, and he found the prevailing ignorance of Londoners of what they owed to the sea appalling.

He resolved to remove that ignorance, chiefly by writing three books on the subject. *The Foreshore of England, or Under the Red Ensign* (1926) tells of the nature of the shipping trade, the effects of modern changes on sailors, and the political and economic influences on marine commerce. *Below London Bridge* (1934), illustrated with photographs, provides a tour of the London Docks. Tomlinson's text is an appreciation of the Port of London Authority (PLA), the role of the docks in English history, and the changes brought to the docks by modernity. *Malay Waters: The Story of Little Ships Coasting Out of Singapore and Penang in Peace and War* (1950), in addition to showing Tomlinson's lack of concision in his titles, relates the history of the Straits Steamship Company and its adventures in the Orient. His interest in his subject began when he was still a child, and it endured even after his vision of progress and warfare became a disillusionment that dulled his interest in other aspects of modern life.

Tomlinson could hardly have avoided his abiding interest in the
sea. It was in his blood. His maternal great-grandfather was an officer
of the East India Company, and his grandmother eloped to marry a
gunner in the Navy. Tomlinson's father was a sailor and his Uncle
Dave was once a bo'sun of a China clipper. One of his early memories
was the portent of a portrait falling from its place while its subject,
Tomlinson's uncle, was at sea.[2] After the death of his father compelled
Tomlinson to contribute to the livelihood of his mother and three
younger brothers, Tomlinson found himself a clerk in a shipping firm,
where his imagination naturally turned to the sea.

I am thinking now of a periodical, quarto size, with orange covers, which was
renewed upon it weekly, and reported the name of every ship then loading in
the Thames, the port to which she was bound, her tonnage, her class in
Lloyd's Register, her captain, her loading brokers, and the date of her
departure. I gave that periodical attention as close—and for no better
reason—as I gave to Ballantyne's "Ungava" and "The Young Fur Traders." I
used to choose my voyage every week. That took time—the firm's time.[3]

The firm's time also suffered whenever Tomlinson was to pass a
shop—Hughes of Fenchurch Street—which displayed navigational
instruments in its window.

Tomlinson's duties also occasionally took him to the docks.

One day, I remember, a boy had to take a sheaf of documents to a vessel
loading in the London Dock. She was sailing that tide . . . . It is unlucky to
send a boy, who is marked by all the omens for a city prisoner, to that dock, for
it is one of the best of its kind.[4]

Invited to join the improbably small ship on a voyage to the Brazils,
he turned down the offer.

And observe what we may lose through that habit of ours of uncritical
obedience to duty; see what may leave us forever in that fatal pause, caused
by the surprise of the challenge to our narrow experience and knowledge, the
pause in which we miserably allow habit to overcome adventurous instinct! I
never heard again of the Mulatto Girl [sic]. I could not expect to. Something,
though, was gained that day. It cannot be named. It is of no value. It is, you
may have guessed, that very light which it has been admitted may since have
gone out.[5]

The same fascination that caused him to regret not having boarded
the *Mulatto Girl* ultimately led him to his adventures as a traveler,

notably on the voyage up the Amazon which he described in *The Sea and the Jungle*.

Tomlinson became an historian of shipping deeply aware of the loss of a tradition, and although he recognized the value of such changes as the addition of wireless and improvements in navigation, he mourned its passing. In an article entitled "The Ship Herself" Tomlinson presented the history of the ship's transformation in that context:

Over sixty centuries of maritime history ended with the passing of sail at the beginning of this century; that is something like a revolution, yet it has barely been noticed. In Lloyd's *Register of Shipping* for 1880, most of the ships are sailing craft, and the superior steamers listed are rarely above 2000 tons. Now the steam engine and the engine that explodes oil are obsolescent. The new word is atomic.[6]

His article reveals that he has done his homework, tracing the history of ships from the early days of sailing and noting such events as the *Great Eastern*'s being the first screw steamer to cross the Atlantic, but most of Tomlinson's writing about the sea came from living sources. Returning to Hughes of Fenchurch Street,[7] Tomlinson met Mr. Hughes and

learned that his shop was a sort of club for navigators and explorers, even of the air. Sir Clements Markham, the explorer and once president of the Royal Geographical Society, used to call, and H. M. Stanley, and Grenfell of Labrador, and Captain Slocum, the first man to sail round the world single-handed, and the Antarctic men, Scott, Shackleton and Evans. After the seamen came the pioneers in the air. In fact, in the history of Hughes, the associated famous names include Cody and Hamel, of the early days of flying, and Bligh of the *Bounty*; and back of that, too, for it was whispered that an ancestor of Mr. Hughes was a 17th Century privateer, and was sentenced to be hanged for acts upon the high seas. Could there be another shop in London like it?

Such sources of information were more agreeable to Tomlinson than written records, and most of his history reflects his love for anecdote.

Discussing the elusive problem of finding the longitude and the inability of a navigator even to determine latitude "When the weather is dirty, without sun or stars," Tomlinson reports:

A great reward was offered for a clock that would keep a constant rate for a long period in any temperature, wet or dry, and no matter how a ship was tumbled about; a riddle to make good clockmakers laugh, and pass on. John Harrison, a Yorkshire carpenter and mechanician, took up the matter seriously, and claimed the prize; though not for many years later, in 1761, did a chronometer of his invention go in *H.M.S. Deptford* for a voyage to the West Indies.

At this point, he shifts to the anecdotal style which so frequently enlivened his travel narratives:

Nine days out, by the ship's log and dead reckoning, the ship was at longitude 13°50′ west of Greenwich meridian. A son of Harrison was aboard, and denied it. He stood by his father's watch. He said that the ship was 15°19′ west, and that tomorrow Madeira would be sighted; and on the morrow there the island was.

Tomlinson's love for anecdote often invigorates his narrative at the expense of the continuity of his article. For example, after discussing the chronometer and noting that "the value in a new idea takes long to become common sense, [so] it was as late as 1825 before chronometers were ordered to be part of the outfit of all ships of the British Navy," he discusses the development of the compass from its possible use by Norsemen through Columbus's report of variations of the needle to devices to compensate for adverse influences which would deflect the needle. After finishing with the compass, Tomlinson shifts to Nathaniel Bowditch, who wrote *Practical Navigator* in 1802, which "remains a standard work to this day." Later, as master of the *Putnam*, Bowditch returned from the West Indies to Salem, in Massachusetts, eager to spend Christmas at home. December 24, 1803, however, was a day of impenetrable blizzard.

There can be no sights in a snowstorm; and the storm increased in violence and density. It was time to heave to and wait for a break; the New England coast is highly dangerous if a lookout cannot see the end of the bowsprit when heading for land. Bowditch, however, was so sure of his reckoning and his position that he sailed right in, and made his Salem wharf on Christmas night.

Although most of his shorter pieces on shipping attempted to provide history in leisurely reading, aiming more at entertaining than at informing, they reveal Tomlinson's continued preference for an anecdotal style.

    When Tomlinson considered the role of a chronicler, he related it closely to a sense of place. He knew the Docks and London in the perspective of their tradition, and he frequently reminded his readers of the history behind sights common to him.

There are many Londons. There is one for each of us. A chance glimpse of the right place, the legendary London with its sonorous name, the view my friend desired, of the city itself, with the river that saw the coming of the Romans, the crowning of William the Conqueror, and the departure of the ships to form in Virginia the first permanent English colony in America; the streets that Shakespeare walked; where Milton was born, that was full life to Doctor Johnson, Lamb, and Dickens; a view of that London putting into the traveler's heart the faith that now he knows more than can be told, that prospect comes not of precise direction but of a happy conjunction of events in the hour.[8]

When he speaks of Bankside, on the south side of the Thames, he combines his description of the place with a comment on two renowned London artists.

Bankside is wharves gone out of shape, an ugly power station and a brewery, warehouses, and a tavern or two that suggest survival from a remote past. It is not delectable. You won't find tourists there. Rembrandt could have made a priceless picture of it. Shakespeare knew it well; but it was different in his day, with bear-baiting, and profuse provision for other unholy delights. When he was not busy at the Globe Theatre, which stood here, he learned nearby at leisure, from sailors of experience, the right words for the harsh opening scene of *The Tempest*. When Sir Christopher Wren wanted to know how his new cathedral looked, as it was going up, he crossed to Bankside to view it.[9]

Whenever he describes the London Docks, he tries to communicate his feeling of kinship with England's past to his reader.

You will then pass Wapping Old Stairs and the place of Execution Dock; and Rotherhithe (Swift tells us that Lemuel Gulliver lived there) marked by the tower of St. Mary, its parish church, where lies Christopher Jones, master of the *Mayflower*.[10]

Tomlinson conveys to his reader the sense that England is so steeped in its past, which is inseparable from the sea, that one cannot avoid the sense of lasting tradition.

Although he remains fascinated by Britain's naval tradition, Tomlinson is as eager to dispel myth about it as he was insistent that a traveler be honest in his accounts. The sea may have romance, but it does not derive from the myth of the "bluff sea-dog," which Tomlinson attributes to Parson Fletcher's *The World Encompassed*, "That quaint and pious narrative by Fletcher of Drake's circumnavigation of the globe."[11] Tomlinson's objection to the Drake legend is its injustice to Drake. Fletcher's narrative provides "an early indication of the simple man's instinctive aversion from the attributes of a mind which is superior,"[12] and Tomlinson proceeds to discuss the intellect required to accomplish a voyage such as Drake's,

in uncharted seas where the problems were so abruptly challenging, so different from the commonplace of home waters, that the natural fearful doubts of crews had to be allayed with the continual successful determination of lurking shallows and unknown landfalls. Such a task required the maintenance of an art, and a faith in loneliness amid an alien world, possible only to men able to think and live apart.[13]

He would prefer his readers to examine such legendary figures as Drake in terms of what their monumental tasks required of them.

Drake must have known, as Cook certainly knew, that it is the incompetent leader, or the ill-advised leader, who is almost sure to meet in his enterprise with those tragic happenings that bring a venture to ruin, and make what romantic commentators call "an epic story." Drake understood, as did Cook, that the chance of tragedy frustrating a venture may be lessened by prudence, good knowledge, and bold judgment. Such explorers do not set out to find an epic story, but to add to verified things and the welfare of their fellows. Drake was an imaginative man, but his essays with the unknown were under the control of a patient and calculating mind.[14]

He would require his readers to view the characters and events of history in the light of reality rather than in that of romance.

Despite his denigration of romantic notions, Tomlinson was aware that something valuable had been lost as a result of modernity's encroachments on the sea. Edward Weeks, editor of the *Atlantic Monthly*, described Tomlinson's reaction to the sight of the Docks during World War II:

"Look there," said Tomlinson, and he pointed to the quadrangle. "The American clippers used to dock there. On those quays were three tiers of warehouses with arcades and pillars. The ships lay along the walls beside the big arcades, with the masts above the top—and it was a sight. I've seen so many ships there you could walk from deck to deck, half across the water. Their bowsprits were like the boughs of trees." Now there was not a ship in sight. "Gone—it's all gone," said Tomlinson.[15]

Twenty-five years earlier, however, Tomlinson noted the passing of a feeling of kinship among voyagers who could escape the "cruel misery of man" by going to sea. "All men at sea were his fellows, whatever their language, an ancient fraternity whose bond was a common but unspoken knowledge of a hidden but imminent fate. They could be strangers ashore, but not at sea."[16] The ability to isolate oneself from the woes of the world has passed with the introduction of the wireless:

But all that is gone now. The sea is poisoned with a deadly sorrow not its own, which man has put there. The spaciousness of the great vault above the round of waters is soiled by the gibbering anxieties of a thousand gossipers of evil, which the ship catches in its wires, to darken the night of its little company with the gloom of distant malignity and woe. It is something to retain a little of the light of the days at sea which have passed. They too had their glooms, but they came of the dignity of advancing storms, and the fear which great seas put in the mind of men who held a resolute course nevertheless, knowing that their weird was one which good seamen have faced since first the unknown beyond the land was dared; faith, courage, and the loyalty of comrades, which all the waters of the world cannot drown. But the heart of man, which will face the worst the elements can do, sickens at the cruelty of his fellows.[17]

Tomlinson notes the passing of something important which was not based on romantic fancy, but was once part of the reality of the sea and made it attractive.

For Tomlinson, the shipping trade was an inseparable part of London's tradition, and he often relates it to his own parish, Poplar.

The flags which Poplar knew well would puzzle London now—Devitt and Moore's, Money Wigram's, Duthie's, Willis's, Carmichael's, Duncan Dunbar's, Scrutton's, and Elder's. But when lately our merchant seamen surprised us with a mastery of their craft and a fortitude which most of us had forgotten were ever ours, what those flags represented, a regard for a tradition as ancient and as rigorous as that of any royal port, was beneath it all.[18]

Although many Londoners may have forgotten this part of their heritage, it has not disappeared. He ends his reminiscent essay, "An Old Lloyd's Register," with a description of the present:

And there in that light was a laden barque, outward bound, waiting at the buoys. She headed downstream. Her row of white ports diminished along the length of her green hull. The lines of her bulwarks, her sheer, fell to her waist, then airily rose again, came up and round to merge in one fine line at the jibboom. The lines sweeping down and airily rising again were light as the swoop of a swallow. The symmetry of her laden hull set in a plane of dancing sun-points, and her soaring amber masts, cross-sparred, caught in a mesh of delicate cordage, and shining till they almost vanished where they rose above the buildings and stood against the sky, made her seem as noble and haughty as a burst of great music. One of ours, that ship. Part of our parish.[19]

Tomlinson, looking over the Docks with Edward Weeks, commented that "you can't see it as I see it. . . . All you can see is what's left."[20] His numerous chronicles of the shipping trade were his attempts to enable us to see it as he saw it. Not all of it was pleasant.

II *The Seamen's Lot*

Against the nobility of ships and the achievements of Britain's historic sailors stood the lot of the common sailor. In 1911, on the occasion of a strike by sailors, Tomlinson wrote his account of the reasons for such a strike.[21] After commenting that no one had expected the strike, he stated:

Only a vast unrest, an anger smouldering under an accumulation of grievances, a rankling injustice generally felt, explains that strike. Right at the back of the matter, the public, which really has reasons for alarm at the state of industrial conditions in the merchant service, if it but knew, must thank the Shipping Federation—as representing the majority of the shipowners— for this revolt of the sailors and dock workers. The men, in their own words, "have had about enough of it."

He then complained that "Most of what is known of the lot of the merchant sailor is got from novels and books of romantic travel," and he described a more realistic sailor:

The life of a sailor is more monotonous, squalid, and repellent, especially in the usual tramp, than that of most badly paid labourers ashore. It is not in the least chromatic. His hardships, too, which read so engagingly when treated by an artist who has suffered, are really hardships after all.

To make matters worse,

The conditions of life afloat are keeping good men away from the sea. What shipowners offer for service is such that it would be impossible to find enough experienced Britishers to man all vessels under the red ensign in port to-day. First the Britisher was driven to hate the handling of ships, and now, largely, he has lost the knack of it. The work is so uninviting to-day that Lascars and Chinamen are getting to be the only men who will accept it readily.

For Tomlinson, the problem is that the Shipping Federation is a powerful association of shipowners who "have enjoyed a control over their business which masters in other industries must surely envy." While other industries, such as cotton mills and coal mines, had to conform to "the influence of the improving social ethics of the community," shipping has not, partly because Parliament regarded "the problems of shipping . . . as so intricate and profound as to require experts to understand them."

The public's unwillingness to apply its attention to ships, as it had to the mills and mines, has resulted in neglect of the sailor.

For years there had been efforts to include Merchant Jack with those who benefited under the Acts ordering compensation for accidents. Other workers, represented in the House by the delegates of powerful unions, had long enjoyed that benefit. But the argument against it for the sailor was actually that he required it more than the others, because his trade was so dangerous. This was seriously advanced, in the form of an argument showing what a great expense it would be to shipowners.

In addition to refusing to allow sailors compensation, Parliament has in fact worked to increase the sailor's hardships. The Marquess of Salisbury, for example, opposed measures "to save life at sea by prohibiting, under some circumstances, the carriage of deck cargoes of timber across the Atlantic in mid-winter," a practice which frequently results in the loss of a ship. The Marquess expressed his feeling that "the loss of one steamer a year and twenty-five lives in each case does not appear to me a very large and formidable evil." Tomlinson comments that "One has to imagine the violent death of twenty-five peers per annum to see the humor of this small evil."

Even when politicians provide assistance for the sailor, they do so for some ulterior motive.

Mr. Lloyd George gave the sailor a better food scale, greater space in his living quarters, and the compensation clauses. We heard much of all this. But we did not hear so much of what the shipowners got in return. It was this. Mr. Lloyd George added a vast sum to the shipowners' capital by Act of Parliament. Overloading was made legal by altering the Plimsoll mark. The men got more provisions, and some of the benefits which all other workers have; and the Government gave to the owners in return vessels of greater cargo capacity.

Tomlinson scoffs at

how the Press commented on the humanity of the shipowners, who allowed these reforms to go through with so little opposition and discussion. Yet I myself have witnessed at sea, and have heard other witnesses describe, what happens to a ship when she is loaded with more cargo than she was designed to carry.

He then summarizes a position he took consistently when sailors and owners seemed in opposition:

There you have the present position. On one hand is the shipowner, explaining that his employment of cheap alien labor is because it is more reliable than that offered by his countrymen; and on the other hand is the class, which at one time took some pride in supplying the British shipowner with the rare and right material, with the men whose fine work helped to build up our maritime reputation, looking upon sea-work now as so unremunerative and disagreeable as to mark the man who accepts it as fit for nothing else.

Tomlinson blames the accompanying decline in the quality of British sailors on the shipowners' insistence that the profit motive come before all else, and he predicts that since the class that provides sailors has become more educated and accustomed to a better environment, "If we will not pay for the right men, we cannot have them."

III   The Foreshore of England

The Foreshore of England or Under the Red Ensign (1926) won high praise from Captain David W. Bone, who reviewed the book.

Mr. Tomlinson visited the seaports of Great Britain and Northern Ireland in the winter of 1925 to gain first hand impressions of the state of shipping affairs. "The Foreshore of England" embodies his conclusions. The book is, necessarily, planned upon the lines of journalism, and if ever proof were needed that the gap between journalism and imaginative literary work is small and negotiable, it lies between these covers. Very few writers, however, could invest the stark and sober details of such a survey with the dignity and glamour that Mr. Tomlinson imparts.[22]

The book consists of Tomlinson's investigations during a depression which left thousands of sailors and shipworkers out of work, and while it occasionally refers to the glories of England's maritime past, the emphasis remains on the dreary present. Tomlinson has bitter words for shipowners, whose rapacity he blames for the depression. As Bone pointed out in his review, Tomlinson's interview approach was somewhat slanted since "those questioned by this author were rarely other than the manual workers, the sufferers—as always—in any industrial depression."[23] Tomlinson describes miners out of work, deserted quays, and idle shipping offices in Liverpool, and he records the bitterness of the sufferers, but he avoids making his book dreary by maintaining his anecdotal style, describing scenes in objective detail, commenting on economic and political influences that have harmed the working man, and occasionally enlivening his pages with a wry humor.

What, in other hands, would be but a gloomy recital of plants of industrial stagnation in the seaports, is by him rendered strangely arresting. His facts and figures can be read in objective description of dockside street and palatial shipping offices, of poverty and squalor in Welsh mining villages and "vanity bags" behind the plate glass windows of Queen Street in Cardiff.[24]

One effect of *Foreshore* is to increase public awareness of the nature of the shipping trade and its importance to England.

When Tomlinson describes his walk across lifeless docks, he applies his irony to the owners of shipping companies:

Sailing time is near, night has come, the city is distant and its sounds are but echoes; and all this stuff about quays and Long John Silver is rosy only when seen in a theatre. The reality is nothing like it. Besides, John Silver does not frequent the quays; not in these days. He has learned much since he ended his business with Stevenson. He knows an easier way to the treasure than all the fuss with stockades and muskets against competitors who also are after the doubloons. His present chart is a company prospectus, but with no clue worth mentioning. We shall not meet him here.[25]

At first, *Foreshore* proceeds like his travel narratives, but he opens his second chapter with a description of his childhood admiration for the story of Samuel Plimsoll, who

thought the lives of men were more important than cargoes, and his vehemence so scared in the House of Commons the traditional defenders of that human right to do what we like with our own that they agreed not to allow ships to be overloaded any more. (*Foreshore*, 12)

The result was the Plimsoll Line, which prevented overloading. However, Lloyd George was able to undo Plimsoll's work "without a debate in Parliament, or a protest of sufficient consequence from any quarter to draw our eyes to a cynical reversion" (*Foreshore*, 12–13). Lloyd George introduced

a Remeasuring Order. Beyond sinking some ships which should not have been "remeasured," and making many others so unseaworthy that they were dangerous in heavy weather, this order, incidentally, increased the earning power of the capital of the shipowners. By a stroke of the pen their money became more. There was no public outcry, no remorseful alteration of the school books; for the mysteries of capital, commerce, navigation, and seamanship are not attractive mysteries, as are spiritualism and night clubs. (*Foreshore*, 13)

Tomlinson often contrasts the owners' interests with workers' poverty.

In the village of Blaina I heard that most of its people are living on the rates and taxes. Still, not everybody is so unlucky in Wales. You may hear there of one shipping company which, in 1920, on its capital of £350,000 distributed £1,050,000 in War Bonds. But the barefooted children of the miners appear distinctly undernourished. (*Foreshore*, 38)

He also frequently mentions as sources of the economic crisis the profits which many made by selling ships at the height of the postwar boom.

In contrast, Tomlinson presents the situation of the common man as a hard lot. He invites his reader to see Conrad's

Narcissus for what she was—a machine for profit-making, ill-designed, cranky, meanly found, cruel in her exactions, and beggarly with her hard tack and pence to the fellows who pulled her through for owners and underwriters. She well provided a scene for drama, but as a carrier of cargo and a home for men she would have been suffered only by creatures so slovenly in mind and casual in their habits that they even failed to apply the best they knew to their chief interest—the making of money. (*Foreshore*, 42–43)

The men of the *Narcissus* were not so much noble as desperate. When he addresses the condition of the working class in contrast with that of shipowners, Tomlinson begins to resemble Bernard Shaw:

Though let us not bother ourselves too much about the woes of the seaman.

Let us say a fellow is a fool who endures conditions which could be improved with a little resolution and common-sense on his part. Poverty, we know, is a crime. Yet it is more certain still that we need not pay more attention to the current woes of the shipowner. (*Foreshore*, 54)

World War I may have brought ruin to Europe, but not to the owners of the ships. Tomlinson cites *Fairplay* to show that the value of a ship has increased, between December, 1913, and March, 1920, from £50,250 to £258,750.

The fruit of victory! But who shared it? We do not really know; but we know who did not. Not the man on deck, not the look-out on the destroyer, not the fellow in the trenches. None of those fellows. (*Foreshore*, 55)

When Tomlinson finishes his chapter on Liverpool, which ends the section of his travels away from London, he states what he feels is the significance of his observations:

For Liverpool, like our other great and wealthy cities, has its dreary desert where humans exist only as a sort of plasm which permeates dismal reefs of bricks. Is there no engineer of genius who can invent a way to convert the potential richness of that life into something as gracious as guns, as profitable as docks? Or is our science only for concrete and steel? Because there is no telling what the chance words may do of that nobody outside the shipyard gates when the warship was launched, no guessing where they went, and what fire they may light. As the story goes, Dagon fell. (*Foreshore*, 90)

In the current economic woes of England Tomlinson sees dire portent.

Beginning with Chapter XI, Tomlinson focuses on the London area, and his writing becomes more varied and more historical in its nature.

London is the oldest and greatest of our ports and the most difficult to see and understand. It is more than a port, as everyone knows. It is a world market. There is nothing which is the work or produce of a distant country that you cannot buy in London. What all the world makes is there. It used to be Carthage, Venice, Bruges, and Amsterdam; but the market now is London. For how much longer? (*Foreshore*, 91)

He proceeds to describe the long tradition of London as a seaport and to establish the significance of the London River. He then writes at length of the Port of London Authority, established in 1909, and notes that "The history of the development of the port is more romantic than most picturesque novels" (*Foreshore*, 97). He proceeds to provide his reader with a tour and history of the Docks, and after he has finished, he begins to address the modern world's problems by referring to Eliot's *The Waste Land* and "The Hollow Men," which he finds indicative of the modern dilemma.

In one period of human history, I suppose, the more thoughtful youngsters, after such an experience as ours, would not have written "Hollow Men," but would have escaped from the world into monasteries; shut themselves off; devoted themselves, in a way which then would have seemed right, to a contemplation of the verities which remained undefiled by a transient and secular horror. There can be no such escape to-day. What then? What are such men to do?

They do nothing. They mix with us, their familiar and friendly masks hiding scepticism we never question, for we do not know it is there; they do whatever task is theirs, but contribute to society nothing of the invention and energetic curiosity of the young. They appear to think it is not worth their while. They write, when they are poets, such verses as "Waste Land." (*Foreshore*, 174)

His book ends on a note of guarded optimism, that perhaps the Beatitudes might kindle the human spirit, thereby threatening "the altar of drums, . . . the hand of the bomb-maker, . . . the nature of our commerce, . . . the national temple dedicate to St. Paul. Our affairs might go completely wrong." (*Foreshore*, 195)

Foreshore is less an objective history of the depression and its effects on shipping than it is an opportunity for Tomlinson to air his grievances against the injustices inherent in the system of ship ownership. He resents the profits which many made from the war, the reluctance with which an owner will devote part of his profits to the welfare of his employees, and the malign influence of politics and economics on members of the working class. That Tomlinson was more interested in rhetoric than history occurred to Bone, who commented on the apparent bias:

In his mood (always his mood) of intense sympathy with the manual worker, Mr. Tomlinson is somewhat heated in his attitude toward the shipping employer. He makes no mention of the National Maritime Board, a "Board" that has been instrumental in maintaining seamen's wages and service conditions at a level with which few industrial occupations ashore could compare.[26]

Some of Tomlinson's conclusions regarding the means by which owners profited from the war might not bear close scrutiny from the perspective of a serious historian, but *Foreshore* has lasting value as an accurate description of the state of shipping during the 1925 depression.

IV Below London Bridge

Below London Bridge (1934), illustrated with photographs, is Tomlinson's appreciation of the London Docks and the Port of London Authority. He attempts to convey to his reader a sense of the significance of English shipping, the tradition of London as a seaport, and the history of the Docks. Although he comments frequently on such changes as the disappearance of the Limehouse which was the subject of a Whistler painting, he is less strident than in *Foreshore* and seems content to restrict this book to its professed subject. His writing includes sensory description of the London Docks, where he saw "a group of Jewish women, who knew nothing of Dickens, Conrad, or the Torrens, but knew something, it seemed to both of us, of poetry,"[27] and a description of the *Cutty Sark*, with something of its history. He writes frequently of the age of the clippers and comments on its passing:

I would not decry the clippers. Many men still at work remember when the up-river docks were full of their gracious forms, side by side along the jetties. We could reel off scores of their names, and have done so, for the joy in it, because they were as familiar and good as the high street of youth. Recently, when we returned to look for them as usual, they had gone; and it was 1914. (*Below*, 18)

Among the memories which the Docks inspire in Tomlinson is Lloyd's,

with its new offices on the old site of East India House. It is not easy to explain what is inherent there. But where is the merchant or shipowner on a far coast who would dare question the word of Lloyd's? The Corporation of Lloyd's does not invite our interest. It is more circumspect than most admiralties. It is content with the skilled attentions of marine surveyors, actuaries, engineers, and navigators. Do you know its *Shipping List*? The racing news is not scanned more carefully than is that newspaper by those who know it: by shipowners, and by people in unlikely streets (who borrow it from a local tavern); and those readers put their trust in what it tells them as they never would in the common run of news. (*Below*, 22)

After describing the extent of commerce which occurs by way of the London River, Tomlinson states the importance of the Thames's docility:

> The Thames, however dark and threatening it may appear to a solitary watcher at dusk, is to shipping a friendly stream. There is a rise at high-water spring tides of 21 feet at London Bridge. The bed of the river is amiable to even large steamers aground. They may rest comfortably alongside a wharf at low water. Nor, at the flood, does the stream unduly test their moorings.
>
> This confidential behaviour of their river is worth more to Londoners than the ownership of every gold-mine on earth. They ought to keep in mind, those Londoners, that they live in a city in which the streets are continuous for a space that is thirty miles long, with a breadth of twenty-five miles. (*Below*, 30)

He estimates that London could survive approximately ten days without the produce brought inland on the Thames, and he tries to impress his reader with the Londoner's dependence on the sea.

Once he has established the importance of the Docks to London, Tomlinson presents thirty-seven photographs, each with a paragraph on a facing page. He emphasizes the historical and literary events associated with each of his scenes. "A Bastion of London Bridge, from the Steps on the Surrey Side," for example, is identified with Herman Melville, "who wrote our greatest story of the sea, [who] leaned on this parapet to consider the ships, the morning he arrived in London" (*Below*, 42). A photograph of the Angel Tavern in Rotherhithe faces a description identifying this as Lemuel Gulliver's neighborhood and the last resting place of Captain Christopher Jones of the *Mayflower*. Unlike *Foreshore*, *Below London Bridge* stays with its purpose—to acquaint the reader with an area important to Tomlinson from boyhood. It is consistent in combining the organization of a walking tour with commentary on the historical, commercial, and literary significance of various sights.

V Malay Waters

Malay Waters: The Story of Little Ships Coasting Out of Singapore and Penang in Peace and War (1950) is the most satisfying of Tomlinson's chronicles. It follows the history of the Straits Steamship Company in eighteen essays. While the essays are not arranged in chronological order, they tell the story of the company's origin, its early development, and the difficulties it encountered in the Orient during World War II. The arrangement of chapters is at first confusing, for "Origins" is the seventh chapter, and many of the essays tell of adventures of the company's employees as they try to avoid capture by the Japanese. However, Tomlinson follows the process by which he discovered his story rather than the order of events themselves, and he warns the reader early that the reader might not find *Malay Waters* a history in the ordinary sense:

there is a great deal of personal reminiscence in this history, so I doubt it will pass muster with sticklers for what is called true history. Yet what is that? Is it like pure art, and inhuman? I shall have to be reminiscent, or else a reader who does not know the Far East would find these peculiar ships in their tropical setting no more related to verifiable life than abstract poetry, and my purpose would fail. [28]

He then describes the company as one whose ships are rarely seen in home waters—Tomlinson first saw the house flag in Singapore, despite his long acquaintance with the London Docks, during his 1923–24 voyage to Malaya for *Harper's*.

Tomlinson explains his motive for assuming the role of the historian:

Are we ever likely to have an official account of the general contribution of the Merchant Service to our welfare, though without it the defence of our country would have utterly failed? Experience warns us that we are not. Whitehall historians will not feel constrained to record the doings of those ships and men whose voyages and fidelity fed us all the time, and kept going workshops and factories with the material for war; that conveyed the armed forces to all parts of the world, and brought home the inflammable stuff without which our planes would have stayed on the ground. We shall not have that history. (*Malay Waters*, 17)

One reason we will not have that history is the reluctance of Whitehall to release records to civilians.

When Whitehall is begged for particulars of events that have more precision than the imperfect memories of seamen should be expected to retain after a lapse of years, the answer is: "I am commanded by My Lords Commissioners of the Admiralty to acquaint you that it is contrary to the practice of the

Admiralty to grant access to official records, they regret that the facilities desired cannot be afforded." So, as the saying is, "We've had it." (*Malay Waters*, 20)

The difficulties were compounded by the Japanese, who destroyed all the records of the Straits Steamship Company during World War II. The company, as a result, had no idea of which ships were still in operation, or even the names of their masters. "We had to be like Micawber—wait for something to turn up. The surviving ships appeared afterwards in all sorts of unlikely ports, where we had nobody to watch our interests" (*Malay Waters*, 55). As a result, "The recollections of servants of the Company were invited, and their notes and memoirs began to drift in from places as far apart as Edinburgh, Mombasa, Australia, and Devon" (*Malay Waters*, 56). Tomlinson was thus able to piece together a history of the company which began in 1890.

Mr. Bogaardt began the new service of the Straits Steamship Company to the west side of the Peninsula, Malacca, Port Dickson, Klang, Teluk Anson, and Sumatra, and directed it from Robinson Quay. If you care for the names here is his fleet: *Sappho*, 328 tons; *Will-of-the-Wisp*, 166 tons; *Malacca*, 405 tons; *Billiton*, 195 tons; *Hye Leong*, 296 tons. (*Malay Waters*, 63)

After describing the era in which this fleet would not have been strange and commenting on the Company's growth for approximately thirty pages, Tomlinson brings his account to the beginning of Japanese involvement in World War II and describes the effects of Japanese enmity on the firm.

Tomlinson drew from the men who experienced them the events of the Company during the war. When the fleet was in convoy, the *Klias* posed problems to its engineer, a Free Frenchman: "Me, I am a Diesel man, and thees sheep and engeens is a beetch" (*Malay Waters*, 107). Anecdotes abound. Mr. Horn, the Chief Engineer of the *Hua Tong*, suffered a broken leg when the ship was hit. He was picked up by a Dutch launch shortly after the *Hua Tong* sank, eventually transported to a hospital in Palembang, subsequently evacuated with the Dutch, and although the Dutch ship was attacked by the Japanese, he eventually reached Java, and survived to participate "in every major operation from Arawe to the retaking of New Guinea, the Philippines, and Borneo" (*Malay Waters*, 115). In another chapter Tomlinson describes the adventures of the *Jarak*,

which fled Singapore and spent three days successfully evading the
Japanese; then the crew switched to a native boat. When a Japanese
fleet of three armed oilers was sighted, everyone went below except
one Malay, who remained at the tiller.

It was when the fleet was, very thankfully, three miles astern, that one of its
ships put about. She approached, and fired a shell across the bows of the *Setia
Berganti*. She closed the prahu and ordered her to come alongside. The
refugees had to board the *Sinkoko Maru*; and its captain, a venerable man, in
good English, told them how sorry he was they had failed. It was his duty to
make them prisoners of war. In another minute they were on their way back
to Singapore. (*Malay Waters*, 145)

Similar tales concerning the Japanese abound in the book, and Tomlinson also described a Japanese atrocity—the murder of unarmed
civilians, male and female, with bayonets and automatic rifles. One
nurse survived:

She was shot through the thigh, fell into the water, and floundered out a short
distance. She was left for dead. After the soldiers had gone she scrambled
ashore through the bodies of her friends, which lay in and out of the water,
and escaped into the woods, but in a few days hunger and exhaustion forced
her to give herself up. She survived to be released, at the end of the war, from
the misery and humiliations of a prison camp, with twenty-one other nurses
of the original company. (*Malay Waters*, 172)

Most of these stories are anecdotal, reported to Tomlinson by the
survivors of several close calls and near misses.

The final chapter of the book, the story of Captain Brown of the
Circe, provides a slightly lighter touch. Captain Brown found himself
in difficulties with military seamen.

He always forgot formality when considering what had better be done next,
and so he was ticked off once more. He explained to me, in excuse, that he
often "forgot to salute the gangway." He never had felt that respect for
gangways. (*Malay Waters*, 175)

He encountered frustration because, as an expert navigator of the
Straits Settlements region (including Penang, Malacca, and Singapore), he ventured to give advice to Authority only to be told "that
when his information was wanted it would be sought" (*Malay Waters*,
175). Bureaucratic ineptitude resulted in a shortage of cooks and

stewards for the ships, a spoilage of cheese which was transported on top of pigment powder packed in paper bags, and confusion concerning which ships carried what. An officer boards the ship with a demand to count the sheep—"It was well known that she had 900 sheep on board" (*Malay Waters*, 199)—and is acutely disappointed to learn that the ship lacks a consignment of mutton:

the master had the hatches taken off to satisfy a stout disbeliever. The American, who was aware of the need for live meat, stood gazing down at pigments, cordage, cork, and hides; a commercial cargo for the Italians. (*Malay Waters*, 199)

In addition to comparatively harmless bungling, Captain Brown often had to resist orders that seemed designed to sink the ship, such as the order to anchor and wait, thereby becoming a sitting target. Tomlinson declines to follow the Captain through the entire war:

All we need know is that she did at long last arrive in the Thames, her decks still awash, for she was deep with iron ore from Huelva; it was 5th May, 1945. The war had ended, and forgetfulness was beginning to set in. (*Malay Waters*, 199)

Although *Malay Waters* relies heavily on others' reminiscences and therefore concentrates on the history of the Company during World War II, the book provides a diverting and faithful picture of the development of the firm, from its founding in 1890 through the war. It also enables a reader to become familiar with a company as British as any shipping firm, but normally inaccessible to Londoners.

As a chronicler of London and the sea, Tomlinson occasionally allows his social and political opinions to displace the informative purpose of historical documentation, and his preference for people over books contributes to the anecdotal quality of his accounts. Nevertheless, within the limitations imposed by his personal vision, his histories are fairly accurate, and they are much more readable than the usual accounts of the past. His chronicles allowed Tomlinson to combine those forms of writing he enjoyed best—the informative and entertaining essay, the commanding story of action, the descriptive narrative usually associated with travel writing, and the examination of human character, generally the prerogative of fiction. His chronicles allowed him to combine his love for the sea, his Cockney identity, and his knowledge of maritime commerce with his desire to increase public awareness of England's shipping tradition.

CHAPTER 6

The Enemy of Progress

I The Modern Decline

ALTHOUGH Tomlinson never devoted an entire book to the purpose, much of his writing was directed against the shortcomings of the modern age. For Tomlinson, the modern age is characterized by a general decline in the quality of life, a denial of the human spirit, a loss of direction, an ignorance of the humanities, and an unreasonable worship of mechanism. His articles and sections of many of his books addressed the problems of the common man in the Age of Science, and he tried to restore a system of values that regards man as an end rather than a means. Many of his pronouncements resemble the socialism of the Fabians.

Tomlinson's dislike of progress, according to Helen and Richard Altick, stemmed from his early years.

"Down Poplar way," in the 1870's, was no place for a congenital romanticist to be born. It was the twilight of the gods—twilight of the era that had seen tall-masted ships by the score thrusting their bowsprits far across the wharves and waterside streets of the East End. But the funereal pall of smoke had not yet settled so thickly over London River that Tomlinson as a youth could not know the glory that had been the sea in the days when his own father had found satisfaction and prosperity in sailing his bark to the corners of the earth. Darkness, however, fell: his father came home for good, and ugly slab-sided steamers elbowed the graceful clippers from East India Docks. Tomlinson early sensed the meaning of "progress," and he did not like it.[1]

He witnessed the detrimental effects of progress in the changes his own family suffered, and he had little patience with those who chose to celebrate the mechanistic achievements of the moderns.

The poets, unluckily, do not oblige us; not convincingly; not even Whitman. We are beginning to suspect that much of Whitman's celebration of the Modern is a bluff. Whitman bluffed himself. He shouted himself down, deafening himself—for he did not want to pause, even for a moment—with

115

lusty iteration of the naturalness of ugliness, of the native attraction of
barbarities and squalor, and the intimate hairiness of chests and legs.[2]

Tomlinson would prefer to see things as they are, and to make his
view prevail.

For Tomlinson, modernity represents a decline from a bygone age
during which life had more meaning and fewer dangers.

Some onlookers are sure the world of men, despite the newly acquired
menace of its heaven, once its promise of bliss, gets better and better. I have
tried to believe this, tried hard, but it is too much for me. My experience in
watching the goings-on in that world has been fairly long, and my recollections as a journalist point to the probability that the commonweal, though its
fund of skill, gadgets, and knowledge has increased miraculously in my day,
makes collective noises more like Bedlam than ever, and louder.[3]

Reporting a conversation that occurred after an air raid, Tomlinson
indicates that he is not alone in his feeling:

[a young woman] remarked, reminiscently, "You know, as far back as I can
remember, all the news of the world I've ever heard has been bad." There
was a hint of reproach in her manner, as if we had deliberately cheated her of
good tidings.

We turned to her. What she had said was, in its way, more startling than
the raid.[4]

The woman remarked that one of her earlier memories was being
awakened by her mother to be taken to the cellar during Zeppelin
raids during World War I, and

A smash of glass still frightened her. She then went on to give us a casual
selection from the news of many nations since the 'twenties.

What of general good, she asked, could we set against that uproar? A few
books and poems, and the excellence of orchestras? Little more, she thought,
except the work of physicians and surgeons, aided by pharmaceutical
chemists and research workers; nothing whatever from religion, and not
enough from any source to prevent serious people from speculating on how
long it would be before the ground gave way under us all.[5]

When Tomlinson reported this young woman's statements to "an
elderly man of religion,"

[the elder] was silent for a while, and then said her indictment was not only just, but the responsibility was his; and that others, if they felt like it, could share the blame. And what ought we to do? Because, he remarked, if the earth continues to be such a place for the young that its beauty is meaningless to them, if the earth is to remain a place where it is difficult to rejoice, even over the first swallow, then God's purpose is lost.[6]

The elder was willing to allow individuals to determine their own responsibility, but Tomlinson was more specific in assigning blame.

Like Jonathan Swift and Bernard Shaw, Tomlinson attributed the actions of malefactors to two motives, malice or incompetence. For him the evils of the modern world derive from the greed of businessmen.

The unseen masters of the British public are the financiers and industrial magnates. We always forget them, of course, while admiring Mr. Baldwin's leisurely and reassuring pipe. National policy in any industrial society is shaped nowadays to the advantages of the people who are in the advantageous positions . . . .

Then those naval and military experts! Those gentlemen, of course, are always energetically preparing for war—for the last war, as a matter of fact, never for the next.[7]

Tomlinson places the interests of industrialists and military men in opposition to the common man's desire for peace:

We cannot trust either the elected politicians or the established military experts to give body to our common and natural desire for a world in which we may do our work in peace.[8]

Describing the effects of World War I, he notes:

. . . some things have gone irrevocably out of Europe. There is, for example, a whole generation of young men, that very stratum of society where chiefly resides its dynamic power, its invention, its enterprise, its poets, artists, and musicians. That is gone out of Europe. The men who still direct Europe's affairs are the very fellows, for the most part, who brought Europe to its disaster.[9]

As long as England's "unseen masters" remain in a position to serve their private interests over public good, the barrenness of modern life will become worse.

Tomlinson also admits that those who affect the affairs of the world are not capable of meeting the challenge. After deploring a news-

paper's subscribers' selection of "men of action" as the world's
greatest men, Tomlinson comments that no one tried to "throw any
doubt whatever on those awful benefactors. Well, we've no doubt of it
now. Look around the world, that prospect of the devotion to our
welfare of those great men of action! What are we going to do about
that? Does it not need action of another kind, quite differently
inspired? And who will start it? He must be quick, or it will be too
late."[10] He becomes ironical when comparing the failures of honored
men of action with failures of other public figures.

We talk so freely of financiers, and statesmen, and men of business, as Great.
At the same time we know perfectly well that a musician who tripped up
when playing a piece, and did that not once but often, would never again be
asked to play in public. If you are a musician you must not make mistakes. But
the great financiers are never right. The great men of business are as helpless
in this present mess [the Great Depression] as their golf caddies. They don't
know. And every guess they make about it is no more valuable than if they
had diced for a solution.[11]

After citing such failures as World War I and the Great Depression,
he concludes

Great Statesmen! Great Diplomatists! The war ended, and we see now that
nothing was achieved of all their aims. They were all wrong. Not one of their
ideals was reached. They were all wrong, all of them, and all of the time.
Their astute activities, their realism, their patriotism, and the outpouring of
wealth and labor in support, succeeded in the end in overturning nearly
every throne in Europe, releasing Lenin to power, and beggaring the lot of
us. Men of action! If only these fellows were born with a bit of red worsted
tied to the great toe! Then cunning midwives could recognize them, and
would know what to do.[12]

Between the self-serving interests of the industrialists and the failure
of so-called statesmen to maintain economic prosperity and peace,
the world of modern man has become intolerable.

II   *The Loss of Perspective*

Tomlinson cites several errors in the thinking of moderns which
have contributed to the modern plight. One is the modern denial of
the joys of living: "We have become burdened by the marvelous.
Knowledge and experience have made us indifferent not only to the

things of the spirit but to the adventures of the body. Our machines are treasured and oiled with devotion, but life in general has lost its joyous worth."[13] According to Tomlinson, we have lost our sense of direction. "Life is more hurried than ever, but has lost its sense of direction and forgotten its traditional values, excepting the certitude of what, without irony, we call progress."[14] By focusing our attention on the marvels of machinery, we risk losing our power of reason itself:

Our dire need is for grace to save us from a general preoccupation with mechanics, with immense speedy things, with marvelous enormities, with nuclear fission and its dismaying purport; this latest desire of mankind to rise nearer the moon, and even to attain complete lunacy.[15]

Tomlinson places this lapse of man's value system outside morality, claiming that

whether or not there is a principle of good, and another of evil, this is indeed a mysterious universe, and it ought to be plain enough to everybody today that our cleverness has leased from it powers which may be the undoing of human society, unless we can discover pretty soon a way to safely bottle them up, and use them only as we need them.[16]

Man's lack of reason, allowing his invention to outrace his ability to control it, has resulted in his rejection of the true value of life and of his world. Matthew Arnold once related the role of culture to seeing things as they are and making the will of God prevail. Tomlinson draws a similar connection.

Man's preoccupation with material progress has resulted from his denial of religion, his indifference to culture, and his ignorance of sociological perspectives. Modern man has turned to a new deity:

The State and its edicts have been substituted for God and a moral order. The State is an impersonal monster with a heart of gun-metal and bowels of steel piping. Its only rule is expediency.[17]

The absence of a Christian value system has resulted in a lapse in man's attention to the humanities.

We have to remember, for instance, that art and letters, once of the first consequence in a civilized community, have sunk to the level of intricate plays for intellectual circles. We might have expected that lapse. When religion goes, out goes art. When there is no faith except in material power, how raise a joyous song about it?[18]

Tomlinson reports that

One of the Brains Trust, an eminent politician, asked the other evening what difference it would have made to mankind in general if Plato had never existed, answered boldly, "No difference at all."

He was prompt. There could be no doubt about this. Doubt may exist as to what flies do with themselves in winter, and anxious listeners still await a word on that; but listeners learn at once they need have no doubt about Plato's value to us. There isn't any. It would have made no difference had he been still-born. From this simple and honest answer we learn also that as our knowledge increases so we grow in confidence. A driver of a tank knows what Shakespeare never knew.[19]

After deploring that "philosophy, which is something near religion, can be dismissed at 'the mike' with the indifference of a Nazi throwing petrol on books,"[20] Tomlinson comments on the significance of the wholesale rejection of culture.

What really have we to go upon? Nothing much, except the faith that Plato's extension to mankind's outlook may be almost as good as the full benefit of the news this day on all wave-lengths. What difference to mankind has Confucius made, or Zoroaster—what difference any and all of the few superior minds? . . . For that matter, what difference has been made by the understanding of men and things of that best mind of them all—from Europe to the South Seas, where is the influence of Jesus Christ?

While considering this, doubtfully, let us admit that the speaker at the Brains Trust answered in accord with the spirit of his age. Athens is out. Bethlehem is out.[21]

He attributes many of the modern world's ills to this rejection of religion and art, and he states that the science of the moderns has contributed nothing with which to replace religion and art.

The truth is, we know more about the secrets of the coral reef, the ant hill, and the beehive than we do of the laws which give health or cause sickness in the human industrial community. Very few bankers or great organizers of industry have much knowledge of the hidden springs of their profits. They understand the machinery only when it is running freely; and generally it runs so freely that they imagine their profits are the gift of the good God who ordered a world so favorably for them.[22]

Man has rejected the sources of wisdom that derived from religion and art, and he must suffer the consequences.

Tomlinson is specific concerning the fruits of modern man's rejection of his traditional values. The Alticks remind us in their essay,

From the first, both by instinct and by circumstance, he was the enemy of mechanization and amalgamation—two words ugly in themselves and with overtones infinitely uglier to a young man of Tomlinson's disposition. "Commerce" in all its significances was anathema to him. [23]

In the course of addressing himself to the failures of mechanization, amalgamation, and commerce, Tomlinson included his observations and applied them to virtually every modern ill which came to mind.

We have been left in no doubt as to the things that repel him—trade's transformation of Poplar from a cheerful, prosperous port to a grimy slum; the greedy agents of British imperialism as they seduced Nature's brown children with bribes of tinned meat and oil; the brass-hats of the war office happily applying in 1915 the lessons they learned in the Boer War. [24]

When he addressed himself to the fruits of modernity, he was most insistent in presenting the contrast between mechanism and science on the one hand and life's positive values on the other.

We have heard, till we are weary of hearing it, that this is the Age of Science. Yes, it is. We know it. Air-raid shelters and gas masks for infants did not come like the flowers in spring; they developed as the thoughts of man progressed. This scientific age began, we may say roughly, when, with the Industrial Revolution and the inventions that mechanized human effort, reason advised us, at the same time, on all the new evidence at its disposal, that the universe itself is a mechanistic affair; a series of cosmic accidents chanced to bring about things as they are, and that means, of course, we are under no obligation to any superior authority, save the State. All we have to do is to survive, as the fittest to survive; and if not thus qualified so much the worse for us. The only imperative necessity men need acknowledge is circumstance. If they want to get along nicely, they make the most of circumstance, while taking precautions to keep out of the way of the police. [25]

The moderns' mistaken belief that mechanism is good in itself is responsible, for Tomlinson, for the worst events of the new age: "the war . . . was the inevitable outcome of the everyday opinions of the society which thinks scientific industrialism is as right as little apples."[26]

To illustrate the ways in which this attitude influences the modern public, Tomlinson cites a war memorial, in the classic form of an immense bronze figure of a youth wearing but a fig-leaf and a huge sword, and you might wonder what it symbolizes. Well, it pretends to be a tribute to the men of the British Machine Gun Corps who fell in the Great War, but on its pedestal you may read these words: "Saul hath slain his thousands, but David his tens of thousands."

Now, the fig-leaf is a silly evasion and a snigger. David was not of the neuter gender, nor was any machine gunner that I ever met; but that inscription, for me, proves the cruelty, the essential ugliness, of the whole conception. David slew his *tens* of thousands! You see? That image is not at all a tribute to the men who fell, as it pretends to be, and as its artist thinks it is. It is the glorification of Carnage. It is a tribute, not to the poor machine gunners who died, but to the Machine Gun itself. It says so, though without conscious intent. Instinctively we worship the machine, in these days. The inscription might just as well have been in German, for certainly most of our own men were slain by the German David.[27]

He deplores this misuse of art, and he cites the influence of a humanistic artist, Thomas Hardy, in countering the evil effect of the worship of the machine.

While Hardy lived he justified the least of us, who serve humbly in Athena's temple. His presence did much to redeem this new age of mechanical science, in which the swarming Barbarians, who never doubt their appetites as men of civility question the difficulties of wisdom or falter at the exactions of art and learning, appear again to have taken control of the destinies of our cities. The Barbarians come this time, not in skins and with crude swords, but armed with the awful powers which engineering and chemical science have given them. We are compelled to submit to the discipline of their bristling tanks, and to the moulding of public opinion in the machinery of the popular newspaper press to the forms of thought which money finds most profitable; and to the reduction of our aspirations to a few simple and standardised desires that can be satisfied easily with public pomps and games, with music by mechanical apparatus, and a criticism of life by cinematograph drama.[28]

Tomlinson blames progress for the decline of the humanistic in modern life, resulting in his warning that "The mental climate of our age is pestilential."[29] He can only offer the hope of men like Hardy:

In such a world a great poet is unique, and definitely alien. His presence is a challenge to its powers. He keeps in heart the lesser men who oppose the things of the mind, though with no apparent success, to both the insolence of authority and the noise of the market place.[30]

III   *Modern Economic and Social Inequity*

Tomlinson, with his characteristic sympathy for the common man, also finds the modern age at fault for its indifference to the basic human needs of all people. In an early essay he records the heroism of common men in the face of a mining disaster:

I have a new regard for my fellows since Great Barr. About you and me there are men like that. There is nothing to distinguish them. They show no signs of greatness. They have common talk. They have coarse ways. They walk with an ugly lurch. Their eyes are not eager. They are not polite. Their clothes are dirty. They live in cheap houses on cheap food. They call you "sir." They are the great unwashed, the mutable many, the common people. The common people! Greatness is as common as that. There are not enough honours and decorations to go round. Talk of the soldier! *Vale* to Welsby of Normanton! He was a common miner. He is dead. His fellows were in danger, their wives were white-faced and their children were crying, and he buckled on his harness and went to the assault with no more thought for self than great men have in a great cause; and he is dead. I saw him go to his death. I wish I could tell you of Welsby of Normanton.[31]

To contrast the heroism of Welsby, Tomlinson describes the events of the next morning at Great Barr:

Children, who could see no reason about them why their fathers should not return as usual, were playing football by the tiny church. A group of women were still gazing at the grotesque ribs and legs of the pit-head staging as though it were a monster without ruth.[32]

Tomlinson was ever sensitive to the economic plight of the working class in the midst of supposed prosperity and peace.

I remember in particular one distressed Welsh mining town, which had the look of a community crumbling after a disaster, never to be set straight again. A man stood at a street corner, to whom I spoke. He was spruce and upright, but his clothes were thin and threadbare on a cold day. He was haggard but stern, and his grey eyes met mine as if he were a master of his craft, though now he did not practise it. I wanted to know how long he had been out of work. He held up three fingers. "Months?" I asked. "Years," he said. That sort of fellow, now proving his mettle in Italy, as he did before at Ypres, was one of the victims of the social lie with the fine name "economic necessity."

Let us clear our cities of that before we ever complain again of barbarity in our midst.[33]

He recognized the indifference of modern politicians and industrialists to the plight of the working man, and he bitterly resented it.

When Tomlinson considered the lot of the working classes, he saw dire implications for the future of democracy itself. He states that "Industrial civilization, based upon the simple motives of private profits and national advantages, is fairly sure to wobble badly on its foundations, this year or next."[34] He remarks:

Democracy has not failed, for as yet it has never tried to do anything, except what it was ordered to do, or was cajoled into doing. It leaves all to its statesmen. And its statesmen, ignorant of the inherencies of a world unified at last by science, and obviously afraid to face the powers for evil which have taken control of mankind's affairs, still continue to placate us with the platitudes of political and economic notions that now have the same chance of fruitfulness, conditions being what they are, as the planting of wooden nutmegs in Fifth Avenue.[35]

"What is the matter with the world," Tomlinson asks, "that the experts cannot set it right?" and decides that it is the profit motive. He supposes

an experimental botanist, who at last evolves a wheat he has imagined. Thereupon wheat will grow two hundred miles nearer the Arctic circle. A wheat-belt is added to the world, say three thousand miles long by two hundred wide; and some of it is at once used by hopeful and adventurous pioneers. It is then easier to feed the multitude? It is not. The problem of feeding people becomes more difficult, for two reasons: we can easily increase production, but all we have done toward the just distribution of harvests is to put hindrances in the way, because food is not grown for food, but for profit.[36]

Tomlinson concludes that to expect concrete benefit from progress is folly.

. . . why expect the man of science and the enterprising pioneer to benefit us? When the result of their good work comes along we do not feed children with its excess, but locomotives, though coal miners are unemployed.[37]

His assessment of the misplaced values of the moderns is direct:

We have had no time yet to learn what the inherencies are of production by machinery, but an immediate revision of old notions about them is now essential. I suggest that the only trouble with the world is that we have given no thought to the means of the just distribution of that abundance of earth the machines have so greatly multiplied.[38]

He offers no specific advice for these "means of just distribution," but he implies that should statesmen fail to consider the solution, they might regret it: "Our statesmen are not unaware of that growing and universal impatience over their delays, nor of that dust-bin; they might go into it, with the litter."[39]

Such statements of the need for the just distribution of wealth and the eradication of social injustices met with cool reception from several contemporaries of Tomlinson. Among these was Stuart Hodgson, who regretted that Tomlinson so much as brought the subject to print.

I am a little doubtful whether his fierce zeal for social reform has not done something to check as well as something to forward the causes for which he crusades so passionately. It leads him at times into the merely tiresome trick of the Bellocs and the Chestertons: the mechanical dodge of extolling times past for virtues which did not exist in them in order to condemn more effectively evils in the present day which, in the exaggerated form in which they are stated, do not exist in them either.[40]

After noting that slum dwellers' "relative contentment is one of the great difficulties and perplexities of the practical reformer,"[41] Hodgson asserts:

Mr. Tomlinson is wrong in supposing the slum dweller to be as a rule inordinately miserable; he is fantastically wrong in conceiving that he feels as Mr. Tomlinson himself would feel if he were condemned to live in a slum. It is horrible that in civilised communities such social conditions should continue to exist: it is odious that men should be found willing to make money out of their continuance: but to suggest that the slum is a place of torture (which in fact, to those who dwell there, it is not) deliberately devised by avarice (when most slums are a perplexity and a sorrow of heart to their owners) is to darken counsel.[42]

Since Tomlinson had some experience with poverty as a youth and Hodgson apparently has not, I would be interested to determine whether Hodgson's opinions might alter should he be given the opportunity to dwell in a slum.

Tomlinson's social criticism suffered greatly from his failure to provide a solution to the problems he illustrated. Helen and Richard Altick refer to the "essentially negative character of his thought" and cite a major flaw in his social criticism:

> How can we save ourselves?
> If he had had a positive, well-developed credo with which to answer that question, Tomlinson would have won for himself a position in contemporary literature far higher than that which he now holds. He would be remembered as a crusader *for* something, rather than as an indefatigable rebel *against* something. As it is, literary historians are inclined to dismiss him as an exponent of "a somewhat tiresome middle-aged liberalism."[43]

Tomlinson frequently commented on the absence of a concrete solution to the problems of modern life, including the failure of escape.

> And the feeling to-day seems fairly general that, though the cheat in the compulsion of our materialistic society is plainly manifest, yet nothing can be done about it. There is less chance of escape for us than there was for the soldier in the old front line. The war was certain to end some day, but he would be a bold man who would hint a period to the dominion of the money-power, of the rule of Mammon.[44]

Occasionally he raises the question of a solution, only to disappoint the expectations of his reader.

> How are we to mend the matter? We have our statesmen and men of business, and that appears to be all. They worked well enough when the turning of the wheels of the factories seemed to be from eternal motion, and no official folly, however monstrous, could do society serious harm. The momentum of the wheels was too great. It might slacken, but never fail. It carried us ahead, whatever the politicians did. All went so easily that even the captains of industry never asked, as would an intelligent child, why the wheels went round. The wheels were going round. That was enough. To inquire into the springs which motivated society profitably was sheer pedantry. Yet now the wheels are slowing, are even still, and over vast areas of the globe communal life begins to stagnate. Yet the only remedies that statesmen and the captains of industry can suggest, to quicken the flow of life, are the devices of administration which, we cannot help noting, are the very cause of the breakdown.[45]

The subject of this essay, the sad state of world economics during the

Great Depression, fixes blame for the crisis without suggesting what should have been done.

Commenting on his antiwar writings, Helen and Richard Altick identify a characteristic trait of his social criticism as well.

And so, as the whistling-in-the-dark tone of his essays written during the Battle of Britain reminds us, Tomlinson contributed little more to the anti-war literature of our era than a sense of comprehensive horror. All he could do, after writing one terrible indictment after another of commercialism and militarism, was to indulge in a pleasantly nebulous and thoroughly unconvincing confession of faith in the ultimate victory of man's goodness. His writings against the war were heavy with a conviction which he never squarely faced: a conviction of futility. He could offer no positive program for the redemption of modern civization, because he could not believe in any. His disillusionment, begun in Poplar's tangle of spars and rigging, was too complete. His magnificent mission was doomed to failure.[46]

Part of this failure resulted from Tomlinson's narrow personal vision. He was quick, and perhaps too simplistic in his assessment, to attribute blame to the malicious greed or heedless ignorance of financiers, industrialists, and military men, and he was content to describe the modern world in terms as depressing and pessimistic as the contemporary view expressed in Eliot's *The Waste Land*. However, except for the conspicuous absence of a solution, Tomlinson was comprehensive in his examination of modern life. He identified several prevailing views of the moderns—their denial of the human spirit, their lack of direction, their indifference to culture, their rejection of God for the State, and their worship of mechanism in an Age of Science—and he related these to several pressing conditions, including the economic distress of the lower classes, the apparent inevitability of war, and the pestilential mental climate of his age. His description of modern life in the light of the values of a past which may or may not have existed communicates his sense of horror, disillusionment, and disgust with the actions of modern man.

CHAPTER 7

The Pacifist

I *Early Development of Antiwar Stance*

TOMLINSON had an abiding hatred of modern warfare. He was twenty-seven when the Boer War ended and was fortunate to have been mature enough to resist the war fervor that swept England during that military fiasco, comparable to America's Vietnam. When World War I broke out, Tomlinson was dispatched to Belgium by his newspaper, and he later served as war correspondent in France until the war ended. He had ample opportunity to observe at close hand the difference between the recruit's expectations and the soldier's reality. The impact of these years appeared in all his subsequent writing. His travel writing included encounters in remote places with veterans of the war, his novels dwelt on changes the war had brought to his characters, and his essays examined the causes, nature, and consequences of the European conflict. He also became something of a crusader against the mechanistic spirit of the modern age and against warfare itself. For many, he became the most strident and insistent voice raised against the enormity of war.

When the modern age reached the point at which numbering world wars became necessary, Helen and Richard Altick considered the effect of Tomlinson's antiwar writing on the military force of the Allies.

Henry Major Tomlinson in the era-between-wars was one of those writers against war whom Mr. [Archibald] MacLeish has categorically accused of having contributed much to the so-called "psychological disarmament" of the democracies. History will decide whether eventually he will be sanctified as a passionate but unheeded prophet or assigned a particularly bleak station in the outer darkness as an unwitting but effective saboteur of democratic morale.[1]

The Alticks point out that Tomlinson was disillusioned before the outbreak of World War I, unlike Hemingway, Remarque, and Dos

128

Passos. "Tomlinson . . . had drunk his bitter draft long before Sarajevo, and the war merely added desperate emphasis and urgency to convictions he had long entertained."[2] Tomlinson described his attitude toward warfare in similar terms, comparing his uncertainty in his childhood years with that of the atomic age:

I suppose my antipathy comes of being born early enough to be in the midst of the spectral doubts and fears loosed over Europe by the Franco-German war, Sedan, and the Commune; those shadows have increased to what we now contemplate, for this day the blue of very Heaven has darkened to the perennial menacing loom of the atomic age.[3]

He once remarked that the twentieth century was ushered in with the sound of bullets, and he comments on his life in terms of constant warfare:

Always a war, or the threat of it. I can still sense the dubiety in an early home because of British battles with Zulus, Afghans, Egyptians and Soudanese. To make matters worse, just as I married, a Boer War began. It was then that some of my friends advised me, quite genially, yet with heartfelt conviction, that though I would not improve a lamp-post, if hanging to it, that was a proper place for me.[4]

By the time he began his career as a pacifist writing against modern war, the subject was an old one to him.

Tomlinson identified his rhetorical stance as a pacifist with a humorous resignation to the view of his audience. "For as to the subject of war it may easily be that I am a pathological case without knowing it."[5] He recognizes that his voice might have become somewhat tiresome to his readers.

As for this subject of the war, and especially of literature as it relates to the war, it is said that some of us are a bit crazy. It would not be easy, and it would not be worth while, to deny it. I was asked once—there was a kindly thought, perhaps, that if I tried I might lay my ghost—why don't you write about it? That idea I considered—it looked attractive—but when reflecting the bright hope, it occurred to me that a cynical enemy could accuse me of having written about nothing else since 1914. He could make a sound case, too, I fear.[6]

Tomlinson admits that he feeds his "pathology" regarding the war:

I must confess, though, that I am a bibliophile with War books. Any book about the Great War is good enough for me. I am to that class of literature what little boys are to stamps. Yes; I know well the dread implication. I am aware of the worm in the mind; that I probe a wound; that I surrender to an impulse to peer into the darkness of the pit; that I encourage a thought which steals in with the quiet of midnight, and that it keeps me awake while the household sleeps. I know I consort with ghosts in a region of evil. I get the horrors, and I do not repel them. For some reason I like those ghosts. Most of them have no names for me, but I count them as old friends of mine; and where should I meet them again, at night, but amid the scenes we knew?[7]

The extent of this passion for war books is impressive—Tomlinson noted that "I have a catalogue of all the books and documents prompted by the War and published before June, 1916. It runs to 180 pages of small type. It contains the names of about 3,500 books and pamphlets."[8] This passion for war books is not a passion for warfare, however.

Speaking for myself, no matter how the subject is doctored to disguise its odor, with the traditional incense of national honor, with solemn anthems, with the epitaphs of heroes; no matter how, to keep our attention diverted from the highly repellent nature of this plague, we are cheered with brass bands, ornate theatrical costumes, cocks' feathers, banners, and the sobs of ladies who love good lads but don't mind seeing them go off to get mutilated (an exalted emotion, theirs, quite genuine, though its instinctive stirring in good Christian souls had better not be too closely investigated); no matter with what national songs and patriotic airs the reality of war is disguised, so that we may not guess or remember what we are really considering—for all that, it is a subject and a reality which I loathe as would anyone else the existence of a gas escape in a morgue.[9]

Tomlinson recognized the reaction against his preoccupation with the war and chose to deflate that reaction by addressing his preoccupation directly.

II *War and Literature*

When he regarded his role as staunch pacifist, Tomlinson objected to the presupposition that a pacifist could not be an historian. When he encounters a statement in William McFee's biography of Frobisher indicating that "he doubts that scholars of a peaceful temperament should attempt to write history,"[10] and then wonders why the Elizabethans did not romanticize such events as the defeat of the

Spanish Armada and the adventures of Drake's *Golden Hind*, Tomlinson finds a connection between Shakespeare's failure to glorify Elizabeth I's reign and his understanding of human nature.

For the man who wrote *King Lear* is silent about it; he ignores the sensational events which must have caused nearly all the talk on Tudor quaysides and in the taverns of London. Can there be a complete and satisfactory answer? Clearly we dare not say that Shakespeare was what is now called, disdainfully, a "pacifist," and that therefore he was aware—he was aware of most of the things which disturb us, which check us with doubts—that as a historian he would be mean and inadequate. Yet, even so, he might still have celebrated the triumphs of his great contemporaries? Well, he did not.[11]

The failure of an artistic genius to glorify contemporary events is also evident, for Tomlinson, in the few successful books about the war. When he considers the role of the soldier as an author, he cites Ardern Beaman's *The Squadroon*. The book was surprisingly good, but

To induce readers to buy it it has a picture on its dust-cover which kept me from reading it for weeks. This wrapper shows a ghostly knight in armour leading a charge of British cavalry in this War. I should have thought we had had enough of that romantic nonsense during the actual events. The War was "written up" for the benefit of readers who made a luxury of the sigh, and who were told and no doubt preferred to believe that the young soldier went into battle with the look we so admire in the picture called The Soul's Awakening. He was going to glory. There are no dead. There are only memorial crosses for heroes and the Last Post.[12]

To Tomlinson's surprise, however, "Mr. Beaman's book is not like war correspondence. It can be commended to those who were not there, but who wish to hear a true word or two."[13]

"To hear a true word or two" is unusual for readers of war books, even when the authors have been soldiers.

These authors who were soldiers faced the real War, but they dare not deride the noble and popular figments which lived but in the transports of the exalted. They write in whispers, as it were, embarrassed by a knowledge which they would communicate, but fear they may not. To shatter a cherished illusion, to expose the truth to a proud memory, that, I will confess, is always a task before which a sensitive man will hesitate. Yet it is also part of the test of a writer's courage; by his hesitation a soldier-author may know that he is in danger of failing in his duty.[14]

One barrier to the fidelity of the soldier-author's account is the misplaced fastidiousness of the reading public:

He is astonished by the reflection that if he were to reproduce with enjoyment the talk of the heroes which was usual in France, then many excellent ladies might denounce it indignantly as unmanly. Unmanly! But he is right. They not only might, but they would.[15]

Twenty-eight years later Richard Aldington, introducing James Hanley's *The German Prisoner* (1950), made the same point:

"But," it will be said, "there are so many dreadfully dirty words in the talk of these two men. Even though they are tortured to madness, we cannot sympathise with men who talk like that."

Well, you ought to. You were not afraid to send men to that hell, you did everything you could to get them there, and congratulated yourselves on your patriotic fervor.

Gentlemen! here are your defenders; ladies! here are the results of your charming white feathers. If you were not ashamed to send men into the war, why should you blush to read what they said in it?[16]

Tomlinson, as he had insisted in his travel writing, demanded as the minimum an author's scrupulous veracity to detail.

Tomlinson would insist, above all, that an author recognize the passing of glory from modern warfare. In an age when the casualties of warfare include the victims of indiscriminate bombs, war cannot confer honor:

When Flanders Fields take in the Marylebone Road flats, a romantic vista is lost. When the battle-ground includes all nurseries and infirmaries there comes not exaltation but a grue. The privilege of sudden death is for the infant as well as the paladin; and lifeboats and battleships share the same glory. Wonder goes out of war when it is on the doorstep and everywhere, when all seas, all back streets and coral strands, all tropical forests and London suburban gardens, have commonplace investments in "old unhappy far-off things and battles long ago."[17]

This will be as true of later wars as it was of World War I: "War now would be not only between soldiers. In future wars the place of honour would be occupied by the infants in their cradles. For war is not murder. Starving children is war, and it is not murder"[18] As a result of World War I, the European now recognizes that victory in war is synonymous with ruin, and that glory is only a common frustration of every effort towards civility, [and] he dreads that the new vast power in the west may gather some day into an overwhelming mass at the call of a noble and inspiring word, to another blessed crusade to compel righteousness among reluctant and alien men.[19]

The dread of the European, which Tomlinson described in 1931, resulted from the impressive power of the United States.

III   *Tomlinson's Antiwar Rhetoric*

Tomlinson's war writings, far from appealing to man's desire for glory, focused on the horrors of destruction. Describing his view of ruins, he found himself unable to comprehend it until

there, lying in the road, was that corn-chandler's ledger. It was the first understandable thing I had seen that day. I began to believe these abandoned and silent ruins had lived and flourished, had once a warm kindred life. . . .[20]

Tomlinson contrasts his personal vision of warfare with the dispassionate discussions he hears regarding future conflict:

As for me, I know what war is, though I am not going into so personal a matter; it merely prompts me to speak up when careless and thoughtless souls would discuss a future war as though it were an academic dispute over the probable finalists of the intercollegiate football matches. Calm talk of that sort is more than a man can stand after he has seen what happens when soldier boys get chlorine gas in the lungs, or what a group of children looks like when their bodies have been dispersed with an aeroplane bomb.[21]

One sight of reality will forever dispel the glorification of war:

Ypres is within the region where, when soldiers enter it, they abandon hope, because they have become sane at last, and their minds have a temperature a little below normal. In Ypres, whatever may have been their heroic and exalted dreams, they awake, see the world is mad, and surrender to the doom from which they know a world bereft will give them no reprieve.[22]

The War

provoked the emotions which assembled civilians in ecstatic support of the sacrifices, just as the staff of a corps headquarters, at some comfortable leagues behind the trenches, maintains its fighting men in the place where gas and shells tend to engender common sense and irresolution. [23]

Throughout his articles on the war Tomlinson reminds his readers that their glorified conception of warfare would fall before one glimpse of the truth.

When Tomlinson addressed the discrepancy between traditional views of national honor and fervor for war, he employed irony more often than bald description of ruin. Ashley Gibson, reviewing *Waiting for Daylight* (1922), praises Tomlinson's essays on the war:

we perceive from as many angles how exactly an intelligence far subtler and more sensitised than that of any common or garden Britling's saw the monstrous affair through. Here we have a mind both philosophic and poetic, a spirit sweet and charitable, sorrowful rather than angry over the hideous mess which the "strong men" let the world in for and handed over to the "nobodies" to do what they could by way of clearing up. The poisoned arrows of bitterness are not in Mr. Tomlinson's quiver. The blade of his irony flashes bright and often, but there is no rancour behind those thrusts, however keen. [24]

For Tomlinson, the Nobodies were the source of whatever wisdom grew from the war. He quotes one Nobody as saying to him "Don't tell me, sir, war teaches you a lot. It only shows fools what they didn't know but might 'ave guessed."[25] The Nobody did not necessarily have to go to the trenches to provide his wisdom. Tomlinson reports the verdict of a cobbler shortly after the war began: "You think . . . that this war will be over by Christmas. It won't. It will last for years, and when it is over that will be only the end of the first act in the European revolution."[26] For Tomlinson, "any average Nobody has a cool impregnability to the worst bad luck can do, which is conquering and awe-inspiring. That gives the affair something of the comic. That is what makes the humour of the front."[27] While the Nobody's "betters" cry "Calamity cometh!" the Nobody arises to solve the problem. "A Nobody never seems to know anything, but by the grace of God he gets there just the same."[28] Frequently in his antiwar writings, Tomlinson refers to the rather cynical humor of the men who fought the war:

the Knight-Errant, who also was returning to the front, re-wrote the well-known hymn of Phillips Brooks for me, to make the time pass. It began:

"Oh little town of Bethlehem,
   To thee we give the lie."[29]

Most of the soldier's humor verges on the sacrilegious: "It has become
a common joke that the only man who came out of the last war
with any credit was Jesus of Nazareth."[30]

To this cynical humor Tomlinson frequently adds his own ironical
sense of the reality behind attitudes toward the war. At times, this can
be heavy-handed:

It rained next morning. This was Christmas Day. We were going to the
trenches. Christians awake, salute the happy morn. There was a prospect of
straight road with an avenue of diminishing poplars going east, in an inky
smear, to the Germans and infinity. The rain lashed into my northerly ear,
and the A.S.C. motor-car driver, who was mad, kept missing three-ton lorries
and gun-limbers by the width of the paint. One transport mule, who pretended to be frightened of us, but whose father was the devil and his mother
an ass, plunged into a pond of black Flanders mud as we passed, and raked us
with solvent filth. We wiped it off our mouths. God rest you, merry gentlemen. A land so inundated that it inverted the raw and alien sky was on either
hand. The mud clung to the horses and mules like dangling walnuts and
bunches of earthy and glistening grapes. The men humped themselves in
sodden khaki. The noise of the wheels bearing guns was like the sound of
doom. The rain it rained. O come, all ye faithful![31]

Most of his irony is not so insistent, nor so extended. He comments
that "I have never heard that Americans gave the brewers the job of
settling the little problem of strong drink. Then why expect an
admiral to sink his ships or a general to reduce his bayonets?"[32] Much
of his irony derives from contrasts focusing on hypocrisy not always
perceived:

We attend the vicar's garden parties, and we see nothing curious in a
major-general—famous, naturally, like all generals—telling our youngsters
at the school's annual prize-giving that the privilege in their higher education
is to make foremost fools of them on some battlefield.[33]

Yet Tomlinson, like Shaw, enjoys taking a deeper look at reality than
usual to make a satiric comment on man's irrationality:

I have heard at home an ardent general on the retired list, who had never
made his way through the wire with his pockets full of bombs, and never

would, trying at a school prize-giving to arouse the enthusiasm of boys for the inevitability of war; talking airily but ignorantly of human nature and its proper and its inevitable functioning, and so on. And I wondered then as I listened what the parents of those boys would say and do if a pretty but immoral lady were to follow that general with similar advice to the boys about human nature and its inevitable functioning. That would raise a din, would it not? But the general's speech caused no protest.[34]

He does not hesitate to deride hypocrisy when the subject is misguiding youth to war: "'I wish I were young enough,' their uncles used to say, with a regret that seemed poignant, but was—and the uncles thanked God for it—idle."[35]

When Tomlinson describes the results of such influence, he takes on a Shavian combination of irony and understatement:

A real understanding of our calamity, an idea that the war had dropped on the world as the reward for humanity's common behavior, was even then, the December of 1914, beginning to dawn on the soldiers . . . . It was strange to hear from young British officers of the sort of job they had before them. Nothing like those ideas was ever entertained on the playing fields of Eton.[36]

When he considers the causes of warfare, Tomlinson comments derisively on the state of the world.

Anyone who does not believe in recurrent moods of despair or derision that the present world is crazy, is himself probably in need of skilled attention. We have been told by one of our most acute and attentive critics that humanity gives him the impression this earth is being used by the other planets as a lunatic asylum.[37]

Examining the reasons for man's continuous involvement in armed conflict, he concludes that man himself is irrational: "man is unteachable. He is the most unpredictable and dangerous animal which has ever developed on earth."[38] He notes that "it appears that the lesson of war is that no lesson is learned from it,"[39] and that "youth would march to destruction again, when the bugles call . . . . But youth did not make the last war, though it was the fighting force, nor will it make the next."[40] Tomlinson joins such satirists as Swift and Shaw in deploring the inability of writers to make lasting change, for "First and last, it is in the schools, homes, and newspaper offices that wars are made."[41] People are unwilling to hear the truth and are unable to feel the sufferings of others.

The Irish have a saying that a man may sleep comfortably on another man's wound. And Duhamel tells us that man must suffer in his flesh alone, and *that* is why war is possible. . . .

Yes, he has disclosed a secret. We can so easily bear the sufferings of others, especially if we do not even hear the boy crying in No Man's Land where none may aid him.[42]

Tomlinson argues that the inability of man to abandon war is partly a result of human nature.

However, the unwillingness or inability of an individual to perceive the truth before experiencing it does not absolve other causes that Tomlinson blames for the pro-war spirit of the modern age. He cites financiers and politicians as malign forces that advance the cause of war to serve their private interests: "the powers behind Congress and Parliament are inscrutable and unpredictable in their movements, and appear to be preparing for war. They are doing that without intending war, of course, and, of course, without any consent of ours."[43] Politicians are inherently inept because

Politicians move on the level of the common intelligence, and compete there with each other in charging the ignorance of the commonality. A politician need be no more than something between a curate and a cardsharper.[44]

The causes of war result from the same insidious influences that made Tomlinson an enemy of all progress:

Our own War was inherent in the inventions of mechanical cotton-spinning and the steam-engine—the need to compel foreign markets to buy the goods we made beyond our own needs. We know now what were the seeds the active and clever fellows of [the eighteenth century] were sowing for us. We were present at the harvesting.[45]

Man's folly may be responsible for his continuous involvement in the arts of destruction, but politicians, financiers, and mechanists feed on that folly.

The end of World War I brought little hope for peace, and as early as May 9, 1919, Tomlinson wrote that the Peace Treaty actually made another war more likely. Reasonable Europeans

cannot believe that the War, which they thought began as a war of liberation, a struggle for Europe to free itself from the intolerable bonds of its past, continues in the Peace Treaty as a force malignantly deflected to the very evils out of which August, 1914, arose. Then did they imagine the well-meaning leopard would oblige by changing his spots if spoken to kindly while he was eating the baby?[46]

For Tomlinson, "It was not the War, but the Peace and its Treaty that ruined Europe."[47] In 1930 he could take some encouragement from his contemporaries' enlightenment:

Yet in common opinion we may note now another change coming; for as to war, we are waking up, and we are turning to the sincere records of the last affair. We are growing disinclined for romantic nonsense. We have come through the heroic mood, and are not so moved as formerly by helpless sobs and laurel wreaths. We are afraid that graves are opening and that ghosts are gibbering.[48]

This growing awareness, however, had another side which disturbed Tomlinson:

a youth, an idealist who was broken in the war, thinking of patriotic chants and imperialism, said to me: "The Union Jack! It means no more to me now than a stranger's shirt hanging on the line to dry. I've had enough of that nonsense."

There, indeed, is our task. We have to give that boy, and those like him, another content for that symbol.[49]

Ironically, the youngster's revulsion for the Union Jack was partly the result of Tomlinson's attempts to undermine patriotic fervor. He reported a conversation in which a veteran urged him to

"Write a book that will make people hate the idea that the State is God as Moloch was at last hated. Turn the young against it. The latest priest is the politician. No ritual in any religion was worse than this new worship of the state. If men don't wake up to that, then they are doomed."[50]

The veteran's invitation for Tomlinson to write such a book came in 1920, and the youth's disillusioned statement came in 1922, after Tomlinson had written numerous critical essays deploring warfare. When he wrote *Mars His Idiot* in 1935, Tomlinson heeded the veteran and tried to ignore the youth's rejection of patriotism.

IV   Mars His Idiot

Mars His Idiot is not entirely effective, partly because he had already written so much about the war, partly because he tried to sound reasonable to the detriment of the polemicist's traditionally strident voice, and partly because he had little to offer in the way of a solution. His book also lacks the immediacy and urgency of such antiwar writing as Swift's *Conduct of the Allies* or Shaw's *Common Sense About the War* in that it is written almost twenty years after the war's end, and before the emergence of Hitler in Germany began to assume an aspect of impending doom for Europe. Instead of focusing on inflammatory issues which are immediately identifiable, Tomlinson's book flows in a discursive style which is very easy to read but difficult to recall afterwards. Even the sections of his book are untitled, diminishing the organization of his presentation. In a word, the book is a discussion rather than an argument.

Tomlinson begins his book with an appropriate epigraph from Shelley:

> Power, like a desolating pestilence,
> Pollutes whate'er it touches; and obedience,
> Bane of all genius, virtue, freedom, truth,
> Makes slaves of men, and, of the human frame,
> A mechanized automaton.[51]

Although this passage, taken from *Queen Mab*, would suggest a harsh indictment of the forces of power, Tomlinson adopts a less direct approach. Early in the book he justifies his preoccupation with World War I in terms of what it can teach about the next war.

If some of us are still held by the memory of that last war, it is not only because we had a dose of it; so had the mules. But the idea that innocence should again be caught unaware, caught and lost in the insensate grind of another such mechanical and universal horror, gets between us and the sunlight. We know that mystical stuff about the badness of human nature, which never changes, and that war is an exercise which improves the heart muscles; but we are not bemused. Only fools pretend to believe there was no warning out of the last war and its consequences which told us that men must either discover a better way of life or else clear out. (*Mars*, 11–12)

He states that the first World War was inevitable in one sense:

That war came as the unavoidable consequence of forty years of the intrigues and confident tactics of Europe's statesmen and diplomatists, each of them seeking security and enhanced profit for his nation. Security turned out to be the wreck of a continent. Profit proved to be the same as common bankruptcy. To keep the future safe for the rising generation its blood was poured down the drains. (*Mars*, 25–26)

Tomlinson later qualifies this statement:

But our last great war was no more inevitable than the loss of the *Titanic*. Certainly it was inevitable in the opinion we held and the things we did; but we could have done better thinking and acted with more decorum. It was the result of folly. Only a little reading of the history of Europe since 1870, and particularly since 1900, tells us that we had our great war only because fear and stupidity brought us to it. (*Mars*, 38–39)

In terms of the causes of World War I, Tomlinson has little to offer except the observation that man's thoughts and actions led him to it and that man could have avoided the war had he demonstrated more foresight.

However, Tomlinson is more concerned with the prospect of a coming war, and he finds sufficient cause to expect one. He states that "The Treaty of Versailles was but a bridge of tinder over hell" (*Mars*, 31) and comments that the fruits of this treaty were a "greater complication of frontiers" and a war debt "so fantastic that only the hallucinations of malevolence could have fashioned it" (*Mars*, 114, 115).

The only creative word spoken at Versailles was the League of Nations; and because the United States of America abandoned their own best contribution to the debates, that League lapsed into a group of victors fearful of the security of their victory. Europe was given over to anarchy. Georges Clemenceau confessed afterwards: "the art of arranging how men are to live is more complex than that of massacring them." (*Mars*, 115)

For Tomlinson, the issues of war are never far from "security" and "profit," and he had harsh words for those responsible. The statesmen concerned for security failed:

Of all the ideas shaping the policies of Europe's potentates and statesmen during those forty years [between 1870 and 1910] not one came to anything but skulls. The cunning devices of those statesmen led not to triumphs but corruption. They were all wrong, all of them, and all the time. (*Mars*, 33)

Those motivated by profit were no better: "While goods are grown and made for profit, and not for use, then swords will never be turned into ploughshares. They will be of more service as swords" (*Mars*, 120). Tomlinson argues that since modern warfare can drop bombs on classrooms, war and security are incompatible. He comments that the bombing of civilians is the ultimate insult of man to his Maker: "To procure abortion with a bomb!" (*Mars*, 49), and he dismisses the traditional picture of heroism from modern conflict.

Anybody may be a hero in the future, and instead of with sword and banner fulfil his destiny, little guessing it was upon him, handling a kitchen shovel in his own coal-shed. War becomes serious when we may die though we never joined-up, and while doing nothing more aggressive than attending to the water for the bath. (*Mars*, 53)

After he has degraded the heroism of warfare by machinery, he proceeds to make war an unpleasant prospect from the point of view of those who serve in it.

Tomlinson addresses much of his argument to youth, frequently adopting a stance of talking to a younger generation directly and often referring to youth as his subject. He wishes to discourage an heroic view of the young soldier in the trenches:

We are assured that war ennobles the spirit of youth. A young man armed, and smelling lyddite, looking to the wire where his enemy is hidden and waiting, feels the soul's awakening. I suspect that to be a myth of the boudoirs. War, as we saw it last time, not only breaks the body, but wrecks faith and hope. (*Mars*, 45)

Tomlinson could have proceeded from here to apply his descriptive powers to such foes of a soldier as fear, mud, lice, and boredom, as well as the continuous dread of imminent destruction, but he chooses not to do so. He keeps his discussion on more abstract plane:

When a man must summon the courage, not to meet a champion of his own weight, but to fight an automaton of his own invention, which simply rolls over him unheeding his valor and skill, then he has reached the point of sublime idiocy.

War is even worse than that. It has sunk to a bestiality which, to men compelled to obey orders, is a filthy outrage on the mind. I do not think the effects of phosgene are worse than those of shrapnel. I do not see why, since civilians cheer the progress of war, they should not share the bombs with the troops, as in future they must. (*Mars*, 48)

Instead of providing a vivid picture of a war without heroism or chivalry, Tomlinson prefers to discuss it in more general terms.

It is the day of the national war. Chivalry has gone, and cannot be revived. Chivalry is as remote a solacing legend as Bethlehem, in the year when Mussolini orates before "a splendid display of force," and Japanese soldiers fire trench mortars over Pekin University as a warning to the Chinese that they are "harboring dangerous thoughts." (*Mars*, 165)

He treats chivalry as a luxury which warriors no longer can afford:

When a nation is "fighting for its life" chivalry is preposterous. The foe must be damaged by any means that offers, however hideous the result. There is no rule but one for the right conduct of a national war: obliterate the enemy. So even an infant in her cradle may be a heroine, the equal of standard men, uncomplainingly suffering her cyanide gas or torn bowels. We are all in it, when the clock strikes; there can be no exceptions; and any moral attitude assumed would be an invitation to death, and any high-mindedness in national policy a hostage to fortune. (*Mars*, 166)

Against this picture of war without chivalry, Tomlinson places the soldier without identity. He laments the sacrifice of individuality which participation in modern warfare requires:

It is the person that counts. The multitude is only counted. Why, even in war it is in the mind of a soldier (who might have been one's jobbing gardener) and not between armies, that the battle is fought. The battle is in a man's own heart. The more important outcome of so stupendous a spectacle, with its dramatic thunders and flames, may be unseen and unheard, and more than likely will be forever secret. We forget that. (*Mars*, 59–60)

Once a man becomes a soldier, he loses his personality and his worth as a human being.

His suffering is spilled into an ocean of it, so makes no difference. It is the lives of all those others, "this generation," or "the men in the line" and presently "on the dole," or "the enemy," or "the women and children," lives counted in a mass, statistically, totals of numbers and categories that are bloodless; they are the lives we do not feel as important, except numerically. There can be no feeling for mere varieties of the population. Men and women are lost in generalities that merge into an abstraction called humanity. (*Mars*, 60)

After the soldier has fought, and suffered, and returns a cripple, "His country . . . is intent on something more interesting than a ruined man" (*Mars*, 61).

Part of this soldier's plight is the result of the malice of statesmen and financiers. Tomlinson distrusts multitudes, not because they are inherently inhuman but because they are "that limitless repository of instincts and emotions that can be enlisted for service by skilful men seeking wealth and power" (*Mars*, 151). In the modern state,

Of what value is personality there? It hasn't any. It is a nuisance. It is ignored, and perhaps blown out. Statesmen and other controllers of primary forces do not reckon men and women, but man-power; and the machinery of the State has a control of that enormous energy as complete as a power-station over electrical supply. (*Mars*, 153)

This enables Lord Kitchener to feel "great distress over an early and abortive battle in France. He exclaimed, 'Terrible, terrible!' His colleagues thought he grieved for lost men; but his sorrow was for wasted shells" (*Mars*, 62). The soldier has subjected himself to such indignity because he has succumbed to the appeal of Nationalism as a religion:

And whatever else you may have worshipped, whichever altar you once served, that is abolished; for the Nation is the One.

The Nation is Alpha and Omega. It is the Absolute. Zeus with his thunderbolts was only a nice chubby little cupid to this new god. It has all the attributes of deity, being unbegotten and without form, though omniscient and omnipresent. It is the All Terrible which is unescapable. A man is exalted when he abandons himself to its inexplicability, to its august caprices. (*Mars*, 68)

Man's surrender of individuality to the state can mark the end of all man's essential worth, for "There is no soul now but in the Nation, and no religion but joyous acceptance of the decrees that prompt its instincts into activity" (*Mars*, 68).

Such enormities as those provided by warfare result from the character of a nation, which lacks the positive attributes of individual character. Tomlinson often made this comparison.

A nation has no honor; racial needs and impulses know nothing of it. Honor, like reason, would but confuse instincts that are on the way to the gratification of a viewless appetite. A nation knows no morality, but only what it wants. (*Mars*, 71)

Man's dominance by the state has reached such proportions that Tomlinson can only hope that "men will find they have had enough ot it. It will occur to them that the State is only a necessary instrument, like the drains; it was meant to save trouble, not to make it, and they will see that it dutifully performs its rightful office" (*Mars*, 157). After asserting that "The base of human nature may be depended on; it is human" (*Mars*, 158), Tomlinson compares human nature with the nature of the state, which is "non-human; an august muddle; a loud but indeterminate noise; its motives are low and fuddled. The man is above the State, for the State can claim, as a deified ideal, no more love than we should give to tricky scales for weighing bread" (*Mars*, 159–60).

For an answer to the dilemma of the modern state, Tomlinson can turn only to the individual.

The State never accepts the risk involved in a nobler ethic than that shown by its neighbors, and a man often will; it is the only way by which a better opinion may prevail. The culture of a country, its science, art, literature, and the code of its industrial and merchant class, is the work of individuals, contributing to a tradition. (*Mars*, 160)

He argues that the morality of individual men must apply to that of the nation.

A citizen who murders a neighbor while stealing his property is hung without a recommendation to mercy. When a Great Power does this, however, other names must be found for the crime, because the world does admit a moral order. Murder and Robbery by a Great Power, when enforcing claims no law would recognize, are called Defence; they must be seen as points of Honor. (*Mars*, 203)

The problem with human nature, however, is that it is ill equipped to confront the demands of the nation, even against the better impulses of the individual.

The serious difficulty with human nature is not that it is brutal, but confiding and submissive; it may know the better thing but do the worst, when ordered to it. (*Mars*, 145)

He comments that "There is no reason to despair of human nature because it cannot be changed. Opinions . . . can be changed," and concludes that "Though our nature does not change, our acts are a matter of choice" (*Mars*, 145, 147). Although his optimism may not be convincing, Tomlinson asserts that "Mankind need not have war if they do not want it. Let us be platitudinous; a platitude is only an assertion of a fact too well known to be noticed. We do not want war, and yet it comes" (*Mars*, 221).

His solution to the problem, if it may be called a solution, depends on his belief in the inherent goodness of man. "I cannot believe it is inevitable that owing to the divinity of reason men should become flocks of ready obedience, and so close the book of life. They need not; though it would suit some people if they did" (*Mars*, 156). The problem that Tomlinson does not address is how to prevent "some people," who bear a suspicious resemblance to statesmen and financiers. When Tomlinson discusses the uncertainty of man's change, he begins to sound like the youth who has complained to him thirteen years before the appearance of *Mars His Idiot*:

So we cannot say when patriotism will be God-like. We are still the bond-slaves of realms. The change can come only of saner and milder opinion; out of patience, understanding, tolerance, and the courage that is unimpressed by confident bulk and peremptory noises. We do not know when the dream which came to Hardy will be seen by enough of us to make it a waking reality. We know only that it will not be common while patriots continue to confuse love for their country with pride in its prestige as a Great Power. (*Mars*, 197)

Unfortunately for Tomlinson, *Mars His Idiot*, and modern man, a movement against war rallying around "saner and milder opinion" would have little impact against the more arousing and flamboyant cries of chauvinistic fervor.

When William Harlan Hale reviewed *Mars His Idiot* in 1935, he commented that "A pacifist book is a thing to be automatically welcomed. . . . One hopes, therefore, for some special message. One is not rewarded."[52] Hale felt that

The author places his reliance not in a revolt of the masses against their warlike dictators, but in the conscience of the individual person. It might be unfair to call this a doctrine of passive resistance, but the general forceless-ness of Mr. Tomlinson's conclusion does suggest it.[53]

To this "general forcelessness" the Alticks add that Tomlinson "wrote so persistently about the war (it could not be kept out of even his most Conradian sea-pieces) that it became less of a horror than an unmitigated nuisance."[54] For me, however, the comparative ineffectiveness of *Mars His Idiot* results from its timing. Most of the statements Tomlinson made against financiers, statesmen, the Versailles Treaty, and the horrors of war had appeared as early in his career as 1920. He might have written *Mars His Idiot* immediately after the treaty, attacking it as a probable cause for another war, and thus have reached a much larger audience. He might have assumed the adversary posture so skillfully employed by Swift and Shaw in their polemical writings, directing his audience by arousing its anger rather than appealing for a "saner and milder opinion," which will always be ignored by those in the grip of patriotic fervor. As a tract against war, *Mars His Idiot* fails partly because its tone is as pacifistic as its aims. A reasonable approach in the form of discursive argument appears fairly indistinct beside a pamphlet trying to jar its readers out of complacency.

CHAPTER 8

The Propagandist

I *From Pacifism to Propaganda*

AFTER Hitler invaded Poland in 1939 and Europe became embroiled in another holocaust, Tomlinson wrote several articles in support of the British war effort. Although some regarded this as a disturbing shift in his philosophy, and others wondered how damaging his earlier writing had been to the preparedness of Britain and her allies, in reality Tomlinson's World War II writings were partly a vindication of his pacifist works. Helen and Richard Altick wrote in November, 1943:

The results of the present war must first be in, and the crusade against war given a chance to revive, before we can be sure what the writers of anti-war tracts in the 1920's and 1930's really did to us.[1]

As early as 1922 Tomlinson described one possible effect of the post-World War I attitude on military readiness at "a historic naval base":

A fleet of British warships, from Dreadnoughts to submarines, with all its priceless gear and appurtenances, and many of its vessels "hush" craft of the war, is there decaying at its moorings. The ships are rusty and dismantled; they are rotting. A bare hint of so monstrous an iniquity ten years ago would have swept any government out of office instantly. Yet to-day nobody was interested enough to pay attention to the sad story. It was even considered, by professional pressmen, bad journalism to print it. Let them rot, we murmured.[2]

The Alticks wrote:

The present war has seen Tomlinson for the most part drifting out of control. Superficially what he has written since the rape of Poland reads like a negation of his old principles; for he has proclaimed that this war is different.

147

It is a necessary war—a war against barbarism and the threat of world enslavement.[3]

From here, the Alticks argue that Tomlinson's antiwar writing was without a sense of purpose, making it "heavy with a conviction . . . of futility,"[4] thereby attributing Tomlinson's shift to a defect in his pacifism.

However, even before the outbreak of World War II, Tomlinson indicated that even a pacifist must recognize a need to fight, given one condition. Citing the Kellog Pact in 1931, which attempted to outlaw war, Tomlinson wrote that "There can be no neutrals, when the maker of war is an outlaw; there can be but the rest of the world against any nation guilty of anarchy."[5] At the end of this article, prophetically entitled "That Next War," Tomlinson states that

Even though the cynics are right when they tell us the tide of events on which we drift is blind, yet our course need not be set for nowhere and disaster, unless we shut our eyes and make no effort towards a proper course. That can be made; but let us remember that a love of peace is not mere negation, but is revolutionary; it only begins in a revulsion from dirt and evil.[6]

When Tomlinson wrote in support of the effort against Hitler, he emphasized the need to prevent Hitler from destroying civilization, the pride he felt in his people as they demonstrated their courage in adversity, and the suffering that warfare brings to friend and foe alike.

Tomlinson addressed the apparent shift in his writing as early as July, 1940, when he compared his anti-Hitler article with *Mars His Idiot*:

Some of my friends may be surprised that I write thus of war. I still think war an obscene outrage on the intelligence. I should not be in the least upset by what Communists call the downfall of British Imperialism. I see no reason to alter a line of what I wrote of war and peace in *Mars His Idiot*.[7]

The justification of this statement, for Tomlinson, is the necessity to choose between freedom and dignity on the one hand, and submission to the Nazis on the other:

But this challenge of the Nazis is ultimate. If they have their way then nothing can be discussed. There will be no right or wrong, neither good nor evil; even the priest at the altar may be one of the secret police. Slavery is bearable, but the mind in chains is not. I know that some of our traditions and institutions may perish in resisting this subversion of the mind, but all will surely perish if no resistance is made. That is the choice we have.[8]

For Tomlinson, this conflict between Nazi and Briton shakes the very foundations of civilized values.

He continues to praise the common man in his propaganda, to the detriment of statesmen and "great men" and T.S. Eliot:

> When I hear eloquence, large and loose, on great men and great heroes, I feel as uneasy as when reading of hollow men who end not with a bang but a whimper . . . .
> Have we forgotten what happened when the test of all came in 1940? Looking back, I think we may be forgiven some pride in our people. The bearing of our neighbours in that year, threatened with the loss of their "waste land," threatened that even its ancient and honoured name should be dropped into the mud, still astonishes, when we recall it. They were not hollow. They did not falter. They never so much as repined. They accepted the challenge in quietude.[9]

As in his pacifistic writing, Tomlinson focuses on the common man, the Nobody, as the embodiment of British virtues. When he writes of varied efforts in an attempt to exemplify British heroism, Tomlinson focuses on the fire brigade during the bombings, the seamen who fish in defiance of Nazi plane and submarine, the grocer's boy who has enlisted in the cause of the democracies, and above all his beloved Cockneys.

Although Tomlinson has enlisted in the ranks of war propagandists, he retains his compassion for human beings of whatever nationality and refrains from expressing hatred against all Germans, although his tolerance began to wear somewhat thin after his home was destroyed by a robot bomb in October, 1944. Tomlinson frequently states a reluctance to do unto others which makes his writing much more effective than a frenzied indictment against all Germans. In December, 1941, he remarks that the necessary defense of civilization has some morally unpleasant side-effects:

> It begins to appear that, when deciding war to be far better than to allow our altars and everything else to be kicked over by perverts and morons, much that was inherent in the choice was not seen at the time. Good people, therefore, are now appalled, for they find that getting rid of German war factories also rids Germany of many women and children; yet evidently it has become a plain duty to destroy those factories. Every choice has its inevitable

inherencies, just as though law governs our ways as well as the courses of the stars.[10]

Painful as this may be, however, Tomlinson reduces it to a matter of choice:

Still, what else could we have done, after Hitler's act at Prague? What else was there to do but face him? Tell us that. It troubles us, the horror of it; but what is now going on in the world was as certain to come about as disease following careless dirt . . . our statesmen . . . are telling us now that nobody foresaw the consequences of war from the sky. But that is a lie. It was not only known but it has happened before. It happened in the last war. It was pointed out years ago that the cradle would have the place of honour in the next war; and it is there.[11]

In his accusations against statesmen, however, Tomlinson has not changed, nor has his attitude toward destruction and civilians' death altered. If he exercised his freedom of choice to determine the lesser of two evils, he did not try to argue that the lesser evil was less evil.

In September, 1940, Tomlinson published an article entitled "Propaganda" which lends some insight into his understanding of his apparently new role. After noting that "The variation and uses of propaganda are protean,"[12] he states that "No aspect of social life is free from propaganda, not even religion, literature, and the arts."[13] For Tomlinson, the question becomes one of good versus evil, of good advice as opposed to deliberate manipulation by lies. He cites two examples of propaganda to press his point. First, he mentions the widespread belief of World War I that British soldiers had been crucified by Germans. Tomlinson denied this in a review, only to receive a letter from a soldier claiming to be an eyewitness to this particular atrocity.

The man was alive, his name was given, the battalion of the regiment in which he had served, the date when the crucified Tommy was seen, and the place in Flanders. This was serious. My editor thought we were caught, and ought to own up. But I delayed the apology a little, and discovered almost by return of post that this man's name did not appear on the regimental roll, and that the battalion in which he said he had served was not in Flanders but in India at the time he mentioned.[14]

Tomlinson cited this piece of propaganda not to call the soldier a liar, but to point out that we are ready "to believe whatever agrees with our mood or faith . . . . The absurdity of the tale is only further evidence of the subhuman character of whatever opposes us."[15] He cites another example which the British War Office would neither deny or confirm, the presence of Russian soldiers in England during August, 1914. The rumor readily spread, and Tomlinson's inability to meet and interview these Russians was attributed to their being shifted to the Front.

The right wing of the Germans then, you will recall, was sweeping round rapidly on Paris. Paris was about to fall. Anybody in those days could see plainly that the German right wing was vulnerable, if only a flank attack could be made upon it. And how could the German command decide that such an attack was out of the question? That command had heard as much about the Russians as most of us.[16]

The former example Tomlinson would call an attempt to take advantage of human gullibility, while he would appreciate the latter as a piece that had military effectiveness. He concluded, "There is nothing to protect us but the quality of our understanding and the soundness of our gumption."[17]

Tomlinson's propaganda was different from the extremes of his examples. Assuming the tone of a good man offering sound advice, rarely going beyond the authority of his personal observation and conversations, Tomlinson wrote pro-British articles of two distinct types. Between August, 1939, and August, 1941, he wrote a series of essays for the *Atlantic Monthly*, directed toward an American audience. The purpose of these articles was to arouse American sympathy for Britain, standing alone against the Nazis, and to convince America that America could not remain aloof from the struggle. The later articles, written between December, 1941, and July, 1945, continued to justify the British war effort, described the travails of Londoners subject to German air raids and robot bombs, and affirmed the need for the democratic victors to make this war meaningful by laying the foundations for a lasting peace. As propaganda, both series were effective. By arguing from the viewpoint of a man who deplores war, and by limiting his articles to his direct observations and personal opinions, Tomlinson's propagandistic pieces were effective in a way his pacifist writing was not. A reasonable tone may not be effective in his pacifistic writing, but it must have seemed somewhat refreshing in the midst of rabid anti-German polemicists.

II   The Wind Is Rising

When Tomlinson collected twelve of his articles written for Americans in *The Wind Is Rising* (1941), he chose as his epigraph part of Carlyle's *History of the French Revolution*:

Alas, yes! a whole world to remake. . . . For all is wrong, and gone out of joint; the inward spiritual, and the outward economical; head or heart, there is no soundness in it. As indeed, evils of all sorts are more or less of kin, and do usually go together: especially it is an old truth that wherever huge physical evil is, there, as the parent and origin of it, has moral evil to a proportionate extent been.

The essays are presented in diary form, each dated by month and year. Although rarely does Tomlinson overtly invite the Americans to take their part in the struggle against Germany, this is implicit in his descriptions of England's sense of loneliness in the struggle, his comments that the age of isolation has been brought to an end by modern aviation, and his expressions of cultural kinship uniting England and America.

"Omens" (August, 1939) discusses the impending conflict with Germany and the visit of the German minister for foreign affairs, Joachim von Ribbentrop, to Moscow, suggesting that Russia might cooperate with Germany. Tomlinson begins his essay with almost polemical fervor:

We hear nothing from Berlin but the music of marrowbones and cleavers. We are weary of it. The dire cries and antics which have kept Europe in commotion for years, and can mean only that Germany is possessed, must be ended. But how? We recoil from the thought of war; yet this deadening uproar must not go on. It checks the hand of every man at his task. Growth is stopped. (*Wind*, 3)

When he describes the state of Europe at the brink of another war, Tomlinson focuses on the contrast between "reason" and "each brutal assault on the understanding":

For ten years past, febrile unreason, of the size of a great nation, has been flinging the institutions of its neighbours about like old kettles, bawling at us, and making the general air ammoniac with feral odours. We have been kept thoroughly worried. We are tired of it. It has caused a flight to America of the more nervous of us. (*Wind*, 4–5)

Tomlinson finds absurd

the belief that decency in the future would have much noticeable effect on European politics. Mussolini's piracies and wholesale murders, Hitler's pulverizing of helpless Guernica with his bombers, and his salvoes from a battleship on sleeping Almería in revenge, while nobody did more than shake the head regretfully, told us that honour and all the virtues had been flung, in haste of prudence, into the dustbins of the world's chancelleries. (*Wind*, 5)

Tomlinson places this in the context of history, beginning in 1930:

A doubt occurred to a few onlookers then. If the German people allowed cruelties so foul to be done to Germans, to their own liberals, democrats, dissidents, folk of Jewish birth, trades-unionists, indeed to any man or woman against whom the Nazis had a grudge, what would they care if the same were done to us? (*Wind*, 6)

At the outset of the series, Tomlinson states the reasons why even a pacifist can justify opposing the Germans and sets the stage for what is to come. He remarks that "We still had one genuine reason on which hope of peace could be maintained. There was Russia" (*Wind*, 7), and then dispels hope with the news that Ribbentrop has gone to Moscow.

There it is. The Germans are now free to attack the Poles. If they do, then act we must, whatever Russia does, or be forever damned. There is no return. Our fleet is out, and the French army is in the order of battle. Surely even now Hitler cannot be so confident of the outcome of chaos as to open fire? The world's air is suddenly loud with presidents, premiers, and prelates, beseeching that man of destiny not to pull the trigger. (*Wind*, 9)

Undoubtedly written after the fact, this initial essay provides the rationale for those that follow.

The second essay, "The Black Shade" (September, 1939), reports only one "fact" worth noting—"They've started" (*Wind*, 10). The rest of the essay consists of Tomlinson's reflections of what is to come, based on his memory of World War I. He comments on the irony of modern civilization: "Innocently bent on increasing light, it never entered the head even of Aristotle that light could be bad for man" (*Wind*, 15), referring to the implausible use man has made of reason, and then he proceeds to the blackout "over a continent now" (*Wind*, 16). He speaks briefly of the censorship that had been a problem of war correspondence during World War I:

I remember that in the beginning one was allowed to mention the fact that a battlefield could be reproachful with the strewn results of bullets. Later, only German soldiers were slain in battle. Later still, it was decided by the proper authority that a great battle could leave the floor as tidy as would a curate's sewing circle. We may judge then, from these queer signs, that authority does respect the sensibility and intelligence of the public? (*Wind*, 16–17)

Tomlinson proceeds to comment on the necessity of censorship during war, stating that "Truth, in war, can be more terrible than a flight of bombers. For that reason it is war's first casualty. It must be retired with the enemy aliens, and suitably guarded" (*Wind*, 22). However, he adds that censorship contains a grave danger and reports what occurred after the Germans had exaggerated their reports of victory:

Mark what happened. A day came when the German public had to be told that its armies, marching to victory, were falling back. Then that public, its courage kept by falsities, collapsed. The stimulative propaganda meant to strengthen its heart was the cause of sudden heart-failure. (*Wind*, 24)

"The Cliffs of England" (July, 1940) begins a subtle argument which will end in England's inviting America to join her. Tomlinson describes his location on a cliff where a "young friend" found a flint arrowhead dating back to "about the year when Abraham journeyed south to Egypt," where a "beacon flared, when at last the Armada of Spain was in sight," whence "a ship called the *Mayflower* was insignificant in the distance, bound for what no watcher on this height could say," and whence the *Victory* sailed "west and south, on her way to Trafalgar" (*Wind*, 26). Tomlinson then reports that "An American friend, concerned for my welfare, in a recent letter hoped that I had 'gone inland.' We have no inland. The challenge allows none" (*Wind*, 27). He then notes that the coast of France, once a source of security, now is the home of the enemy, and he moves to his major theme:

What faces us today transcends international war. It is new in history; anyhow, new since the forgotten Tatar invasions. It goes beyond contention over sovereignty, and over ancient rights to tribute. From the beginning of this war its inherency was guessed, and in this hour it is stark. There can be no compromise with our adversary; implacable evil has no good in it to which reason can appeal. Our enemy speaks a language civility does not know and cannot learn. (*Wind*, 28)

Tomlinson then identifies the war not as between England and Germany, but between civilization and barbarism.

The old values, patriotism, philanthropy, religion, kinship, which we thought as enduring as the hills, we have discovered can disappear in a night, as though all we had even innocently trusted was spectral. . . . the German revolution is against all those traditional sanctities acknowledged by fellowship, and without which hitherto we could not imagine communal life. (*Wind*, 32–33)

He then states that his present stance contradicts not a word of *Mars His Idiot* and reduces the struggle to a choice between resistance and the destruction of tradition and institutions, or nonresistance and the destruction of all tradition and institutions.

"England Under Fire" (August, 1940) describes the experience of waiting for enemy bombers and the growing resentment of Londoners toward Hitler:

Ten minutes are bestowed on a shelter, as formal acknowledgment of kindly official instructions, and then, unless ruin has come close, men and women go up to their tasks. Mustn't waste time! But what a cold hatred of the Nazis accumulates! "They shall pay for this!" decided the aged shopkeeper in the by-street, when she came out to rescue from plaster and broken glass what was left of her stock. Many of us are in full sympathy with her, for one reason or another. (*Wind*, 70)

Tomlinson quotes the German Minister of Justice: "Right . . . is what is in the interests of the German *Volk*; wrong is what harms it" (*Wind*, 70) and concludes that resistance is the only answer. He praises the British air fleet for destroying "the legend that German propaganda had created of the invincibility of Hitler's Luftwaffe" (*Wind*, 70–71) and reports that now the English are bombing Berlin, but he does so with a restraint calculated to appeal to reasonable men:

The destruction Berlin designed for others is visiting her own precincts. What Berliners rejoiced to hear had been done to Rotterdam and Warsaw is being returned to them. I do not want to exult. That, too, is hateful. There is cruelty enough in the world without adding to it. Nor could anyone exult after witnessing what may be seen in my own neighbourhood. (*Wind*, 72)

"The Battle of London" (September, 1940) is Tomlinson's tribute to

the common man, who won the Battle of Britain. After describing the
German bombers as "The ride of the Valkyries . . . seen and heard
over Paternoster Row" (*Wind*, 83), Tomlinson describes the result:

As anyone who keeps his wonder over the mystery of human nature would
have guessed—anyone, that is, except men whose faith is based on the evil in
us—the Nazi attempt to break the spirit of the citizens in the centre of the
British Commonwealth has raised an unexpected power against Hitler.
(*Wind*, 83)

This unexpected power is the active resistance of the Nobodies,
which may result in Hitler's losing the war. "Hitler won't know what
he did to himself, when he tried to break them, until he is informed.
There is a blasphemy against life to be exorcized" (*Wind*, 84). Formerly Tomlinson regarded human frailty as ubiquitous,

But I have learned since how common is valour, though when things are well
we do not see it in the strangers about us, because no special call has come.
That, today, is an assurance of a better world, if we survive, and if we will it. It
was not soldiers who kept London steady when Göring's legions struck. Only
one's neighbours were there. They did it. (*Wind*, 90)

He admits that "I was unaware mettled people were so numerous"
(*Wind*, 91).

"Vistas of War" (January, 1941) shifts from the heroism of the British
to the destruction the Germans have caused in the city of London.
Tomlinson compares the present destruction with the London fire of
1666 and draws a conclusion with implications for America:

I have wondered since whether I did well to go over the ground again, after
its second Great Fire. It was not the body that could stand no more of it, but
the eyes, weary of seeing. Nothing tires the spirit so much as a contemplation
of waste, the waste of good. Malice is depravity. All seems undone. London
this day is a warning against attempts to negotiate with the diabolical.
Londoners see and smell daily what happens if you try to appease that.
(*Wind*, 103)

He wants to clarify one misconception that Americans might hold:

I suppose I had better not speak too loudly of other ruins in London, and
elsewhere; we don't want to hear rejoicing in the wrong place. But you may
tell your informant he is ignorant if he says the aim of Nazi bombers is for
military objects. They are attempting to do in London what they did on the
continent, divide the people from their rulers, and turn the anger of the
multitude against the government. A bomb launched on a parachute cannot

be aimed, but if it drifts over an area of tenements for the workers, then presently, on contact anywhere below, it will blast to the ground a parish of rickety houses. This the Nazis do. (*Wind*, 108–09)

After he talks of such traditional London sights as St. Paul's, he shifts his address directly to Americans.

Mr. H.G. Wells is just back with us after a visit to the United States, and he reports—and we always attend to what that great man has to say—that Americans are not interested in stained glass, but only in successes. I feel rebuked. There may be more stained glass in my view of it than is right. (*Wind*, 112)

Once he has used this means to confront his American audience more openly, he uses it to advance his argument.

Tomlinson focuses on the American preference for victory:

As to success, we on this side also are plucked up when we hear of it. Our hopeful eyes are fixed on the horizon for it all day long. It cheers even a pacifist when the grandiose arrogance of Mussolini and his cohorts is deflated by quiet men who were civilians but yesterday. Mussolini today has new and better information about the senility of democrats, and joy may be wicked, but we are joyful. Our successes in Africa, unimaginable some months ago when Hitler was about to march through Syria and Palestine, or somewhere, to meet Mussolini at Suez, look as clean and decisive as the abrupt intervention of Providence when tired of presumptuous fools. (*Wind*, 112)

Tomlinson does not shift his attention from stained glass, however. He tries to make it the more relevant to his audience.

By Tower Hill there was a church which escaped the fire of 1666, mainly because of the efforts of Admiral Penn, father of William, founder of Pennsylvania; and Pepys witnessed that fire from its steeple. It has not escaped this time. The old building held much of London's long story. William Penn was baptized in it, John Quincy Adams married. There is a Roman pavement in its foundations. The Temple off Fleet Street, which was a London sanctuary, will not now bear looking at, if you used to know it. You may not be interested in stained glass, yet it is hard for a Londoner to say what he feels about the loss of it. (*Wind*, 117)

He does not end his article on a pessimistic note, however. He feels that "we need not fear that either war, or the corrosion of the idea of profit, will overcome the sense of the past," for "the form vanishes, the spirit endures. There is continuity" (*Wind*, 119). In his next article he continues to address the American directly, relating it to the issue of continuity or resistance.

"The Wind is Rising" (February, 1941) describes the British spirit of resistance despite the prevalence of darkness, destruction, and doubt. The situation invites discouragement:

In the meantime, most Londoners have not slept in their beds since August last. Many of them have lost home and bed. They snatch food and baths between warnings. And that is only the capital. (*Wind*, 128)

He describes the loss of a cathedral in Coventry,

a right example of a Gothic that was England's own, the Perpendicular. A Nazi in his teens roving the night, not sure of his whereabouts, but anxious to drop his load and get home, who knows nothing of history before 1933, and cares nothing, and nothing of the spirit except Hitler's, and wants to know no more, blasts to dust the best the centuries have given us. (*Wind*, 128)

After considering an English retaliation which might seem appropriate, the bombing of Rome, Tomlinson finds that

We are back in the wilderness. That is the centre of this affair. We are back in the wilderness, and whether for forty years, or less, or for ever, depends more on what America thinks and does than perhaps America cares to acknowledge. (*Wind*, 132)

After focusing on America's possible involvement in the war, Tomlinson pleads for the unity of the democracies against the Nazis:

There will be renaissance. The wind is rising. The knowledge of what we ought to do is at hand, and the spirit which must breathe life into it is the sense of comradeship in a common cause. (*Wind*, 142)

Instead of pursuing this theme in "Ships and the Sea," dated March, 1941, Tomlinson discusses the role of the British sailor in the war effort, notes that the sailor's role seems diminute since the sailor is rarely seen, and describes the dangers that the sailor must face in the normal course of events. Remarking that "The majority of us know little more of maritime affairs than American farmers in the Middle West" (*Wind*, 151), he proceeds to describe the lot of the sailor during war, providing the island with its needs. Tomlinson notes that many of the merchant seamen bear decorations from the last war, suffered ingratitude from civilians between the wars, and gladly suffer the increased dangers of the German submarine and airplane. His essay ends with his discovery that the ship of his last voyage met disaster, only one boat being picked up.

One only?
 She had gone. Where were the other boats? Those ribald messmates of mine were in it again. Which of them had come through? The announcer had no more to tell me. I spent the rest of the evening looking at the wall, and wondering. I am still wondering. (*Wind*, 169)

Tomlinson returns to the issue of America in his next article, "From an Observation Post" (April, 1941). The essay describes his discussion with the new generation, whose representative comments,

"there is more than that fellow over there to deal with," and he indicated the southern horizon. "When we've pushed him out of it, only half the fight for freedom is over. We shall need more than guts for what will face us when the war is won. We won't go back to 1918. No, and we shan't feel like making many polite concessions to 1938." (*Wind*, 170–71)

After a digression concerning Whitman's "Where the Great City Stands" and the influence of progress of humanity ("We are troglodytes again" [*Wind*, 173]), Tomlinson shifts to Franklin Roosevelt's speech of March 16, 1941, announcing that "the hour had struck and America must assemble" (*Wind*, 175). The effect of this announcement on Britain is to cause hope. Tomlinson's younger companion reports:

"Our fellows heard him. They sang afterwards, frying eggs. I say, the cheering in Washington, when the President went all out, did you notice it? It was worse than a raid, that noise. If my knees had been Ribbentrop's, I should have flopped." (*Wind*, 175)

For Tomlinson, the issue is more simply expressed: "Aid was at hand. We were not alone" (*Wind*, 176). Tomlinson, however, does not make this the only point of his essay. He proceeds to discuss the war not as a national or international conflict, but as a civil war between fascist and democratic forces in Russia, Italy, Germany, and Spain. He also alludes to the Brownshirt movement in Britain to emphasize his point, and then shifts to the cheering news that Yugoslavians had revolted "and the ministers who signed the pact yesterday in Vienna are under arrest" (*Wind*, 190–91). Although the mobilization of

America was the chief inspiration of hope in this essay, Tomlinson took care to prevent its being the only sign of hope.

"The Swastika Over Olympus" (May, 1941) discusses the implications for civilization should Germany's successes continue. Hitler's occupation of Eleusis, birthplace of Aeschylus, epitomizes the opposition between Nazi and civilization, and Tomlinson uses it to imply dread implications for the free world. "If Mount Ida, why not Primrose Hill? Why not Bunker Hill?" (*Wind*, 200). However, the thrust of this article is to comment on man's misuse of the fruits of progress and to conclude that "The aspect of the morning sky will remain what it now is, livid with the hue and torment of hell. We shall have chosen death when we could have chosen life, and life more abundant" (*Wind*, 218), unless we realize that "the gifts of the gods could become baneful to whoever used them to secure dominion over his fellow men" (*Wind*, 218).

Tomlinson returns directly to American involvement in his final two essays. "The *Mayflower* Sails East" (July, 1941) is more overt in its argument that the British and American cultures are one.

The Pilgrim Fathers sought isolation from affairs which wearied them past further bearance, and they found it. Their children still have it. Those pilgrims voyaged better than they knew; so very much better that we, whose forefathers stayed home, envy their descendants their precious isolation, which remains intact. (*Wind*, 219)

Tomlinson compares this isolation to the "bombers of the enemy" and other problems on the east of the Atlantic, and then he discusses the unremarked return of the *Mayflower* to England with "the awful addition to the heritage she carried away long ago to Plymouth, Massachusetts" (*Wind*, 222). The *Mayflower* took from Europe conjectures from the Renaissance and Reformation, but she returned with more than the potato and tobacco. Aside from the impact of her production of steel, America contributed "economic compulsion" and "the new rhythm of life" to her forebears. This becomes manifest in the loss of individuality of concentrating many families into vast buildings and the "penalty for specialization, since man's duties amid intricate industrial gearing have become widely separated" (*Wind*, 231). Tomlinson sees many aspects of American life as the very ill effects of modernization which have resulted in the Nazi machine.

He notes that an American might object to his view, saying in effect that "It suits us well enough. We like it that way" (*Wind*, 232).

Tomlinson can sympathize with this view,

But how if he part himself from general human welfare? Civilization concerns him, too? It concerns all who dwell on earth. For that reason, do not suppose it is only steel in bulk which the *Mayflower* has brought back to Europe. (*Wind*, 232)

He attributes much of the world's uniformity to America. Once he has stated his objections, however, he finds three redeeming features embodied in the American republic.

Yet I don't see how America, the origin of technical achievements, can possibly abolish the very virtues without which there could have been no Republic. Abolish her own foundations? (*Wind*, 244)

A second redeeming feature is in America's contribution to letters. After arguing with Tomlinson about the coarsening effect that Hollywood was having on writing, an American declared

. . . that America presently would teach me how to use my language; and then played a trick, with a trifle of typescript. Who wrote that? he asked. I could not place the extract, but suggested that it was from Sir Thomas Browne. Said the Philadelphian, "I knew you would say that. Actually, it is from Melville." (*Wind*, 245)

After praising the literary efforts of Melville, Whitman, Emerson, and Thoreau, Tomlinson focuses on a third feature which becomes an invitation to help England:

Where is the spirit which took the *Mayflower* westward? That might quicken us. A meagre beanfield in peace, and the smell of the morning earth, would be better than great possessions while we sleep in dugouts, fearful of the night sky and the morrow. (*Wind*, 248)

What seemed to begin as an indictment of the New World ultimately results in an argument that the New World may be the Old World's last hope.

The final essay, "A Year of It" (August, 1941), expresses the British situation after one year of German bombing. Tomlinson focuses almost immediately on Roosevelt's exhortation to "cut out the dollar sign" as "unity in a cause" of Britain and America. When Tomlinson describes the effect that the sight of the American flag has had on him in foreign waters, he also finds an opportunity to rebuke America for its lateness:

It has been my own emotion, so I suppose other travellers have felt it, but the sight of the American emblem in strange waters has always affected me as if it were next to my own flag. Do we not know, though we grudge admitting it, that this war, with its corrosion by substantial and mental filth from Shanghai to Bordeaux, would never have begun had others been aware that American and British ships, as sure as sun-up, would have orders for common action should any power hoist the skull and cross-bones? Of course we know it. Then why not admit it? (*Wind*, 258)

He then refers to Hitler's invasion of Russia and Churchill's message of solidarity to the Russian people, and he prophetically offers his hope: "If Hitler could not unriddle the Russian enigma before the snows met him, and no man has done it yet, then he would join the company of great conquerors in the coldest deep of Hades" (*Wind*, 269). Tomlinson ends his essay, and his book, with his belief that this war transcends prior notions of warfare:

This war, we see now, transcends the defence of democratic institutions. It is above self-interest and national interest. It has no concern with frontiers. All social, economic, and political divisions, the miserable signs of personal and national ascendancy, have vanished since it is manhood itself that is threatened. Monarchs, hierarchs, presidents and premiers come down in it to the same choice as the nobodies. Their souls are no more valuable, and that is the simple value which must be defended or go. This challenge is to manhood. This war is the last phase of the war which began in 1914, and is for mastership or fellowship, as was prophesied long ago. (*Wind*, 270)

After dismissing all authority but conscience, he finds that "We have lived a century, and witnessed its events, since last August" (*Wind*, 271).

Tomlinson's book ended at this point for pragmatic reasons. He had published most of it in installments in the *Atlantic Monthly*, but in order for his appeal to be effective, he required a larger American audience. *The Wind Is Rising*, released as an Atlantic Monthly Press Book, appeared in March, 1942, in America. Unlike *Mars His Idiot*, *The Wind is Rising* was timely. It argued reasonably for the justice of British resistance, addressed the necessity for American involve- ment, and stressed the unity of America and Britain in the cause before the Japanese provided a more dramatic argument for American involvement. The effectiveness of *The Wind Is Rising*, ironically, derived from the sources of Tomlinson's ineffectiveness as a pacifist. The voice of studied reason was much more powerful in the midst of frenzied and strident invective than the traditional polemical stance could hope to become.

III   The Turn of the Tide

The purpose of the essays in *The Turn of the Tide* seems less immediate than in the earlier collection. *Turn* did not appear in book form until 1945 in England and 1947 in America, so that its function in book form was to provide Tomlinson's war and war-related memoirs. Realizing this, he included a reminiscent travel piece, "Log of a Voyage, 1935," as the first selection, and not all ten essays focused directly on the issues of war. Nevertheless, most of the essays did serve a more timely function since they appeared regularly in the *Atlantic Monthly*. In this second series, Tomlinson often refers to themes he has mentioned before, and he becomes measurably more angry toward the Germans. Tomlinson's collection begins a less rapid ascent than his earlier collection—the first essay is prewar, the second an account of British justification for resisting the Nazis—and the third essay, "Progress" (January, 1942), continues to discuss the war in terms of causes. At one point he notes that legislators demand freedom of the air and asks "Freedom for what?" (*Turn*, 77) and discusses the causes and conduct of the war in terms of abstractions directed as much against modern mechanization as against war.

The fourth essay, "Back to First Things" (March, 1942), begins with a conversation that Tomlinson might have recorded a year earlier. A soldier remarks, "I wish America would tumble out soon, and pull her weight" (*Turn*, 81). As it happens, however, this statement occurred the day the Japanese bombed Pearl Harbor, so Tomlinson sees no need to pursue this. Instead, he discusses the differences between Japanese and American in terms comparable to the differences between German and Briton. The Japanese, unlike the Americans but like the Germans, have deliberately taken the road to conquest, and this was as evident to those familiar with Asia as the fascist rape of Spain had been to Europeans.

As Mark Twain once pointed out, how deadly is the silent lie! For which of us cried out? We remained dumb witnesses while Chinamen were killed and their goods stolen; and as the wounds were Spanish that had to be dressed with dirty bandages, we felt no hurt. (*Turn*, 86)

He states that "All the peoples of the world are of one body" (*Turn*, 86), and then focuses on democracy as a crucial distinction:

Democracy is the luxury of personal responsibility; and what is responsibility, if justice, through ignorance and neglect, is indistinguishable from wrong? It begins to look as if an enemy were in the house. The democrat who loves liberty seems to have been on easy terms with him. (*Turn*, 87)

Tomlinson also takes umbrage at an American statement regarding the British effort:

An unofficial Washington commentator remarked recently, "the concept of this war is British, and the British, strictly speaking, are not in the war." What sense of responsibility was at the back of that man's mind? . . . The British concept of war! Was that shown at Dunkirk? (*Turn*, 88)

However, he uses this essay to establish the true nature of the war rather than to avenge old wounds:

We are back in this war to first things. The heart and intelligence of the common man take on a significance that transcends the power of the machines. The man himself is again of first importance, as in the beginning. And nobody had thought of that, as another outcome of war waged by engines. May we begin to hope that Frankenstein will at last gain control of his monster? (*Turn*, 93)

He ends the essay by stating that the war is between the creative forces of order and the chaotic forces of darkness, and argues that "Creation never ends" (*Turn*, 94).

"Wreckage at Sunrise" (June, 1942) begins with a survey of the ruins of London but quickly moves to broader issues. For Tomlinson, "the English-speaking peoples are chiefly responsible for the future welfare of mankind. That is our fate. If we refuse it, our fate will be no better" (*Turn*, 97). This fate results from the problem of mechanization: "Enough knowledge was possessed to have crowned a civilization, but good intent would not appear to have gone far enough to correct perversion by cleverness and greed" (*Turn*, 103). Moving to this as his theme, Tomlinson declares that Hitler himself is not the cause of the current problem: "our greater problems would still be here. Hitler is incidental, not a cause but an issue, like the outcome of neglect when the human swarms are disorderly" (*Turn*, 103–04). He returns to an old theme: "it is not easy to forgive our politicals for not knowing, many years ago, what was under their noses" (*Turn*, 107),

but he ends on an optimistic note: "Man's apprehension of circumstance is widening. The possible is enlarged . . . . It is another day,
and we have struck tents and are on the march" (*Turn*, 109).

"Salute to Adventurers" (December, 1942) begins with Tomlinson's
misgivings regarding the American conception of the American/
British alliance.

I often fancy a shake of anxiety in a simple message from a Washington
correspondent. His duty is to report the latest, but he seems worried lest,
meanwhile, I develop a dubious notion of America; or else should trust her
too much—it is sometimes hard to tell which. He fears that while he informs
me of progress towards victory, my sense of being an ally may faint. Probably
he remembers that most of us know just where peace went astray last time. It
was when Americans walked out of the League of Nations. (*Turn*, 110)

Tomlinson dreads mistrust separating Briton from American, and he
proceeds to argue the need for the allies to remain in a single cause.
He also states his belief that "The cause which has brought the United
States, China, Russia, and Great Britain together, to most ordinary
men and women, has the urge of religion, and is limitless in its scope"
(*Turn*, 115).

After dwelling on British imperialism and the rights of such coun-
tries as India to become free, Tomlinson examines the nature of
democracy:

We forget that never anywhere has there existed a right democracy. It is a
form of government still in the experimental stages, and of interest mainly in
the Anglo-Saxon communities. We overlook this, though the shocking spectacle of democratic and republican France ought to be warning enough to
scare the most noble patriot from pursuing his political ambition till it end
gloriously in what he wants, or in the dismay of his people. (*Turn*, 119)

He then states his hopes for the new order to result from the war. The
younger generation's

thoughts will expand to the occasion, and be out of bounds. National frontiers
to them will have lost the old meanings. They will strive to release human
relations from constricting bonds, to free the bounty of earth for the use of all.
The world will be ready again for the enterprise of adventuring minds. (*Turn*,
122)

After commenting that the war was pulling Britain and America out of
the Great Depression, Tomlinson says,

It hurts the mind merely to be aware of such a fact; and to look into the eyes of a child condemned to hunger and withheld from joy is to know that civilization is a falsity, whatever the late architecture of its institutions. Let us cease to lie to each other about hunger and the restriction of life in a disguising scientific jargon. That is what we have been doing, and libraries are full of the clever evasions of the scholarly. But hunger is hunger, dirt is dirt, ignorance is savagery, and hopelessness is death. (*Turn*, 123)

Tomlinson already considers the need to "know beforehand where we want to go" (*Turn*, 125), lest this war, too, end in an ineffective "bridge of tinder over hell."

"The Ordinary Fellow" (May, 1943), published in the *Atlantic Monthly* as "The Common Man," extols the virtues of the Nobody. Tomlinson's statements resemble those in the earlier "The Battle of London." The common man is numerous, unpredictable, and the victim of human folly: "We know it. Man is the only animal to accumulate knowledge, and to reason on its benefits, and the only one to make a fool of itself of choice" (*Turn*, 133). As he has said before, "The chief sufferer from the consequences of ambitious authority and cunning is the common man" (*Turn*, 138), whether he becomes the soldier of war or the unemployed worker of peace.

In "Night Watch" (November, 1943), Tomlinson's thoughts have already turned to the prospects of the future peace. He reflects that a stranger walking the London streets might assume that England had been occupied by America.

It must surprise him that Londoners are either unaware of this clear confirmation of Goebbels's prophecy of American dominion over the British, or else are taking the occupation as their due share in the reordering of mankind's business. In truth, it does not matter which. It is too late to scare us with that stuff.

We are in the mood to accept anything, if it means concord; any dispensation from men of understanding to get release from a nightmare which has lasted ten years. (*Turn*, 146)

Wondering what the future might bring, he shifts his attention to Sir Winston Leonard Spencer Churchill, "unanimously acclaimed by the British . . . . It was our fortune to have a great person to express us" (*Turn*, 149). In one respect, however, Churchill troubles Tomlinson:

Yet we are still perplexed by the fact that, having been given the glad franchise of the folk, he should afterwards have accepted as a crowning honour the headship of the party group which had rejected him a few months before the explosions began, and was largely responsible for the inauspicious conditions in which we entered battle. (*Turn*, 149)

Although he concedes that this might be a sign of Churchill's magnanimity, Tomlinson also expresses his hope that Churchill has read *Utopia* and that the doubts raised by the establishment of the Allied Military Government of Occupied Territories are unfounded. His foreboding of the future, however, receives direct expression:

After victory, if each of the victorious powers should seek its own, we shall have but an uneasy leisure to count our losses, suspect all other men, and wait for the next war while air-transport corporations quarrel over rights, claims, and privileges. It is not an enjoyable prospect. It would be but waiting in the dark, listening for the drone of oncoming bombers. (*Turn*, 157)

The shift in Tomlinson's propaganda, from relief at the American alliance to uncertainty concerning the direction of British and American leaders, recalls the uncertainty of his pacifist writings.

"New Horizon" (March, 1944) retreats to praise of the common man, this time the common man of the sea who has adapted rapidly to the requirements of warfare, and Tomlinson attempts to make a statement of hope:

We have reason for a new song of praise, then, since we have found that the heart of the common man transcends the devices of statecraft and the mockery of the cynics. His virtue, free at the call, is of proved greater value and potency than whatever further power science can discover and release. We could at least depend on him not to go on mutilating our tender planet, for gain, till it is a dead star. (*Turn*, 172)

However, Tomlinson conveys his feeling that the problems that grew from the last war will pale beside the problems that will grow from this one. The final essay in the collection, "Christmas Eve," is more hopeful, but it dates back to December, 1941. It would appear that, in the process of justifying British resistance against Germany, Tomlinson found the seeds of discord that had been sown at Versailles. In a sense, these essays seem to verify his earlier statements that nothing but evil could come of war.

However, if some of the pacifist philosophy appears to surface in these later writings, Tomlinson refused to mitigate his growing sense of hatred for Germany. In October, 1944, he published "Frankenstein in England" in the *Atlantic Monthly* to state his position on the terms of peace. A note informs the reader that Tomlinson's home had fallen victim to a robot bomb, and although no one was hurt, this loss was a source of personal grievance. "It's all a lie, of course, to say that London has stopped, or is even afraid—*you* know better than that; but please don't expect liberals over here to have other than cold jaws when looking Germans in the eye about terms."[18] After describing the intensity of the Londoners' knowledge that such bombing now would not cease with the first light of dawn, Tomlinson states his feeling and the feeling of most Londoners in direct terms: "I think Americans had better know that on this side of the Atlantic a once kindly distinction made by us between Nazis and Germans has gone. Quite gone."[19] After noting that this method of warfare required years to prepare and that the Germans were aware of what they were doing, Tomlinson concludes that "In settling with the Germans, we must remember to be kind first and last to the rest of our fellows on earth. Peace to men of good will. Any other sentiment for guidance would be suicidal."[20] The robot bomb excluded Germany from the realm of good will. A final article on the war, "A Presiding Spirit," which Tomlinson published in the *Atlantic Monthly* in July, 1945, mourns the passing of Roosevelt rather than qualifying his ire toward Germany. He states that "outsiders regarded Roosevelt's existence as an act of Providence at a critical juncture for humanity"[21] and then argues that the invention of the airplane has destroyed isolationism forever. He has returned to a level of abstraction that characterized his between-the-wars writing.

It is difficult to assess Tomlinson's value as a propagandist, partly because he wrote from a conviction that was compatible with his reasons for hating warfare, partly because he eschewed the art of justifying lies in print with a higher purpose. Perhaps the label "propagandist" itself is at fault, for Tomlinson wrote from the heart. Despite the apparent contradiction between his between-the-wars writing for peace and his World War II writing on behalf of the British resistance to Hitler, he wrote in defense of the same values during both phases. If *Mars His Idiot*, *The Wind Is Rising*, and *The Turn of the Tide* appear to serve different causes, all three works emphasize the worth of the common man, the horror of war, and the belief that when the maker of war is an outlaw, there can be no neutrals. The civilization that Tomlinson felt threatened by war was also the civilization threatened by Hitler, and Tomlinson could encourage the Allies with a clear conscience. His direction seemed to change, but his values altered not. In his pacifist writing and in his propaganda articles, he wrote for the same end.

CHAPTER 9

The Early Novels: Autobiography and History

I Theory of the Novel

W HEN Tomlinson published his first novel, *Gallions Reach*, in 1927, he was not entering the profession of letters as a novice. He was fifty-four years old and had earned his living with his pen for more than twenty years. Not only had he won a reputation as a journalist, war correspondent, and literary editor, but he was also the author of two widely known travel books (*The Sea and the Jungle* and *Tide Marks*). In addition he had published five collections of essays which established him as a prose stylist and linked his name with such subjects as World War I, the history of British shipping, and the pitfalls inherent in moderns' notions of progress. However, Tomlinson was still an apprentice in his understanding and execution of the novelist's art, as the flaws of his two early novels reveal.

Rebecca West, commenting on *Gallions Reach* and its winning the Femina-Vie Heureuse Prize the year after the novel's appearance, found Tomlinson's personal charm

a credit to him, since few men have had a more embittering literary career. When he first emerged as a writer on the sea his emergence happened to coincide with the rise of Joseph Conrad to popular favor; and the fact that they both wrote about these marine matters caused him to be labelled an imitation of Conrad. This is fatuous; for while Conrad is (pardonably enough) a loose and inexact writer of English and gets his strength from the images he pulls somehow . . . through the tangle of his language and the rhythm with which he arranges them in his tale, Mr. Tomlinson's gift is for the precise use of words which scoop up so much of reality as he desires and leave it on his page.[1]

However, while West can praise Tomlinson's style, she finds fault with "*Gallions Reach*, a fine book, but spoiled by the violent insertion into it of the conflicts appropriate to a novel."[2] She would have preferred another collection of essays and concludes her commentary on Tomlinson by recommending "Earthshine" from *Old Junk*. Frederick P. Mayer, also on the basis of Tomlinson's first novel, feels that comparison with Conrad is not right, but he also prefers Tomlinson's essays to his novel. Mayer disposes of Conradian comparison in short order:

> The truth is, Tomlinson does not derive from nor resemble Conrad. "Gallions Reach"—the book by which Tomlinson's name is linked with Conrad's and by which Tomlinson is becoming popularly known—has added no inches to Tomlinson's literary stature. As a novel, it is a doubtful success and then succeeds only where Tomlinson reached distinction many years ago in his seven travel books of essays, some of them now quite old . . . . Both Tomlinson and Conrad write about the sea; that is their chief agreement. If that makes them alike, then Jane Austen and Sinclair Lewis are similar, because they both write of small towns; and Felix Reisenberg and Edith Wharton resemble each other because they both write of New York. Tomlinson can stand on his own feet.[3]

West and Mayer both admire Tomlinson's personality and prose style, but both would advise him to return to the essay, which he understands much better than the novel. When Tomlinson, in 1934, discussed the problems of writing fiction as he saw them, he revealed his resentment of such criticism, his preference for the essay form and style, his reluctance to grapple with the elusive nature of the form of the novel, and his annoyance with some of the novelist's techniques.[4]

He began his discussion with a barb:

> Some people write novels, while others are born novelists. The latter, apart from their novels, are recognized with ease when they venture to write anything else. Yet strangely enough a writer who is not a novelist born is expected to make a novel as though he were.

Tomlinson places the "born novelist" outside the tradition of Aristotle, Henry James, and E. M. Forster by insisting that the "born novelist" is not a craftsman. He implies that the "born novelist" thinks only of the circulation of his book and has made the novel "the best known and most profitable of literary products, . . . it has settled into a conventional shape, and so is read by its consumers as readily as the homely label on their favorite breakfast food." Tomlinson, not a novelist born, places himself in a different position, one who "submits to the compulsion of an idea, and allows that to have its inherent consequences." As a result, he "may learn that though his effort, when finished, bears some resemblance to a book, yet it is not seen at once to be a novel." Tomlinson then proceeds to define the novel, but he goes no farther than E.M. Forster's *Aspects of the Novel*, the apparent source of most of Tomlinson's literary theory, agreeing that the novel should tell a story, and that this requirement is a pity.

When Tomlinson moves to novelistic technique, however, he begins to reveal his feeling that contemporary expectations of novel readers restrict the writer. He warns that "we good readers ought not to dismiss a novel in petulance as erroneous because it does not conform in all respects to the style and divisions, say of the restaurant table to which we are accustomed" and proceeds to a more exact definition of the novel's purpose:

For the novel, that difficult form of literature which evades exact definition, is not only and always a transcript of life at once known and easily read. It may be a new expression of life made manifest by the compulsion of adventuring spirit; and so it needs must, as it grows from within, change its outer form.

He proceeds to reflect on the possibilities of the future, antedating Graham Greene by claiming that "the art of the cinematograph will drastically affect the novels of the future." In the process of explaining what these changes will mean, he answers criticism directed toward his own technique. Because readers have become accustomed to techniques of the film, a novelist now can make abrupt transitions, present an episode in a symbol, and employ "the economy of allegory and parable." This, according to Tomlinson, will make life difficult for the conventional novelist, who will find leisurely descriptive chapters, gradual transitions "as though he were afraid his readers would lose themselves unless he led them from one room to another," and "prodigality" of details suddenly out of mode. This will result in the born novelist learning that "he has to give as much care to his writing as is now given by technical experts to the lighting of material in the film studio." Once he has established this, Tomlinson moves to a defense of his particular strengths in the art of fiction writing.

After suggesting that "Perhaps a born novelist has too much to write, to be able to write," Tomlinson "should like to hear what reason there is, then, for the general application of a lower standard of criticism to the novel than to poetry." He attributes this to the novel's commercial purpose and its appeal to a specific market, and then he quotes a popular novelist whose criticism of another's work was that "it was written too well. . . . 'No novelist,' he commented, 'writes as well as that—but then, no novelist wants to.'" Tomlinson finds in this statement both an admission that this popular novelist is incapable of fine writing and also "the annoyance of a tradesman over a comparison which might stultify the usual line of goods—a stock now readily saleable—were readers unfortunately to begin to show a finer discrimination." Tomlinson then offers, as examples of works that were not spoiled by good writing, Hardy's *The Return of the Native*, Wells's *Wonderful Visit*, Stella Benson's *Faraway Bride*, and Bunyan's *The Pilgrim's Progress*, all containing fine writing and all popular in the market. If others find his essay style inappropriate to fiction, Tomlinson would argue that this is to the detriment of contemporary writers of fiction.

He also argues that "The adventuring of the mind in the novel has ceased," and he laments its passing, relating it to a growing need among contemporary readers for release from modern tensions. He describes the novel as "a profitable medicine for the multitude which suffers from speed, noise, and anxiety; readers need soothing, and the purpose of the novel is just for that." Tomlinson does not object to this—"Anything that helps is good to have"—but he sees a possible danger in

the careless benevolence of the critics, some of whom supply the stuff. . . . If they are not watchful they will lose their sense of smell, and good and bad will become the same to them. They plead, rightly, that it is too much to ask them now to judge novels as books. They must lower the standard to save their lives. Life is not long enough for the task.

While he can sympathize with this lament, however, he feels that "with the world as it is the critic of letters, as much as president, premier, and bishop, is under a heavy responsibility; much more onerous than he shows that he knows, usually." He finds this a matter of conscience, and he seems to agree with Bernard Shaw that the purpose of art is to force the public to reconsider its morals, to instruct, and to heighten people's awareness of reality.

While Tomlinson concedes "that any poet, dramatist, or novelist, who declares that he is indifferent whether or not people give him attention, is either an ass or a liar; anyhow, he is not natural," he also demands that literature be "an expression of life." The importance of this demand, for Tomlinson, is the quality of the life expressed. The

proper novel could reverse a trend that has worked to reduce the
stature of modern man:

a revolution against reason; an orgy of violent emotions instead, with good
will an object of hate, as treasonable. Men and women, in the chaos of a world
that has upheaved, have become strangely tired of using the mind. Nothing
but trouble seems to come of using knowledge and intelligence. The mind is
in disgrace, these days.

Since novels, like essays, are essentially "autobiography," and since
"the critical relation of selected experience, should . . . have significance for others," Tomlinson feels that "The writing of fiction should
be classed as a dangerous occupation, unsuited to those who are still
practising upon English with their careless and juvenile hoop-iron."
For Tomlinson, the writing of fiction discharges a responsibility to
society which the novelist cannot perform unless he takes his craft
with the utmost seriousness. Tomlinson's defense of his style, his
purpose, and his understanding of the novel may explain, in part,
why he consistently regarded the novel as a rhetorical mode.

II Gallions Reach

Although *Gallions Reach* (1927), as a first novel, is impressive, it
frequently taxes a reader's credulity and suffers from an episodic plot.
Much of the novel derives from Tomlinson's unhappy memories of the
Scottish shipping firm, his experiences in the jungle of Brazil, and his
journey to Malaya, while the protagonist, Jim Colet, shares several
characteristics with the young Tomlinson. The novel opens with a
short chapter describing the movement of a steamer toward London.
A child, young Jim, responds to the magic word "London!" in the
manner of Stephen in the opening pages of James Joyce's *A Portrait of
the Artist as a Young Man*: "He stared up ahead, as his elders were
doing. He wanted to see what London meant."[5] When his father
comments that he has not "seen this river since the year the *Princess
Alice* was lost," Jim's imagination begins to work on the literal word.
"Who was that princess? It did not look like a place for princesses.
Sometimes his father did not mean what he said" (*GR*, 2). The
introductory chapter ends when an old man announces their arrival at
Gallions Reach, point of departure for ocean-going vessels.
    Tomlinson moves to young Jim Colet, the recently promoted
executive assistant at Perriam, Limited, an import firm founded by

the master and part-owner of an opium clipper, whose descendant now acts as the firm's principal. Like Tomlinson, Jim despises his work; unlike Tomlinson, he derives no satisfaction from the names of ships or of far-flung ports, which are only names to him. Tomlinson's detestation of his former place, however, appears in his descriptions of "the guarded recesses of the cliffs of Billeter Avenue," where "There is no joy in it even for the privileged. A life devoted to the cherishing of this treasure gives to the devotee a countenance as grave as would golf or the obsequies of a dear friend" (*GR*, 5). His descriptions of the realm of ledgers are excessive, as in his introduction of Jim:

James Colet was one of the multitude which entered this region every morning at nine o'clock, and deserted it about six in the evening. Between those hours the arid and hollow limestone, where nothing grows but cyphers, is thronged with a legion as intent and single-minded as a vast formicarium. Before those hours, and at night, it is as silent as the ruins of Memphis, and as empty, except for a few vestals with brooms and pails who haunt the temporary solitude on their ministration to whatever joss presides over numerals. (*GR*, 6)

On this Saturday morning, Jim answers a summons from Mr. Perriam, who had assigned Jim the task of resolving a labor dispute—the men at the warehouse disagree with Perriam on the hours they will work.

Perriam expected Jim to discharge the workers, but Jim cannot bring himself to do this. Periam gives Jim an ultimatum to complete his assignment by Monday. Although Jim is thirty-five and has worked at Perriam's for twenty years (Tomlinson was with his firm for eighteen years), Jim has not become resigned to the practices of his employer and remains unwilling to discharge the workers. When he leaves his office after noon, he decides to do nothing and wanders a bit about London, considering his dilemma (this allows Tomlinson several opportunities to describe the sights).

In the course of his walking, Colet recalls that, as a youth, he had wanted to "trade with Indians from a fort of logs" (*GR*, 17), but that "duty to a father whose influence intrigued a lucky berth for him had marked him for Perriam's before ever he knew the name of that house" (*GR*, 18). Tomlinson recalled, "When I was a little fellow, a nipper, I wanted to go out with the Hudson's Bay Company, . . . But luckily they take only Scotchmen,"[6] and he had found his position in a

shipping firm through the good offices of an uncle after Tomlinson's
father had died. Unlike Tomlinson, however, Jim was single and had
an appointment with Helen Denny (named after a ship whose
figurehead beguiled Tomlinson in his youth), who took pleasure in
the company of literary-minded wits. Joining Helen as she held court
in the midst of her crowd, Jim realized he was an outsider and, after
continuing his musings, left the company. Helen followed him, but
when Jim had taken her to her room, they parted abruptly. Like
many of Tomlinson's central characters, Jim is intensely introspective
and prefers his own company to that of others.

Like Tomlinson, Jim severed his connection with his firm after an
altercation with his employer, but Jim's method of argument was
more severe—overcome with revulsion for Perriam, Jim struck him.
Perriam died instantly, and Jim fled. True to form, Jim sought the
help or company of none but spent the night wandering through
London, and early in the morning met the master of the *Altair*. The
first of several coincidences occurs at this point—Jim owns a statue of
an oriental deity, Kuan-yin, and the master of the *Altair* finds that his
morning duties have become cumbersome because he has purchased
an identical statue. Jim agrees to deliver the Kuan-yin to the *Altair*.
Sinclair, the Chief Officer, conducts Jim to the master's cabin, conve-
niently forgets him, and does not return until the ship has set sail. Jim
discovers that the *Altair* is one of Perriam's ships, and after Sinclair
comments that the *Altair* has had two sets of owners in four years, the
present owners being worse than Perriam, Jim implausibly admits to
Sinclair that he killed Perriam.

Jim learns that the death was not reported as a murder, but he
decides to remain with the *Altair* as ship's purser. Jim becomes
acquainted with Gillespie, the Chief Engineer; Hale, the master; and
the nature of life at sea. In one area of his reflection Jim draws a
conclusion on the sea reminiscent of Stephen Crane's "The Open
Boat": "The romance of the sea had flown off, perhaps, on the wings of
the clippers, and it was lost. It was not there. But the sea and the sky
were unaware of any loss. They were beautiful, but were aloof from
the desires and anxieties of man" (*GR*, 95). He also learns, when he
applies himself to the maintenance of the ship, that "A little concen-
tration with a chipping hammer will do more to the inexperienced
back than to a rusty deck" (*GR*, 98). In the course of the voyage Jim
observes several of the ocean's wonders, frequently resulting in
passages such as this:

Companies of flying-fish were surprised by that iron nose, and got up. They skittered obliquely over the bright polish of the inclines, and plumped abruptly into smooth slopes which opposed them. A family of four dolphins were there that morning. They were set in the clear glass just before the cutwater. They did not fly from it. Their bodies but revolved leisurely before it. The crescent valves in their heads could be seen sleepily opening and closing when they touched the surface, with the luxury of life in the cool fathoms. One after another they rolled belly up; they were merely revolving without progress, yet the fast-pursuing iron nose never reached them. It was always just behind the family, which wove a lazy and gliding dance before the ship. Artfully leading them on, these familiars of the deep? (*GR*, 105)

The tranquillity of such scenes departs, however, when the *Altair* develops an unexpected crisis in a storm—she loses her rudder.

During the storm Jim worked in the captain's cabin on the ship's papers. When the storm became rough, the captain departed, and Jim found himself at a loss until a roll upset the captain's pipes, and Jim had something to do: "They also serve who only look after the tobacco pipes" (*GR*, 115). Deciding that he was useless in the cabin, Jim was about to leave when the papers were upset, and he hurried to save them from the "tongue of water" shooting over the carpet whenever the ship shifted. Deciding that "At least, the ship's papers could be put in order" (*GR*, 116), Jim distracted himself from the tossing of the ship, and Tomlinson presents a fine picture of the workings of the mind under duress. Jim finds his mind going where it will:

"We are but little children meek." The tune of this hymn, for some uninvited cause, was running through his head. The movements of the ship kept it going. "Not born in any high estate." Couldn't very well call this estate puffed up. "What can we do for Jesus' sake?" Well, Jesus, I was checking this ship's manifest when I went down. Sorry it's wet. (*GR*, 117)

Tomlinson's ironic description of the workings of a mind fearing its abrupt ending nicely balances the tension of the ship's plight. Jim is surprised to discover morning has arrived, but when the captain returns to the cabin, Jim does not ask about the rudder: "Perhaps rudders were indelicate" (*GR*, 117). The *Altair* survived the storm only for a short while, and it became apparent that she would founder. A passing ship could not offer a tow because it carried mail, and Captain Hale refused to abandon the *Altair* at that time. However, the ship sank, Captain Hale choosing to go down with her, and the men found themselves subjected to hunger, thirst, and exposure as they trusted to their luck in open boats. Jim's boat was fortunate. A passing liner, bound for Rangoon, picked up the men, and Jim's meeting with Norrie on the liner leads to new adventures.

Norrie seeks "important metal that goes by troy weight; or by the ton" and has little patience with less pragmatic concerns: "Your abstractions," he tells Jim, "wouldn't turn my scales with a martyr's crown as make-weight" (GR, 156). He lends Jim a book addressed to geologists and surveyors and persuades Jim to accompany him on a jungle expedition in search of tin. Jim reaches Penang, where he presents a chit to a Mr. Ah Loi (an unfortunate punning name) to outfit the expedition. As fortune would have it, Jim finds an opportunity to discuss Kuan-yin at length. While waiting for Norrie so that they can depart for the other side of the peninsula, Jim's observations of his surroundings are reminiscent of Tide Marks:

These Chinese boys moved about as though they were disembodied spirits, and unless you were watching they were never more than wraiths in the very act of vanishing. At that moment he was sure that a Malayan sunrise, with some tea just after you had bathed, was not to be exchanged for a halo and a harp. This corner of the earth was a leisured and regal scope, and its jubilant light, with the musky smell of its lush growth, was good enough for the pleasance of an archangel, only he might be upset by a sight of Aphrodite. The crowns of the dominant palms, and the filigree of the upper foliage of the shrubbery, were black against lambent gold, and that tide of fire was plainly welling rapidly to flood the garden. The colours below were already bright; the orange and ruby crotons were separated, and the blossoms on the vines. The sun was so quick that he could be seen moving up behind the screen; he was blazing over the top before the first moment of coolness and calm was forgotten. Wasps arrived with him, to blunder about the joists of the verandah, and they were not ordinary wasps, and knew it. (GR, 189)

Norrie and Jim journey down the coast and remain on fairly good terms, although Norrie chafes Jim for not bringing a corkscrew, essential to traveling. Shortly after Norrie informed Jim that the natives were admirers of the English and easy to manipulate, Jim watched a Malay run amok and became more apprehensive in his observations. After engaging Malays to act as bearers under the supervision of Mat, their Malay guide, Jim and Norrie enter the jungle. Norrie contracts fever, but after he recovers, he and Jim discover an area "as ripe as a freehold in Piccadilly. The floor of this hill is tin. It only wants spades" (GR, 235)

Once this trove has revealed itself to them, however, Jim's imagination and his ethical bent provide him with a rationale for turning his back on their success. Norrie and Jim encounter Mr. Parsell, a well-known and often published ethnologist who seeks the Sakais, a primitive tribe which the Malays call "shadow" in tribute to its elusiveness. Parsell believes that before civilization corrupted, man possessed lost secrets of being which this tribe might retain, and he has become obsessed with learning these secrets. Jim, however, recognizes Parsell's unfitness for survival and feels a responsibility to the man. Although Norrie decides that "We can't go doddering across Malaya behind an inspired crackpot following the Holy Grail" (*GR*, 246), Jim decides that he must. Jim, Mat, and the bearers accompany Parsell, frequently having difficulty convincing Parsell not to wander off whenever the spirit moves him. Once Jim has dropped his vigilance, he discovers that Parsell has disappeared. A search, which takes him into a "forbidden land" feared by Mat, reveals only Parsell's pith helmet at the edge of a gully. When Jim returns, he must first convince Mat that he is not a *hantu* from the "forbidden land," and with Mat's assistance, Jim returns to Penang.

Jim had last seen Sinclair after the sinking of the *Altair*. Sinclair had been in another open boat, and the boats became separated before Jim's was sighted by the liner. However, *mirabile dictu*, Jim finds Sinclair in Penang and learns that Sinclair's ship is bound for London on the morrow. In jest, Sinclair asks whether Jim wishes to return to Gallions Reach, and Jim surprises him by answering in the affirmative. He declares that he wishes to return to lay Perriam's ghost to rest, and he ends the novel with his comment on Sinclair's disbelief that Jim would prefer that to enjoying "the cool and pleasant morning garden of vivacious ladies."

"The ghosts we know govern us. Not always what you're looking at now, Sinclair, so you needn't draw my attention to it. I see it. It would move a heart of stone. But there's no fun for us unless we obey the order we know." (*GR*, 283)

Gallions Reach is a sophisticated first novel, but it suffers from the flaws of an episodic plot, implausible actions on the part of its protagonist, frequent passages of "overwriting," and rather clumsy unifying devices, such as the repeated emergence of Kuan-yin as a conversation piece and the obviously contrived device of beginning and ending the novel with Gallions Reach. Yet *Gallions Reach* has several sources of appeal. Readers of Joseph Conrad and Jack London

would appreciate Tomlinson's version of life aboard ship; followers of
Rider Haggard, Rudyard Kipling, and W.H. Hudson would enjoy
Tomlinson's account of the mysteries of the jungle; those who appreciate action for the sake of entertainment might welcome *Gallions
Reach* as one of the many spawn of the Ruritanian romance begun by
Anthony Hope; readers of Henry James and E.M. Forster would find
themselves intrigued by the workings of Jim's mind as he questions
the validity of his life, his actions, and his values. Following the
dichotomy Graham Greene applied to his novels, one would label
Gallions Reach an entertainment rather than a novel since action
takes so much precedence over character, for the focus of interest in
this work is not on the nature of Jim Colet, but on what happens next.

According to Henry Seidel Canby, editor of the *Saturday Review*,
this question receives no answer. After noting that "Conrad's men
lived to brood and Tomlinson's brood to live," Canby argues that the
early section of *Gallions Reach*, ending with the killing of Perriam,
"sets a problem. It is the beginning of a novel which Tomlinson never
ends. For to this author endings are not important: it is not what a
man does, it is what he experiences that counts."[7] He describes the
novel as "adventure the conclusion of which is spiritual, the conduct
of which is irrelevant except to the psychology of one man," which
Canby attributes to the novel's being "perhaps the last of his pre-war
self that broke from London to adventure up the Amazon, that
savored strange experience in beautiful places."[8] Frederick P. Mayer
sees something of the same spirit, but he relates it to problems of style
and structure: "A repetition of exclamatory delight always loses conviction. That is one trouble with the Tomlinson books," and another is
that "His exuberance of observation makes his style exuberant. He
fills a page with words, when two lines would be more effective."[9]
Mayer feels that *Gallions Reach* "is, at its best, a good travel narrative; at its worst, it is a novel with poor motivation and a creaking and
disjointed plot. . . . [Tomlinson's] personality as an essayist takes
possession of what should have been pictures of other people."[10]

The central character of this novel, however, was Tomlinson in
many particulars, so that, to him, writing this narrative may have
seemed like writing autobiographical essays. In his next novel Tomlinson continued to draw from the circumstances of his own past, but
instead of leaving his plot in the rather chaotic and unexpected order
common to personal experience, he chose to place events within the
larger historical perspective of his time. When Canby concluded his
review of *Gallions Reach*, he dismissed the book as a novel but not

Tomlinson as a novelist. "We shall see what we shall see when Tomlinson writes of the War, whose psychological intensities he knew as did few others. There will be beauty there too and adventure, but no pausing at the final secret's rim."[11] This prediction Tomlinson bore out in part, but not entirely.

III   All Our Yesterdays

Tomlinson appears regularly in *All Our Yesterdays* (1930), but not uniformly in the same person. He applies various aspects of his personal experience to different characters, trying to chronicle the process by which England, between 1900 and 1919, "lighted fools the way to dusty death." The narrative mode that he adopted in this novel was first-person omniscient. The narrator, at times a journalist, at others a war correspondent, is never identified but reflects Tomlinson's role during the history he relates, and the device of describing character and action from his remembered point of observation seems to have been more comfortable for Tomlinson than the assumed omniscient third-person narrator he employed in *Gallions Reach*. Like his earlier novel, *All Our Yesterdays* occasionally lapses into implausibility and some aspects of the plot are clearly Dickensian, but the characters seem more authentic and the author seems to have chronicled the most unsettling years known to his generation. His descriptive powers are frequently evident, but instead of reflecting "exuberance" they focus for the most part on London and on the horrors of the trenches.

The structure of this novel follows British history from 1900 to 1919, divided into five sections, each labelled with an identifying date. The first part, "1900," begins in Dockland when the "topmasts of a few sailing-ships" are in evidence. After two pages of description to set the scene, the narrator treats the reader to a sample of his amiable irony by reporting a conversation between two passengers on a bus:

Two workmen had taken the seat in front of me, and they were arguing. It was about a lady. One of the stout fellows was convinced of her virtue. He declared that she was a beauty. His companion, though he praised, did so grudgingly. He was a trifle doubting; a timid fellow, perhaps, who could not bravely admire because he was not man enough. He hinted that she might not conduct herself as well as some people seemed to think she would. How did they know? Besides, she was too big. He found some courage in the sound of his own opposition. "Damned great thing," he blurted out. "Nice penny she would cost, too."

"An' she's worth it. Besides, you've had some of it, as far as I know."

"Same as you. I'm not saying anything about that. What I mean is, it's a rotten idea, the bigger the better. Where's it going to stop?"[12]

It turns out that these men are not discussing a lady of easy virtue, but the "noblest ship ever built by us, . . . The most powerful battleship we had ever built . . ." (AY, 7). Lady Carroll, wife of shipbuilder Lord William Carroll, was to launch this vessel. After the launching, the narrator met Jones, who sold books and tobacco from a small shop. While in Jones's company Tom Bolt, a master shipwright who worked on the new ship, chafes Jones by saying that Jones looks like a pro-Boer. (Tomlinson later recalled having this label affixed to him by some of his friends "who advised me, quite genially, yet with heartfelt conviction, that though I would not improve a lamp-post, if hanging to it, that was a proper place for me."[13]) Bolt then utters a prophetic warning: "Mark my words, ole Jones, you'll have that shop of yours wrecked by decent people, and serve you jolly well right" (AY, 23). A "local interest" began in this discussion, but nothing came of it, and Bolt departs to a music hall.

Later that evening, the narrator goes to Jones's shop to find a lively discussion going on among Vicar Talbot, Tom Bolt, Tom's son Charley, and a progressive, young radical member of Parliament named Langham, possibly based on C.F.G. Masterman.[14] Their conversation reflects the problems of politics that preoccupied the English in the last throes of Victorian liberalism, including the Boer War, the growing distance between the cities of man and the City of God, and the failure of traditional values to extricate man from his folly. Jones's conclusion is that "Poor old God seems to have his work cut out" (AY, 54), recalling a popular verse Tomlinson quoted in *Mars His Idiot*:

> "God heard the embattled nations sing and shout
> Gott Strafe England, and God save the King;
> God this, God that, and God the other thing.
> 'Good God,' said God, 'I've got my work cut out.'"[15]

Tomlinson's anachronism reveals his purpose, however; he tries to relate the uncertainty of the Boer War years to the later muddle.

Charley Bolt, teacher at the Madras Street school, recalls the young Tomlinson in many respects. Charley posts his resignation, having determined to become a journalist. He harbored no ill will toward his employer, but venerated Mr. Wiley as Tomlinson reported respecting his early teachers, "men of parts" who "did their best."[16] After saying good-bye to his former headmaster and employer, whose advice recalls that of the history teacher addressing Dedalus in Joyce's *Ulysses* and who hopes that Charley can improve the quality of Fleet Street writing, Charley rushes to the mission hall to meet the current object of his romantic fancy, Betty Whittaker. She has been performing volunteer work at the mission, not so much in the interest of those for whom missions are intended as in her interest in Talbot's curate Francis Langham, brother of the radical statesman. When Charley realizes this he withdraws from pursuit of Betty.

After Tomlinson provides a brief glimpse of the daily life of the Bolt family, during which Mrs. Bolt's thoughts summarize her temporary dissatisfaction with the ugliness of her life, and a fleeting encounter with Joseph Chamberlain, "the man who had given us war!" (*AY*, 82), he shifts to a social gathering at the home of Lord and Lady Carroll. Among the guests are Sir Alfred Harmsworth (the noted newspaper proprietor and journalist who subsequently became Lord Northcliffe) and Langham. The guests discuss the Boer War, the uncertainty of the news, and Langham's contention that "Every war is different from the one for which the experts prepare. The war the generals always get ready for is the previous war" (*AY*, 107). On this day, however, the word "Mafeking" came into popular usage, and "the populace . . . was filling the capital with a paean of triumph" (*AY*, 113). Part of the celebration of victory was the destruction of Jones's bookstore by an angry mob, and Jones himself would have been dismembered had it not been for Tom Bolt, who "got poor old Jones out of it" (*AY*, 118). The ushering in of the twentieth century, in this novel, includes the mania of this mob, the general feeling among workers such as Tom Bolt that "fifty-two more paydays" is justification enough for the continuous building of monstrous battleships, the insightful but futile approach of younger radicals, and the failure of English conventions to sustain the country. The first section of the novel has introduced causes that hindsight can identify as sources of the Great War.

Tomlinson shifts to another aspect of England's prewar role in "Part II: 1908." The second section seems a digression from the novel as a whole, but it performs two necessary functions. It contributes an impression of the aspirations and activities of the British between the Boer War and World War I, and it provides a necessary space for transition between the events of 1900 and 1914. Jim Maynard, a journalist and friend of the narrator, for reasons which remain obscure to this reader, takes a consignment of supplies into the jungle of Novobambia to a "friend who was in need of help in his work of medical research" (AY, 129). Such is the nature of political intrigue among colonizing European powers that no one will accept Maynard's explanation for his journey, and Maynard finds himself regarded as an agent of England's colonial interests. A Mr. Broderic, who serves unknown interests in some shady fashion, provides Maynard with natives and a canoe, warning him against the machinations of an American named Hoyt. On the journey Maynard alienates the natives and becomes encumbered alone with his supplies. After caching his consignment and wandering through the jungle half delirious, narrowly avoiding death by arrows shot anonymously from the foliage, Maynard stumbles upon the American Hoyt, who not only helps him but unites Maynard with his friend Buckle, an entomologist who is studying insect pests. Maynard learns that he has become the subject of dossiers in Paris and Berlin despite his nonpolitical intentions. To avoid further complications, Hoyt, Buckle, and Maynard avoid Broderic by taking a circuitous route out of the jungle, and the three succeed in their efforts to reach Mr. Dickson, the British consul.

During his conversation with Dickson, Maynard learns that most of his misfortunes derived from Broderic's perfidy and that the consul is powerless to act. However, he does have mail for Maynard, including an unintentionally ironic letter from Charley Bolt. Charley congratulates Maynard on having chosen the proper time to leave England, describes the activities of "a fellow called Lloyd George" who "is raising Cain for the good of the common people" (AY, 179), and urges Maynard to "drop that lotus bud" (AY, 182).

When Maynard returns to England, however, he finds the quiet boredom of the journalists' office in "Part III: 1914." Charley has submitted his novel to a judicious literary editor and is beginning to move away from Fleet Street, similar to Tomlinson's shift of careers. Maynard, through his association with Charley, has become a member of the Bolt family circle and seems to view Annie Bolt with affectionate interest, although he follows a leisurely, prewar form of courtship. This section of the novel focuses on the unhurried pursuits of major characters before the deluge, and Tomlinson draws from his own experience to direct the movements of his characters. Charley Bolt, for example, goes to Dublin on assignment, and after Charley "abandoned Dublin because he did not know what to do there," the narrator reports that Charley came to him in Belfast for advice (*AY*, 214). (Tomlinson had reported being in Belfast, waiting for civil war, when World War I began.) Charley's problem was that "it was not easy to write in a lucid way of preposterous bogies, still less of a universal, furious, but invisible maggot" (*AY*, 215), and the narrator finds this description apt.

> A necessity nobody understood had emerged us all into a headless power. We were a common flood of mankind hurrying on. The waters were rising. Where, Charley asked, had he better wait? He could not be advised. The confused currents were not of nameable men and women. They were the uprising from sunless springs of ancestral emotions, and already were at the bounds of reason and control. The waters might overpour anywhere, at any hour. Charley disappeared the same day. One place, he could see, was as good as another. (*AY*, 215)

Maynard concludes that all they can do is to wait.

The sudden change of August, 1914, appears when Charley buys a newspaper in the hope that he will not see the news he knew he would read.

> The opening of that paper was as startling to Charley as the loosing of a maniacal yell at his ear. The morning broke into a senseless clangour, as with the cries of lunatics in multitudes terrified and contentious, and the beating of brass and iron. The magnified headlines bawled the excitement of the gathering of millions of armed men, with the alarms of Paris, Berlin, London, Brussels, and St. Petersburg. He could hear under it all, in paragraphs more obscure, the protesting cries of the workers in the capitals; though the alarm of Berlin was cut short in its record, as though stifled. It was consternation smothered before it was articulate. And he then noticed, as though it were a symbolic act, the forewarning of what now would be done in darkness, that the benign and enlightening mind of Jean Jaurès had been put out. Peace, sitting at its dinner in its accustomed seat, had been shot through the head by a madman. Peace was dead. (*AY*, 220)

On the last page of this section Germany enters Luxemburg.

"Part IV: War!" finds Charley Bolt, his younger brother, Jim Maynard, and several others in uniform. Tomlinson's penchant for description finds indulgence in several descriptive passages of the men marching to war, the destruction of modern warfare, and the nature of the soldier's life in the trenches. This section does little to advance the plot of the novel, but it re-creates the atmosphere of the

war in the trenches as few writers have done. The first-person narrator, now a war correspondent, provides the perspective Tomlinson
had in that capacity.

Four abreast marched with us a column of men, newly taken from their
families, for gun meat. It was a motley consignment of respectable fathers,
still smelling of their trades, and raw from the homes they had just left. They
were going to their fate with that docility, caused by the enchantment cast
over us, which became the mark of most Europeans. One notable figure, with
the luxurious girth of the proud whose watch-chains go well before them, and
a ruddy forked beard, which, but an hour or so before, was the mark of his
godhead to his children, glanced at me enquiringly, with something of the
dumb alarm of an ox who is beginning to suspect that all is not well when on
his way to the butcher. (*AY*, 251)

Among descriptions in this section are an account of the difficulty of
rail travel, the strangeness of returning to London after being at the
Front, and the lack of reality which seemed to prevail. Langham finds
the war a new target for his sense of irony, and Charley feels that he
has gained the insight into reality which his earlier attempts at fiction
writing lacked:

I have learned a lot about them [men and women]. Under the stress of war
they have not only undressed, they have got out of their skins. They don't
care if you can see through them. I think the girls about this camp are crazy,
the dear little anarchs, and the men desperately snatch at the life they are
afraid they are going to lose. That may be it. You never heard such loose and
rollicking talk. All the old fences are down, and we rove, and we don't care a
potato peeling. (*AY*, 273)

Charley has become somewhat of a cynic, asking "Is there a War
Office? Or is it a Public Joke? This is highly important, as there is a
war on. I want to know" (*AY*, 273). The narrator's description of the
army's plight adds urgency to such questions:

The troops went underground to live, if they could, and died of mines and
counter-mines, grenades, and of hopeful yet credulous artillery fire, which
not seldom was that of their friends. The whole library of military science and
history was as obsolete by the end of the November of 1914 as the runes of
witchcraft. The generals, though they kept their expressions of stern ab-
solutism, did not know what to do. An army no longer had its legs to use, and
it had no centre to be pierced, and no wings to be out-flanked; and that left
the generals as were the theologians when the gods ceased to be. An army

had become, for the first time in history, a continuous ditch of hidden men, quite unnatural to the theories of commanders in the field, yet still a fact, for it baulked them. (*AY*, 277)

Tomlinson's handling of most of this section might have been lifted bodily from a tract such as *Mars His Idiot*, for only occasionally does he refer specifically to his characters or to their actions. Instead, he writes a general chronicle of the occurrences of the war that would not be amiss in a history book, then shifts to the home front, then to an anecdotal account which involves the narrator without impinging on the lives of the Bolt brothers or Jim Maynard. For someone who awaited an account of their thoughts in the process of survival in the trenches, similar to Ford Madox Ford's treatment of Tietjens in *A Man Could Stand Up* or Richard Aldington's of George Winter-bourne in *Death of a Hero*, this section was disappointing.

Tomlinson moves his attention to Tom Bolt, still working in the shipyards but at the command of the war effort.

[He] had been preparing a transport for sea even while she moved down-river. He and his gang of men had laboured for thirty hours without a break. They had been put ashore, their job completed, where no rest could be had, and no refreshment. There had been the usual heated dispute beforehand with the shipyard officer about money for overtime, which Mr. Bolt had thought just for his good men; but the owners, who were the Carroll Line, had behaved as though expedition in an emergency, if properly considered, was its own reward. Old Bolt, ponderous, tyrannical, and energetic, against his sense of justice, had bullied his men through it. . . . (*AY*, 289)

Tomlinson derived this from an earlier essay, dated by him November 11, 1918, entitled "The Nobodies," in which he discussed the common man's role in the war.

I went to an engineer who would know the worst, and would not be afraid to tell me what it was. I found him asleep in his overalls, where he had dropped after thirty-six hours of continuous duty. Afterwards, when his blasphemous indignation over profiteers, politicians, and newspapers had worn itself out, he told me. His men, using dimmed lights while working on the decks of urgent ships, often forced to work in cramped positions and in all weathers, and while the ship was under way to a loading berth, with no refreshment provided aboard, and dropped long distances from home, were still regarded by employers in the old way, not as defenders of their country's life, but as a means to quick profits, against whom the usual debasing tricks of economy could be devised.[17]

In the essay he describes this circumstance in more vivid and immediate terms than he does in the novel. Tomlinson also decides it is necessary to interject an anecdote of an adventure as a war correspondent, which he published separately as *Illusion: 1915*. He begins this by stating:

A day came when it was necessary for me to see this secreted region to which our younger men were drifting, and at once it was doubtful whether or not I was good enough for so reserved a privilege. . . . A handsome soldier . . . at length agreed, in almost a friendly way, that he knew of no reason serious enough to keep me from the privilege of being shot at or choked by chlorine gas. (*AY*, 296–97)

This results in a lengthy anecdote featuring an old acquaintance, Upcott, with whom the narrator dines and observes extremely implausible behavior on the part of a French officer and his aide. Apparently, Tomlinson forgot his characters as he was caught in his desire to rewrite his own experiences, but he returns to his characters in the next section.

"Part V: 1916–1919" is slightly misleading, since only the last two pages concern themselves with 1919. The narrator describes a visit to Charley, who had been gassed, but this visit seems also to result from Tomlinson's direct experience in France, as described in the essay "Holly-Ho!" printed in *Old Junk*, where the phrase "by the width of his paint" describes the nearness of the driver's misses in the exact phrase used in the novel.[18] However, when Tomlinson begins to place his rhetoric in the mouths of various characters, he returns to his story line. Langham listens to the embittered comments of a young soldier, who resents hearing the war referred to as an adventure:

The cursed war and its pus are just the outcome of the factories and the laboratories—an interlude, to fight over credits and customers—and the serfs go from one part of the great machine to attend to another, by order. And listen to me, Mr. Langham, if everyone not in the trenches got continuous neuralgia till the last shot was fired—if you and Lloyd George and the Kaiser and Clemenceau got fire in your teeth which wouldn't go out till the guns had stopped—or suppose some one important at home dropped dead in the street every time a chap was killed here—how far off would the bitter end be?" (*AY*, 368–69)

Langham's response to a general is "You seem to have a nice lot of anarchists wearing the King's uniform. We don't let them talk like that at home" (*AY*, 369), but the general replies easily, "We don't mind . . . while they do what they're told" (*AY*, 369).

When the narrator encounters Jim Maynard, he learns that Jim met Betty Whittaker in the hospital, and that she had become a nurse who "gave herself out of her merry heart. The fellows wanted her, and she was a giver" (*AY*, 381). Finally the narrator returns to the Bolt family, to learn that Tom Bolt is bedridden. In an attempt to finish his story, the narrator wraps matters up quickly. Mrs. Bolt receives a telegram from the War Office informing her that Charley has been killed in action, and she keeps this information from Bolt. Bolt has received an almost identical telegram from the War Office informing him that Jack has fallen in action, and he keeps this information from Mrs. Bolt. Annie, privy to both secrets, wonders "How long?" (*AY*, 429), and all main characters are accounted for. The last two pages of the novel describe the narrator's and Jim Maynard's return to France, where they observe a group taking a holiday while Jim and the narrator ponder soldiers' graves.

While both *Gallions Reach* and *All Our Yesterdays* are pleasurable reading experiences, they both suffer as novels. Part of their failure results from Tomlinson's willingness to abandon fiction when it suits his purpose, while another part of their failure results from his frequent disregard for the expectations of his readers. Thus *Gallions Reach*, which introduces several possibilities with the death of Perriam, lapses into an episodic series of adventures which occasionally defy plausibility. *All Our Yesterdays*, which seems to build toward its climax as a psychological study of men at war, unaccountably lapses into a mixture of treatise, history, anecdote, and reflection, returning to its characters only halfheartedly. The ease with which this could happen is understandable, for Tomlinson drew so extensively from his personal experiences and memories in both works that he could frequently forget that the focus of the novel is on its characters and their experiences, not on those of the author. Perhaps Tomlinson suspected that this distraction from his fiction by his reminiscences could only weaken his fiction, for in his next two novels, *The Snows of Helicon* and *All Hands!*, he drew very little from his personal adventures. In the process, however, he discovered other problems that required his serious attention.

CHAPTER 10

The Middle Novels: Adventure and Rhetoric

I The Snows of Helicon

I N *The Snows of Helicon* (1933) Tomlinson attempted to write a novel that derived almost entirely from his imagination. His central character's struggle was certainly not his own, and the movement of the plot did not follow the events of Tomlinson's life. As a novel, *Snows* was a failure, but, as E. M. Forster once wrote about Gertrude Stein's attempts to abolish time from the novel, the "failure is instructive."[1] Forster found such failure worthy:

There is nothing to ridicule in such an experiment as hers. It is much more important to play about like this than to rewrite the Waverley Novels. Yet the experiment is doomed to failure. The time-sequence cannot be destroyed without carrying in its ruin all that should have taken its place; the novel that would express values only becomes unintelligible and therefore valueless.[2]

Tomlinson's difficulties in this novel were not results of a similar attempt to abolish time, but an attempt to abolish his individual reminiscences and personality from a fictive work. The result, as most critics reviewed it, was a work almost entirely lacking in plausibility of character or action, but from the perspective of Tomlinson as a novelist, the shift from autobiography to fancy proved to be instructive. As William Blake put it, "the road of excess leads to the palace of wisdom," for "you never know what is enough unless you know what is more than enough." Although *Snows* is in some ways Tomlinson's least successful novel, it served to teach him aspects of a novelist's vulnerability and to direct him toward the proper balance between his observations of reality and his treatment of life in fiction.

Early reviews were generally unfavorable of this novel. Arthur Colton began his review with general observations on Tomlinson's shortcomings as a creator of characters:

190

Mr. Tomlinson cannot make any of his characters say obvious things. A commonplace person may be intended, but in his hands it becomes an oddity, an alien in a duller world. The sea, the fog, the tropical forest, are always whispering and suggesting.[3]

After commenting on the "musing" nature of Tomlinson's protagonist, Colton relates this trait to flaws in the novel's structure:

The vagueness of the dreamer finds its way into the story. Space and time are jumped between chapters. It is the mind and not the outward event that is important. The story is exciting in places, but it moves in the shadow of curious thought.[4]

While Colton does not dismiss the importance of the mind, he feels that Tomlinson, by ignoring externals such as time and space, has made it far too difficult for a reader to suspend disbelief.

In his conclusion, however, Colton identifies a trait of Tomlinson's work that partly compensates for the lapses in the novel, although the same trait may have mitigated Tomlinson's urgency to develop as a novelist:

Mr. Tomlinson does not often write fiction, and with him it does not greatly matter what thread his mind follows, whether fiction, or travel, or a theme. He is a companion worth going with wherever he goes and as long as he chooses to go.[5]

In this novel, "theme" is more predominant than travel or fiction. In another review of the novel, Harold de Wolf Fuller identifies that theme: "Travers, the hero, . . . knows secretly that in creating these huge structures he is compromising with life as it is now lived. He knows that classical beauty is what he craves and will fight for."[6] Fuller notes the novel's "slender plot" and that Travers, after his demise, has "sacrificed himself for his ideal of beauty."[7] Despite the contrived plot, implausible protagonist, and lack of reality in the vague shifts of time and space, the theme manages to unite the novel by providing a sense of purpose, but the reader frequently finds himself bemused, if not puzzled.

As the novel opens, John Travers, an architect of some reputation, has decided to retire. He is sailing aboard the *Cambodia*, bound for Liverpool from New York. His thoughts are full of classical Greece and he laments the moderns' abandonment of classical beauty: "No Phidias was needed, not when all that was asked for was whacking

great containers of concrete and steel. Still, you could do a scrap of
relief with a colonnade of red and green petrol pumps."[8] When
Travers meditates on his situation, his observations become wry:

Now he had to do that new London hotel. It would be wonderful. Its fabulous
cost would justify it. Who would have the nerve to doubt the loudest and
most extravagant thing ever done? That was the stuff to give them. Nobody
supposed that anything but benefit could come of what was elephantine and
costly. The greater buildings which arose because material desires enlarged
with the quickening rhythm of life always did look as though they never could
topple. They were rightly set to the finer calculations of science, which was
always ready to gratify desire. They were from everlasting to everlasting.
Everybody banked on them and in them. They towered ever higher and
spread ever farther. They were prodigious. They had audacious and conquering severity, as though their foundations were sunk in the rock of ages and
their parapets true to the aligning finger of God. What but money's worth
could ever come from them? Good old towers of Babel! (*Snows*, 10–11)

Travers has met a younger man named Mantell, educated at Harvard
and Oxford, and has taken an instant liking to him, partly because
Mantell is a scoffer. The two men share several ironical reflections on
the nature of man and of modern life, and the younger man's comments ("funk makes brothers of us all" [*Snows*, 24]; "Rouse our fears
and we're human" [*Snows*, 24]; and the like) inspire similar unspoken
observations from Travers. As he observes a woman at another table,
he reflects that "Compared with the original sap and essence of such a
woman, wasn't his art as inconsequential as a parlour-game?" (*Snows*,
25), and he confirms his desire to be quit of his profession.

When the *Cambodia* arrives in Liverpool, Travers is met by his
wife, Fannie, who is considerably younger than he. While Travers
goes to a newspaper shop, leaving Fannie amidst the luggage, he
begins to behave implausibly. His watch has stopped, and when he
"sees" that little time has passed, he decides to leave the terminal to
browse in a bookshop he recalls. Unfortunately, on the way he finds
himself on the periphery of a crowd which formed after an omnibus
bumped a boy on a bicycle. Travers makes a comment that embroils
him in a dispute with the crowd, but he is extricated from this
difficulty by a man named Quirke, who owns a flower shop.

Quirke offers Travers the use of his shop to freshen up before
returning to his wife and luggage, and, after another look at his watch,
which still shows the same time, Travers accepts. Quirke, however, is
no ordinary florist, for he uses his shop to discuss the business

dealings of Lord Snarge. These plans include razing a temple to Apollo. Assuming Travers's ignorance, Quirke discusses Snarge's proposed destruction of the temple with other Snarge minions. Travers, like the reader, finds this development hard to believe.

Travers felt a need to speak, but he could not ease away a congestion of words to express astonishment, alarm, protest, and disbelief, so he was fixed in silent dismay. Somehow he must be mistaken. Surely what he had heard could have no real meaning? It wouldn't give any trouble, that building, though it was all marble. It was a temple to Apollo; that they didn't know. It would be easy to shift it; of that they were sure. Steel masts would go there, instead of a sign to the leader of the muses. It was easy to destroy the peace, the aromatic herbs, and the white colonnade; they had dynamite. It wouldn't take long. For over two thousand years the god of light had kept his house for those who could face the light. The light would go out. Another need had arisen. Not here, O Apollo! Who now? Lord Snarge. (*Snows*, 80–81)

While the others continue to pore over the map, Travers takes his leave. Instead of returning to Fannie and the luggage, however, Travers determines to undertake a quest to save the temple. He resolves to pursue Lord Snarge to "stick a spoke in this wheel," apparently quite forgetting his wife.

Fannie, however, has not forgotten Travers. After waiting beyond the limitations of wifely patience, she accepts Mantell's assistance in moving herself and the luggage to a hotel room. She determines on her own quest, resolving to find her husband. Unaccountably, at least from the narrative, she travels to New York, where she meets Lord Snarge and Quirke. She assumes their interest in her husband is kind, although they have other motives for wondering about Travers's whereabouts. She remains convinced that Quirke and Snarge know where to find Travers, while they believe that she can locate Travers for them. In either case, Quirke indicates the source of their interest, if not a plausible reason for its intensity:

"Lord Snarge hasn't seen him—not yet—but let me tell you that they'd better not meet. Your husband's interest in his lordship's business is too close, and it isn't wanted. Where is he now?" Mr. Quirke's mouth took an ironic twist. "Anyhow, tell him from me to keep out, wherever he is." (*Snows*, 122)

When Fannie inquires into the nature of "his lordship's business," Quirke becomes more insistent: "Mrs. Travers, that's all we've got to say to you. He'd better keep out. Men in business don't like having their interests meddled with. It makes trouble. You understand what I mean?"(*Snows*, 123). The meeting proves mutually unsatisfactory to all parties.

Travers, meanwhile, is sailing to Santa Maria, where he hopes to find Snarge. He sustains himself with reflections such as this:

The fire stolen from Heaven was handy and docile in that original hollow tube of Prometheus, but it held chances beyond the guess of the first benefactor of men. The tube is blowing great guns and small arms now. Man contrived to steal power from the gods, but, the fool he is, he forgot to bring with it the clue to its right use, and here is Chaos come again. (*Snows*, 93)
1, 93)

Travers, in the company of a bosun named Bert Byles, finds his way to Santa Maria and talks with Glenthorpe, the British Minister. Glenthorpe informs Travers that Lord Snarge was "here not long ago," but that he has since proceeded inland. Undaunted, Travers decides to follow Snarge, but first he engages in a vague and some-times rambling conversation with Glenthorpe that leads the latter to surmise "I don't think he is quite all there, . . . yet there's something in what he says" (*Snows*, 153). Travers, with Bert Byles, travels inland by train. The train, however, is intercepted by revolutionaries, whose rifle fire makes no impression on the imperturbable calm of Travers, who seems oddly lacking in the Life Force. When the smoke clears, Travers finds himself in the company of Byles and an American engineer, who, in the manner of Buckle, Maynard, and the American Hoyt in *All Our Yesterdays*, make their way overland by an improba-ble route. The Travers party, however, benefits from the particular experience of this American—having murdered a man, the American had crossed by the same route in record time to establish an alibi.

Fannie has also arrived in this part of the world and Travers, from a secluded vantage point in the jungle foliage, catches a glimpse of her. However, as he is on the verge of revealing his presence to her, Travers sees Mantell, and he infers from the observed relationship that he ought not to interfere. His inference is fairly accurate. Earlier, accompanying Fannie on her voyage to the Bahamas and on to "Paranagua, wherever that was" (*Snows*, 198), Mantell resents Trav-ers's neglect of his wife at the moment before a fortunate list of the ship places her in his arms. She sees no need to resist. Travers, oblivious to his domestic fortunes, proceeds to Colonna, the site of the fated temple. He learns, as he might have guessed, that his lone interference is unlikely to alter Lord Snarge's plans or the complicity of his hirelings, and that the plans to dynamite the temple have reached the eve of their fruition. Travers, in a gesture of sacrifice to classical purity and beauty, enters the temple and remains there until the explosion reduces it to dust. Later, Bert Byles meets Fannie at the Alcazar Hotel, one which Travers had designed, and they talk briefly. After arguing that perhaps Travers's death was suicide, perhaps not, Bert remains emphatic in his insistence that Travers was aware of what he was doing.

The Snows of Helicon includes passages that rank with Tomlinson's travel narratives, instances of his ironic wit occur frequently in the exchanges of Mantell and Travers, and many of Travers's reflections equal similar discursive essays on the subjects of art and misguided progress. Yet, as a novel, *The Snows of Helicon* is an instructive failure. The reader may not object to the movement across the world that bothered Colton, but the inexplicable and immeasurable gaps in time pose a different problem. The reader (or, at least, this one) might appreciate knowing how long it took Travers to reach the British Minister Glenthorpe, or to complete his trek across the South American interior, or to reach Colonna, or to climb to the temple, or to experience the adventures covered in the novel. Other questions of pertinence arise: How long did it take Fannie to discover the connection between Travers's disappearance and Lord Snarge? To reach Snarge in New York? To strike out for the Bahamas? To become romantically entangled with Mantell? To meet Bert at the Alcazar?

The issue of plausibility of character and action raises several other questions. It would be convenient to explain Travers as obsessed by a noble purpose to the extent that it has upset his mental balance, but unfortunately Tomlinson spent approximately thirty pages to establish the values and philosophy of Travers in a sympathetic light, and such a convenient explanation contradicts the evidence of much of the text. Also, how can one explain the machinations of the nefarious Lord Snarge being conducted in a florist's shop, or Fannie homing in on Snarge and Quirke in New York with the unerring instinct of a migratory bird, or her being drawn toward the approximate location of Travers in South America, or Snarge and Quirke considering Travers a serious enough threat even to consider? When one encounters Americans at home in unknown territory because they have previously traversed it to establish an alibi for murder, one begins to suspect that coincidence is being strained to its limit. Tomlinson seemed to learn from this excess, however. In his next novel, he moved back to a life with which he had been familiar since his youth, resolved the problems of character and plausibility within a larger perspective than an individual's idealism, and seemed to overcome the novelist's problem of time.

II All Hands!

All Hands! (1937), published in America as *Pipe All Hands*, was much more successful as a novel than *The Snows of Helicon*. The subject of the novel is the conflicting ethics of a ship's captain and the owner of the ship's line, and the story takes place on board the *Hestia*, which is not only subjected to the worst of the alien winter sea, but also to the commercial machinations of its owner, Sir John Dowland. This novel was received much more favorably than its predecessor, one anonymous reviewer beginning,

It is rare to find in modern fiction well written, unromanticized stories about ships, officers and men of the merchant marine. *All Hands* is such a book and the author's name is a guarantee of authenticity.[9]

Once Tomlinson returned to writing about what he knew, he became more successful with characterization.

Mr. Tomlinson has drawn good types. The captain, reserved, quiet, lonely, with a working knowledge of Persian rugs and pottery; the chief officer, saturnine and disgruntled; the second, young, capable and courageous; the third, sensitive to criticism and feckless; a chief engineer, growing stout and elderly in the oily clamor of the engine room; his second, more concerned with repairing some defect in the engines than in seeing the mosaics of Montreale above Palermo.

The reviewer regrets that Tomlinson did not more fully develop a theme based on "the present-day system of ownership, a system in which an owner may be more concerned in preventing his ship— which probably he has never seen—from getting a cargo than in finding one," and he claims that Tomlinson "uses it merely as a thread and settles down . . . to describe a major Atlantic storm." However, as we shall see, this transition from the owner's motives to the major Atlantic storm is not a digression. Tomlinson needed this storm to advance his owner/ship's master theme. It becomes the means by which Dowland perceives the reality of the ships he owns and the men who serve them.

The novel begins in Malaya, where Jerry Barton, a young officer, goes ashore to perform a death watch over the ship's master. Jerry tells the steward that the *Hestia* has a good name, for Hestia "was the goddess of the sacred fire of the altar and the hearth. Though you might not have liked her. You see, she was an obstinate virgin, or so we're told."[10] Jerry feels that this is a lucky name, but the steward has another opinion:

> "That wasn't our ship's first name—was it, Chief?—and take it from me, leave the gods alone. Don't use their names. They're no good. You never know what you're asking for, with them. I wouldn't name a ship after a god. She ought to be called after the owner's daughter, or his aunt, or his lovely lady, but these gods are a sticky lot. This Hestia—you say she was goddess of the sacred fire? Then you can lay your extra-master's ticket they used to offer up the best good-looking lads to her, to keep her smiling. She wanted her rake-off with the sacrifices, the same as any god would. The Chief says that ship had a good launch. I should say she did. She was about satisfied with a riveter, for the time being." (*AH*, 7)

In *The Sea and the Jungle*, twenty-five years earlier, Tomlinson had remarked on ships' names and sailors' superstitious regard for them:

> I learned why a ship has a name. It is for the same reason that you and I have names. She has happenings according to her own weird. She shows perversities and virtues her parents never dreamed into the plans they laid for her. Her heredity cannot be explained by the general chemics of iron and steel and the principles of the steam engine; but something counts in her of the moods of her creators, both of the happy men and the sullen men whose bright or dark energies poured into her rivets and plates as they hammered, and now suffuse her body. Something of the "Capella" was revealed to me, "our" ship.[11]

Several similar conversations among the sailors of the *Hestia* establish the quality of the sailors' lives.

After the ship's master dies, the *Hestia* receives a new master, Captain Doughty, no doubt named after the author of *Arabia Deserta*, admired by T. E. Lawrence as well as by Tomlinson who called it "the greatest book of travel in our language."[12] Shortly after Doughty's arrival, Adams, the Engineer's second, performs a ritual of fighting with his men to convince them of their duty to raise steam. Victory is his, but as the ship prepares to move, one of the men shouts an insult at his chief. Captain Doughty, while the Chief debates tackling the man, calls "Who is that man?," and the men have their first sight of their new master:

> They saw a lean and elderly stranger up there, on the captain's bridge, regarding them mildly but regretfully. He suggested a man in a pulpit, taking a first view of his flock, which he had surprised, and they could see he did not think much of his luck. His ascetic face, clean-shaven, was contemplative and friendly, though the furrows by its mouth hinted at ironic toleration; that of a man whose task in life was to keep his fellows on a course away from folly, if that could be done; and he had accepted it, perhaps not with rejoicing, yet without repining. He would do what he could, and expect little.
> "Bring that man to me," he said. "I shall log him." (AH, 28–29)

Once Captain Doughty has established his authority, he begins to make himself known more fully to the reader, if not to all his men, and Jerry's wry reflections introduce the conflict between owner and sailor early in the novel.

As the ship passes The Little Paternosters, Jerry muses:

> Wasn't it about there that the skipper and owner of the *Mary Gloster* dropped his wife? The hairy savage! It was he who should have been dropped overside, not his wife. Why did Kipling admire that swine of an owner and skipper instead of drowning him? (AH, 39)

Doughty begins to reveal the variety of his understanding to Jerry, pointing out to the young officer that Celebes is not only older than Java and Borneo, but it is also the home of butterflies shaped differently than most, with a "bolder curve" in their wings. He informs Jerry that "It has taken longer to better that wing than to build civilisation" (AH, 46). Robin, the ship's third officer, reveals another dimension of Doughty's character. Robin admits "I'm no good on the bridge, not a bit, trying to run the ship ashore every time there's trees about," but instead of the stripping down he had expected from the captain, he reports that Doughty has a different manner: "All the captain did was to warn me that steamships nearly always have engines. Have you ever noticed that?" (AH, 57)

The *Hestia* begins to behave oddly, and the men find this extremely unsettling. The men examine the ship's gear for faults, looking for

a silly muddle that was human, familiar, and rectifiable with patience, one that would bring her giddiness within the bounds of reason. It was not there. She had been perverse, but could offer no excuse for her conduct. This worried them. Would it happen again? (*AH*, 62)

As the men continue to worry, Tomlinson comments on the nature of their concern and how it contrasts to an owner's interest:

She was a ship, and so she was more than home and work to her crew. It is not for nothing that a master-mariner is sometimes called a ship's husband, and, if he is specially commended, a good one. Her men are married to their ship; thus they accept the measure of their undertaking. Her owner, whatever his standing and repute, is of less consequence when she is on the high seas than a hatch-cover. She is the first charge. Her safety comes before that of her guardians; so rigorous an unwritten law must never be questioned. Her protectors may leave her only when the last thing possible has been done for her and they see it is of no avail, for she is about to go down under them. (*AH*, 63)

The men's concern for their ship goes beyond such pragmatic issues as survival to become a religious experience:

She embodies a mystery. There is in her a value which never shows in a charter-party. Nor is it helpful to examine her for it, or to question her people about it. A ship may share with art and religion the trust men repose in a hidden purpose which ignores our mortal lot but lures our fealty; a purpose that cannot be named, for it cannot be proved, exacting labour and life, though promising no more than the honour of martyrdom. (*AH*, 63)

The men "may know enough to hate her owner, and to feel sorry for her captain; yet when they board her they are ready to put an idea which cannot be expressed above their lives," and the ship has "the power to exact from her people a service authority dare not command and money cannot buy" (*AH*, 64). In terms reminiscent of Melville's description of the *Pequod*, Tomlinson summarizes the relationship between the *Hestia* and her men:

The *Hestia* was a microcosm, separate but destined, her fate within herself, her welfare sustained by the unity of her company in a common cause, with the chance of frustration through the adversity of the elements, the falsity of material, or errors of the mind. (*AH*, 67)

Having described the principal characters of the *Hestia*, their relation to the ship, and their manner of life, Tomlinson proceeds to unfold a plot based on the ship's perverse behavior and the distant perspective of her owner.

The ship has passed through the Java Sea to Sourabaya, where Doughty expects to take on a consignment of sugar for transport to London. However, he meets an old friend, Paterson, who tells him that Doughty will not be able to pick up his consignment, for a cartel is holding sugar to await rising prices: "Your owner, though I suppose you know it, wants to help the racket more than he wants to ship the cargo" (AH, 106). Paterson suggests that Doughty obey his owner's orders to wait, but Doughty has received no such instruction and intends to load his cargo and proceed to London. He talks to the agent Paget and learns "They must let me have it if I insist? Well, I insist" (AH, 112).

A month later Mr. Nye, the manager of Dowland's shipping line, finds himself forced to discuss Doughty's insistence with Sir John Dowland. Nye had trusted to the *Hestia*'s customary knots and habits, feeling that they would ensure the delay of sugar without specific instructions to Doughty, but the *Hestia* had broken her former records, thereby upsetting the plans of her owner. This recalls a similar experience Tomlinson had as a shipping clerk.

I recalled . . . that once, when my business was concerned with bills of lading and freight accounts, I was advised to ship four hundred cases to Sydney, New South Wales; and one-half of that consignment, my instructions ran, was to arrive a month before the other. The first lot went in a modern steel barque, the *Cairnbulg*. . . . More than a fortnight later, being too young to remember that the little *Cutty Sark* had been one of the China tea clippers, I shipped the last half of the consignment in her. But she disordered all the careful plans of the consigners. She got in a fortnight ahead of the *Cairnbulg*.[13]

Perhaps reflecting Tomlinson's role in a similar situation, Nye is more sympathetic to Doughty than is Dowland, praising Doughty as one of the best in the fleet and reminding Dowland that:

" . . . we sent no advice to the ship."
"Of course we didn't. What's the matter with you? We don't tell our shipmasters everything, or they'd learn enough to order us about. That man must have heard at Sourabaya what we wanted, and ought to have known we couldn't tell him." (AH, 118)

Dowland suggests first that the *Hestia* sail across the Atlantic in winter, even after Nye points out that the steamer is "not in shape for a North Atlantic passage on winter marks," but Dowland relents and sends the *Hestia* to dry dock. In the course of this conversation Dowland reveals an exaggerated indifference to his ships, saying at one point that "a ship is only the last implement applied to trade, and . . . she needs no more sentiment than a coal-bucket" (*AH*, 119), and he advises Nye to stop worrying about the *Hestia*, which is "only a parcel—an untimely parcel" (*AH*, 121).

The *Hestia* goes to dry dock at Bridstow in Devon, where Doughty meets Myles Tennant, a scholar whose chief claim to fame rests on his treatise, *The Evidence for Pre-Glacial Man*. He and his romantic adolescent daughter, Lyn, stay with Chope, the shipbuilder. When Chope examines the rudder of the *Hestia*, he sees something he does not like, but he cannot persuade Dowland's man, whose primary concern is expense, that anything is out of order: "There's an ugly mark on the rudder post, up by the top gudgeon" (*AH*, 156). With no alternative, however, Chope can only hope that he is mistaken, but he also hopes that the *Hestia's* next run is a fair-weather voyage. Meanwhile Lyn, whose fancy has been attracted by Jerry Barton, convinces her father that they should accompany the *Hestia* on its voyage to Crete, and Tennant agrees. The crew receives this news with misgiving, partly because a woman aboard bodes ill luck as well as restrictions on sailors' freedom of language, but mostly because Tennant is a friend of the owner.

The voyage begins uneventfully, as Tennant regrets being severed from the world he knows, and Lyn manages to offend deeply the second engineer by mistaking him for a mere stoker. However, Doughty receives orders to change his course to Boston, thereby crossing the North Atlantic in midwinter. He is piqued and tells Tennant,

"If ever you meet the man who invented the wireless, look round first to see whether the police are about, and if the coast is clear, strangle him. Since he did it we're never alone. An office boy a thousand miles away can deflect a ship and make hash of the plans of her company. There's no privacy and independence any more under the sun. Wherever we are, we are subject to the ceaseless twitterings of epileptics." (*AH*, 205)

Tennant, who has adjusted to the rigors of traveling by steamer, finds himself enthusiastic at the prospect of an ocean voyage and asks Doughty:

"How long will it take, this crossing to America?"

Doughty considered the moon, now sufficiently buoyant to have risen clear of the dark earth. "In the log of my ship, Tennant," he said after a pause, "the phrase used—I'll show you presently—is that she is bound *towards* a place, not to it. You see? Towards it! We'll do our best." (*AH*, 234)

Despite Doughty's attempts to dissuade them, Tennant and his daughter remain on board for the ocean crossing.

Mrs. Doughty, waiting at home, muses that her husband Jack has not been home for Christmas in fifteen years and reflects on the many times she has waited in suspense for him to return. One memory recalls an instance of conflict between Jack Doughty and the authorities:

She had kept several old numbers [of shipping news]. There was one which reported his ship beached, full of water, in the Red Sea. It had struck a rock the day before, which Jack swore was uncharted. A total loss! The Admiralty said no rock was there. Luckily, another ship ran on it after the experts had denied its presence, and was still there when they went to search for her. Jack's ticket had a close shave that time. (*AH*, 242)

Tomlinson, in *Tide Marks*, reported the original of this memory, which also occurred in the Red Sea:

A steamer, the *Avocet*, where the chart, the Admiralty chart, and Mr. Potter's *Pilot* allowed her master to rest on the comforting knowledge of deep water, struck a rock. "Naturally the Court of Enquiry," commented my captain, bitterly, "as much as told that man he was a liar about that rock." Our own master exhibited the sort of displeasure which good craftsmen reserve for theorists and experts—the learned men who would debate such a subject as the Red Sea in the Law Courts of London. But even then he did not begrudge them a fair word. "But they didn't suspend his certificate." They sent a gunboat from Aden to search for the rock. The gunboat cruised and dragged for it for three weeks, but the rock had gone. "Got tired," suggested my captain, "of waiting for another ship, I suppose. Went down below for a rest. The gunboat said there was no rock. And there you are, sir. That proved the *Avocet*'s skipper was a liar. Couldn't be plainer. Ten months later another ship found it, though she wasn't looking for it."[14]

As Mrs. Doughty waits at home for news of the *Hestia*, Mrs. Whitchelow, wife of the Chief Engineer, also follows the reports of the ship's progress.

For a while the news is uneventful, but Sparks, who operates the

Hestia's wireless, learns that ships between the *Hestia* and the American coast are encountering heavy weather, and that Sir John Dowland is aboard the luxury liner *Catalonia*, bound for London. Sparks takes news of the owner's location and of the weather to the captain, and it becomes known that the *Hestia* is bound for the worst of a hurricane. As the *Hestia* braves the storm, Mr. Tapley, an underwriter with ten thousand pounds riding on the *Hestia*, ignores the newspaper to read the "memoirs of an admiral discursive of the Battle of Jutland" (*AH*, 280). Ironically, while the *Hestia* is fighting for her life, the underwriter finds drama and adventure, conflict and tragedy only in these memoirs. However, he finally notices a paragraph in a column reserved for late news:

DOWLAND LINER'S SOS

Wireless report from the Cunarder *Catalonia* eastward-bound says this evening she is proceeding with all speed to the assistance of the steamer *Hestia*, out of control south-east, hurricane blowing and high confused sea. The *Catalonia* reports that she has been unable to get a reply from the *Hestia* since her SOS was received. (*AH*, 282)

The underwriter, who had trusted the ship on the reputation of the Dowland house flag, suddenly wonders who the captain might be since, "whoever he was," he "was important now" (*AH*, 282).

Sir John Dowland takes the news with relative equanimity until he learns that Tennant and his daughter are aboard. When the *Catalonia* reaches the *Hestia*, Doughty dispatches Lyn and Jerry Barton in a lifeboat, but the *Catalonia* loses sight of the *Hestia* and fails in her attempts to find the steamer. Dowland, with Lyn and Jerry, lands at Queenstown and finds two reasons why, for the first time, he is disturbed by the loss of a ship. He has lost Myles Tennant, and Tennant's fame has aroused widespread curiosity about the *Hestia*'s fate. Nye and Dowland lack faith in later reports that a Spanish vessel wired having sighted a steamer eastward-bound, and that a Cardiff trawler sighted a steamer heading for the Irish coast, but a few days later the *Hestia*, defying the elements, reaches port. Dowland, in an unprecedented gesture, approaches his ship.

She had all the marks of having been in the wars, and her funnel was grey with salt. The steward was at the bulwarks, near where a length of them was torn out. He was trying to believe the calm light of that beautiful harbour, with its hills so emerald and softly confiding to men just escaped from the danger of

the Atlantic. The steward knew who this approaching visitor was, and sought
the captain. (AH, 332)

Dowland surveys the men, who do not know him:

A group of scarecrows watched him, mildly speculative as to who the little
fellow was with the big head; the kind of roughs Sir John read about at times,
but never met, when they were makers of trouble for him through their trade
union. (AH, 333)

Doughty and Dowland are both uncomfortable at their meeting, and
Dowland stiffly informs Doughty that "You're late, and her voyage is
uncompleted, but you've got my ship in" (AH, 333). Doughty merely
states that he had a rough passage, and then Sir John "overcame the
reluctance of old habits and moved uneasily forward, his hand out-
stretched. 'By God, Doughty, you've brought her home'" (AH, 333).
At the end of the novel, the owner has come to realize the human toll
of his shipping and to respect the achievements of his men.

In All Hands! Tomlinson has had much better success in creating
believable characters, presenting an authentic picture of the merchant marine, and unifying his plot. His mode of narration, shifting
from the point of view of Mrs. Doughty to Mrs. Whitchelow's to the
underwriter's to Dowland's, also reaches a new level of sophistica-
tion. Once Tomlinson has presented the Hestia, rudderless, at the
mercy of the waves, he maintains suspense by giving the reader news
of the vessel as the news reaches shore. The device is extremely
effective in holding the reader's interest, and it also supports the
owner/ship's master theme by portraying the solely commercial
interest of the underwriter followed by the growing concern of Dowland, whose parsimonious attitude toward ships' repairs and interest
in profit have contributed to the Hestia's difficulties.

In The Snows of Helicon Tomlinson relied almost entirely on his
imagination, with results far removed from plausibility. In All Hands!
he exercised his imagination on events of which he had heard. Tomlinson wrote an article in 1948 entitled "The Master of the 'Rockingham,'" which reveals the source of All Hands! Earlier, we have seen
how Tomlinson's experiences have provided such touches as the
importance of a ship's name, the commercial havoc wrought by a ship
arriving in port ahead of schedule, and the difficulty a master may
have preserving his license when the Admiralty refuses to acknowledge the existence of a rock. Eleven years after the publication of this
novel, Tomlinson provided (without identifying it as such) the origin

of *All Hands!*[15]

One December evening he happened to notice that a ship, the *Rockingham*, was posted as missing in the *Lloyd's Shipping List*. While Tomlinson sympathized with the plight of the ship, he put it out of mind until the ship unexpectedly returned to the news.

The S.S. *Torridon* put into Falmouth, and reported that a thousand miles to the westward she had sighted the *Rockingham* out of control, her boats gone, her bridge structure wrecked, rolling her bridge ends under, with a gale from northwest increasing to squalls of hail and sleet of hurricane violence. The *Rockingham* had requested a tow, but the *Torridon*, it seems, had not the power for it in such weather, which threatened to grow worse. She had therefore signaled the impossibility to the *Rockingham*, and added, "You had better abandon." The master of the steamer in distress answered, "Decline. Will remain till end." The *Torridon* therefore resumed her voyage.

Like the *Hestia*, the *Rockingham* had lost her rudder, and the captain of the *Torridon* claimed "he had never seen the Atlantic in a worse mood." The following Sunday Tomlinson was hastily introduced to a Mrs. Dyson, who turned out to be the master of the *Rockingham*'s wife. Mrs. Dyson, to Tomlinson's surprise, "showed no sign of anxiety," and Tomlinson concludes that she has learned, over the years, to weather such uncertainty. Tomlinson's friend Meredith tactlessly commented that the next time the *Rockingham* was sighted, the master could leave her. In the spirit of Mrs. Doughty, Mrs. Dyson whispered, "Abandon? . . . Jack won't do that. He won't do it." Eventually, like the *Hestia*,

the *Rockingham* did reach port. She was already written off as uninsurable, when she surprised everybody by appearing off Ireland. The gales were still hard at it, and a pilot could not get out to her. A tugboat put into Queenstown to report the ship helpless, dragging her anchors, and sure to strike the rocks. Yet without a rudder, without a pilot, with only searchlights to show her the breakers on either side of the passage in, broadside on most of the time, and carried along by the wind and tide, she kept off the reefs by going ahead and astern, and miraculously arrived, with a few minor casualties, hull and engines sound, and her 4000 tons of cargo intact except for grain burned as fuel because coal had given out.

The details of the *Rockingham*'s problems, particularly the loss of her wheelhouse and her rudder, mirror those of the *Hestia*, and the character of Jack Doughty owes much to that of Jack Dyson. When Dyson appeared before a company of underwriters, Tomlinson perceived him as an ordinary passer-by in the street, middle-aged and nondescript, wondering why he was wanted here; shy and embarrassed; nervously turning his hat about. The sight of his lean face, showing no emotion, his eyes at first straightly questioning a company that had risen and was cheering him without pause, eyes then lowered to look at his shoes, was one of the severest rebukes to the stupidity of pride and self-importance I have ever met.

Tomlinson regarded

the master of the forgotten steamship *Rockingham* . . . emblematic. He still lives, in my experience, as the figure signifying better than most to what human nature can rise in a prolonged test, and hope not there. I never knew him. I never saw him till all was over, and Lloyd's underwriters were giving him a welcome home, and then he surprised me. After that ceremony, which was not public, he put on his bowler hat and went back into the multitude, all distinction lost. He was once more a nobody; his ship's bright news-value was extinguished.

Tomlinson's use of the *Rockingham*'s story is revealing, and it seems to have taught him the proper relationship between history and fiction, at least as he was to continue writing it. He took the story from the records and used his imagination to people the ship, the office which sent it to its travail on the waves, and the shipping parishes eagerly awaiting news at home. Not content merely to tell this story, Tomlinson sought its meaning in the power and attitudes of shipowners, contrasted with the hardships and loyalty of the men who serve the ship herself. The result is a novel that commands a reader's interest, presents its story in terms of significance from several opposing points of view, criticizes the manner of ships' ownership in the merchant marine, and remains a gripping reading experience more than forty years after its initial appearance. Once Tomlinson recognized the relationship between his observations and experiences of reality on the one hand, and his fiction on the other, he found the novel form more congenial to him.

CHAPTER 11

The Late Novels: Historical Fiction

I Problems as a Novelist

TOMLINSON'S early novels, *Gallions Reach* and *All Our Yester-days*, suffered from the inharmonious yoking of his personal experiences and reminiscences with the novel form. Partly because he had previously developed a readable and familiar expository style and partly because he vividly recalled the events which he presented as fiction, Tomlinson was less careful than he might have been of some of the problems peculiar to the novel form. These include the distinction Forster drew between "time in life" and "time in value," the difference between plausibility in fiction and reality in life, and the different expectations held by readers of essays of travel and by readers of novels. Perhaps recognizing that he had been distracted from the problems of a novelist by the intrusion of autobiography and anecdote in these books, Tomlinson shifted to the opposite extreme in *The Snows of Helicon*, the plot and characters of which seem deliberately removed from his own experience. In this work Tomlinson encountered new problems concerning plausibility and the handling of time in fiction.

In *All Hands!*, however, Tomlinson seemed to find a balance between fiction and reality. Working from an account of the perils of the *Rockingham*, an informal chance meeting with the master of the *Rockingham*'s wife, and an opportunity to hear the master of the *Rockingham* address a gathering of underwriters, Tomlinson combined the approach of the journalist with that of the novelist. From the actual event he took the major structure of his plot, and from his imagination embellished it to account for the owner's interest in the ship's fate, the witting and unwitting duplicity of the ship's owner in effecting the ship's difficulties, and the reactions of the master's wife, the chief engineer's wife, the underwriter, and the owner as they await news of the beleaguered ship. From his varied travels, his Cockney origins, his experience as a clerk in a shipping firm, and his reading, Tomlinson drew his understanding of owners' interests, the commercial aspects of shipping, and the roles of ships' officers and men. From his imagination, he provided his characters with credible and authentic personalities and backgrounds. Once he had succeeded, from an artistic point of view, in *All Hands!*, Tomlinson apparently discovered his *forte* in historical fiction. His last three novels attempt to achieve the same balance between his observations and historical perspective on the one hand, and his desire to provide his readers with plausible, instructive, and entertaining fiction on the other.

II   The Day Before

The Day Before (1939) returns to the subject of *All Our Yesterdays*, written nine years earlier. The earlier novel had presented several problems to its readers, and Tomlinson chose to handle his subject with major changes in technique. From a novelist's point of view, the differences are instructive. One major flaw of *All Our Yesterdays* was the first-person narrator. Although the narrator lacked formal identification beyond the pronoun "I", his movements corresponded to Tomlinson's during the prewar years, and his digressions into anecdote distracted from the main characters of the novel for little apparent reason. *The Day Before*, however, has a third-person narrator who follows the novel's protagonist for the most part and rarely leaves the protagonist for long. Another major problem of *All Our Yesterdays* was the inexplicable shifting of focus from one character to another in the novel's sections, making Jim Maynard's adventures in the South American jungle seem gratuitous at best and irrelevant at worst. *The Day Before*, however, tells its story almost entirely from the perspective of Clem Venner, thereby presenting its history with greater unity. Another flaw of *All Our Yesterdays* resulted from Tomlinson's attempt to chronicle English history from the Boer War to the aftermath of the Great War. As he discovered, he had chosen far too great a subject for one novel, and the result was to treat each section with less completeness than the original design required. *The Day Before* partially resolves this problem by stopping on the day of Sarajevo, and Tomlinson also reduces the scope of this novel by setting most of the action in London. Each of these changes improves the latter novel, but, as we shall see, *The Day Before* presents new problems regarding the handling of time in fiction, plausibility in plot, and credibility of characters.

Clem Venner, a supervisor of workmen at the shipping firm of William Davenant, Cheapside, takes advantage of his boss's absence to read Marie Corelli's latest novel. While he reads, he is the subject of Julia Marshall's scrutiny, and she takes this opportunity to reflect on Clem's relationship with the firm: "He only gave the impression that though with them he did not altogether belong to the place. What nonsense! After all, he had been at Davenant's as long as she had. She resented his detachment, slightly . . . ."[1] Julia, Davenant's chief secretary, fails to distract Clem from his novel or his discovery that "Miss Corelli's unrestricted uprush of pink and purple was the kind of thing the public adored . . ." (*DB*, 5). Davenant returns, and after angrily pointing out that the men in Clem's charge have stenciled the wrong shipping destination on a large consignment of crates, fires Clem. After this episode, an exaggerated version of the circumstances under which Tomlinson left his shipping firm, Clem wanders about London to enjoy the rare pleasures of idleness. When Clem returns to his lodgings much later, he learns from his landlady that a young lady has called and has left a message for Clem to do nothing until receiving her note. Clem accurately assumes that the lady is Julia and inaccurately concludes that Davenant wants Clem to return to his job. Clem, however, has decided to take a holiday, and that night he leaves for Portalland.

Clem takes a room in a hotel at Portalland, but his holiday is far from uneventful. Responding to the cries of a panic-stricken maid, Clem goes to another room and cuts down a suicide, a Mr. Winslow. Winslow has been in a romantical intrigue with Mrs. Pitta, but her interest has been to obtain classified secrets of naval design from her paramour. Once she has done so, she leaves, and Winslow, overcome with chagrin and remorse, has hanged himself. Journalists flock to the scene of this story, and Clem's name becomes associated with the incident despite the accidental nature of his involvement. One journalist, Hankey Todd of the *Morning Echo*, takes Clem under his wing and they pursue the elusive Mrs. Pitta, hoping for an interview or for at least a sight of her. Todd has a reputation for being in the right place at the right time, and a rival journalist, Parsons of *The Daily Sun*, follows Todd and Clem as they motor away from Portalland. In the tradition of Evelyn Waugh's *Scoop*, Todd sabotages Parson's automobile and travels where he pleases, filing stories of somewhat doubtful authenticity based on rumors regarding Mrs. Pitta's probable whereabouts.

One evening Todd returns to the hotel room intoxicated, and

announces that he has seen Mrs. Pitta. He writes his story on telegraph forms, takes them to the post office to be telegraphed to his
paper, returns, and passes out. Clem, however, notices that Todd had
reached the end of the

final sheet of his long message, had continued, ended and signed his story on
the marble itself. It was possible to decipher the tragic import of Mr. Todd's
epilogue, but Mr. Todd had forgotten to take the stone slab with him to the
post-office, so now the end of his story would not be telegraphed to London.
(*DB*, 52)

After considering the matter, Clem rewrote the end of the story and
took it to the post office the following morning. Todd, the next day,
reads his story and comments that he has no recollection of seeing
Mrs. Pitta or of writing the story. He also comments,

"It's a good story, though, . . . That's a fine touch at the end, even if the last
paragraph isn't the usual place for a scoop. That was artful of me. I wonder I
thought of it so late at night. Ours is the only paper with the discovery. But
did we see her?" (*DB*, 53)

Clem explains what has happened and Todd feels that the two of them
deserve a promotion, but he adds that success has unpleasant consequences. Having found Mrs. Pitta, Todd and Clem must keep her
alive, and they receive a telegraph from Scotland Yard asking for more
details.

   After about a week, however, the story dies down, and as soon as
Todd and Clem have traveled to Buxton at the newspaper's expense,
they present themselves at the *Morning Echo*. Clem meets Parry,
the editor, Allport, the news editor, and Donald, the general overseer of the printing presses. Clem is told that the paper wants a man
"able to tell a story," and he finds himself working as a reporter for the
paper. He is accepted by the other reporters and listens to various
anecdotes, including one reporter's complaint about an assignment to
interview a centenarian. Expecting to hear about the Duke of Wel-
lington's funeral, the wedding of Victoria and Albert, the Indian
Mutiny, the Crimean War, and other noteworthy events of the past,
the reporter was asked "Where have you come from?" The reporter
states that he has come from London merely to interview the old
man. "'Bloody fool,' he said, when he was comfortable. Then he went
to sleep again" (*DB*, 67). Clem also learns from Todd that the
latter has found Mrs. Pitta, but Todd minimizes the importance of

whatever she learned from Winslow, and Clem agrees to keep Todd's secret.

Julia, meanwhile, has continued to work for Davenant. Her sister has married Joe Killick, a supervisor who is becoming embroiled in a labor dispute. Julia's sympathies are with her sister but not with the workers: "Workers of the World! Much they knew about either work or the world. If they knew more about the world they'd use better sense and do some work" (*DB*, 85). Julia had mentioned her brother-in-law to Clem, and partly out of consideration for her, Clem writes a sympathetic piece on the sufferings of strikers' families. As Joe Killick described it, a strike is a contest consisting of a boss sitting on a baby's stomach to see which tires first. Clem writes his article and expects to see it in print the following day, but the article does not appear. Clem visits briefly with Parry, the editor, who, surprised at Clem's personal interest in this article, deigns to print it. The article, without changing the world, does arouse surprising public interest and sympathy, and the increased sales of the *Echo* result in Clem's being assigned to do a series based on his original piece.

However, the *Echo* plans to cover the current year's naval maneuvers, which are to be of more than usual importance. The editor assigns Hankey Todd to cover the maneuvers, but Todd, who cannot abide the thought of boarding a small ship, suggests that Clem go. When the editor points out that Clem will do a series of articles based on his sympathetic look into a striker's home, Todd, of necessity, becomes "moved to write those parables for the people and as if the sorrows of the poor were his own" (*DB*, 125). In the face of Todd's flat refusal to cover the maneuvers, the editor gives Clem that assignment, and the series of articles appears under Todd's by-line. Julia is disappointed. "How she would have rejoiced had she known this noble lift had come from her word to Clem! . . . Very likely it was for the best that Clem had kept out of it. She did not think he could have done it as well as this. It wasn't in him" (*DB*, 124). Assuming that the original article was also by Todd, Julia continues to work for Davenant and puts Clem out of her mind.

After a considerable but unspecified period has elapsed, a novelist named Hilary Tootal visits Parry, the editor of the *Echo*. Regarding the "new lot" of novelists as "a variety of female," Parry admits Tootal and learns that Tootal plans to write a novel based on Mrs. Pitta and Winslow. Tootal assumes that Mrs. Pitta has died in the intervening years, and Parry warns Tootal of the dangers of lawsuits should his assumption be wrong. After Tootal departs, Parry approaches

Donald, the overseer of the presses, and asks,

"That daughter of yours, Donald, where's Helen now?"
"She was in this morning to see me."
"The devil she was. Here again? She has a nerve. She's dangerous. I've been seeing a fellow upstairs who wants to write a book about her. He thinks she's buried." (DB, 141)

Thus the reader learns that while Todd was ostensibly chasing all over England after Mrs. Pitta, he did so with the complicity of his editor and deliberately threw others off the track.

Clem remains ignorant of this development, for he is still on naval maneuvers aboard the *Forfar*. When he prepares to return to his paper, however, he has a conversation with the captain, who describes the ship as "weak, and out of date. Yet I think she will last long enough for it. Yes, she will be in time . . . . Yes, still in commission, my friend, on the day" (DB, 184). This enigmatic phrase recalls a conversation Tomlinson had with Horace Hood, shortly before "Admiral Sir Horace Hood [led] his battle-cruiser squadron into action at Jutland."[2] The phrase intrigues Clem:

What day? He made to question Captain Hood, but the little man had turned, and stood waiting, in apparent melancholy, for the steps of the landing stage, which were nearing them under the pull of a bluejacket's boathook. (DB, 184)

Unexpectedly, Clem encounters Julia but the meeting is not satisfactory. "The years were between them" and Clem learns that all has not gone well with the Killick family. Julia asks Clem what he has seen of striking families, assuming that Clem has forgotten the strike that had inspired him to write his sympathetic article, and Clem, at a loss for what to say, does not explain the true state of affairs to Julia. Julia tells him that her sister has died, Julia has taken the child, and Joe Killick has lost his job because he sympathized with the strikers. Julia attempts to justify her continued employment with Davenant as economic necessity, but she also describes losing her temper and telling Davenant exactly what she thinks of him, thereby losing her job. Concluding that "You and I are good for nothing while we serve a low purpose" (DB, 201), Julia has become involved in political action. She also hints that she may join the Pankhurst movement to fight for feminism. The meeting leaves Clem somewhat confused, and he has done nothing to resolve Julia's ignorance of his true involvement in the affairs of her striking relations.

At this point Tomlinson begins to bring matters together to end his novel, and the strain on a reader's credulity becomes great. Hankey Todd has been sent to Belfast to cover the launching of the *Titanic*, and when Donald approaches Clem to have him address a letter to Todd, it becomes apparent that Todd and Mrs. Pitta know each other very well. Meanwhile, Clem goes to a political rally which had, as its "chief entertainer, the Welsh wizard," Lloyd George. A woman makes a disturbance, and Clem recognizes Julia as the disrupter. When a scuffle ensues, Clem fights his way to the center and successfully diverts the stewards' pummeling from Julia to himself. Julia and Clem become reconciled after this episode. Meanwhile, Todd has covered the launching of the *Titanic*, and he somehow becomes a passenger on the ship's fated voyage. With him is Helen Pitta. The ship strikes the inevitable ice, and although Helen is helped into a lifeboat, Todd goes down with the ship. The novel ends with two pages, set two years later, describing how Clem comes home to his wife, Julia, and their son with the news of an assassination at Sarajevo. As the novel closes, the world is not yet aware of the conflagration immediately to follow.

The Day Before is much more consistent than *All Our Yesterdays*, particularly because the third-person narrator is more appropriate to this type of chronicle, the action is unified by the point of view of Clem Venner, and the novel covers a shorter historical period than *All Our Yesterdays* attempted. However, *The Day Before* develops other problems. First, Clem Venner and Julia Marshall often seem almost wooden. Despite the third-person narrator's attempts to rectify this by explaining the workings of the minds of Clem and Julia, their actions remain difficult to accept. Julia, torn between a sympathy for the economically downtrodden and her belief that all must accept the work ethic, communicates her dilemma without convincing a reader that a human being could think in her fashion. Clem compounds the reader's difficulty in accepting Julia by his naïveté and his reluctance to behave plausibly, as when he refrains from telling Julia that he did indeed write the article sympathetic to the strikers. One does not expect a novelist to develop fully such lesser lights as Parry or Todd, but the major characters should be more than caricatures or platitudes enfleshed.

Second, while the coincidence in the novel partly seems to derive from the problems of ending the book, a reader often finds his credulity strained. The series of events which includes Clem's cutting down the body of the lover whom a newspaper employee's daughter has duped into revealing state secrets, Clem's becoming involved with a journalist friend of the daughter and eventually becoming part of the staff which includes her father, and Clem's journalist friend sinking with the *Titanic* while the above-mentioned daughter survives in a lifeboat is strained enough to make the events at Sarajevo appear almost commonplace. The Dickensian plot seems incompatible with the historical perspective of this novel.

Third, and more unsettling to a reader, is the problem of time in the novel. As a reader follows Clem through events which, in real life, might occupy little more than a year, he requires some indication of time passing. Tomlinson does not provide such essential transition, and unlike the section titles of *All Our Yesterdays*, which solved the problem by identifying the year of the action, the references to contemporary events are too infrequent and too inconsistent to offer much assistance. Since Clem is reading Marie Corelli on page 5, one can infer early that the novel opens before World War I, but after that the reader must watch closely. A reference to Sir Alfred Harmsworth and to the Russian/Japanese War occurs on page 20, thus placing the date firmly in 1904/05, but a reference to Ramsay MacDonald is too vague to be helpful, and a later reference to Blériot's successful flight across the English Channel seems out of place. When the novelist Tootal refers to the Mrs. Pitta/Winslow episode as having taken place long enough ago for him to assume that Mrs. Pitta has died, the reader wonders where the time has gone, and the reader can ask the same question when Clem, meeting Julia, reflects on years having passed.

During the last third of the novel, perhaps aware of the difficulty of following his time-scheme, Tomlinson began to make more specific references, including one to the death of King Edward, but, two pages later, a reference to McKinley's assassination is followed by a reference to President Taft so abruptly that the clues lose their meaning. The *Titanic* is comparatively easy, although late, and only in the last chapter, describing the morning of Sarajevo, does Tomlinson try the useful phrase "two summers later." A reader's inability to recognize the duration of events and the intervening time between them can distract from his appreciation of the novel. *The Day Before* reveals how much Tomlinson learned about the problems of the novelist in the course of writing novels, but it also demonstrates how problems of handling time continued to plague his fiction.

III   Morning Light

Tomlinson's *Morning Light: The Islanders in the Days of Oak and Hemp* (1946) returns to the world of maritime commerce, but instead of the modern shipping of *All Hands!*, this novel treats shipping when steamships were beginning to replace sailing ships. The central character, David Gay, is visiting his aunt Ruth Penfold at Branton, where Miles Darton, owner of a line of sailing ships, is discussing shipping with his brother-in-law and Mr. Denny of London. Despite the more progressive notions of the others, Darton remains adamant in his insistence that steamships are merely a passing fad.

"I don't like it . . . . And fire in a ship's belly! That's the last place for it. Good can't come of it. Look at my little fleet. It does what ships have always done. My craft get their power from Heaven, and get it for nothing. There's no cost except that of canvas to catch the wind, and a few of the best of them make eight knots with it. And Denny, that's where I have you. Your new-fangled steam-ship, you can't deny it, has to carry so much coal to get her along that she has no space left for cargo, no room for profit. With her it is all cost."[3]

This discussion pauses when the owner's daughter Lucy appears in her father's study to claim the model of the *Lucy Darton*, the newest of her father's ships, and then darts off.

David chafes under the restrictions of his aunt, who constantly opposes his restlessness. Unbeknownst to David until later, his aunt has lost her father, her husband, and her son at sea, and she discourages any tendency in David which might compel him to sail. Eventually David evades his aunt's well-meant surveillance and wanders off for an adventure. He encounters Lucy, whom he does not recognize as the daughter of Branton's most powerful and rich citizen, and he accords her no more respect than she would receive on her own merits. This reaction intrigues Lucy, and she talks with him. David learns that his Aunt Ruth has lost her son on the *Ebeneezer*, one of Darton's ships, and that she continues to await the ship's return although even Lucy knows that the ship is lost.

Lucy offers to show David a way back to the village that takes them through a seaside cave. When the tide rises, the cave fills with water. David and Lucy discover some debris, and Lucy reveals the rather mercenary nature of this village. The villagers refuse to put a lighthouse on the Five Maids to warn passing ships. When David asks why, Lucy responds, "What a stupid you are. If a ship could see a light ahead she wouldn't carry on till she struck, would she? Of course not. And then the pickings wouldn't wash ashore" (*ML*, 45). Because they tarry, the cave begins to fill as the tide comes in, but David and Lucy manage to save themselves without encountering much danger. Meanwhile, both Aunt Ruth and Miles Darton have been worried about the youngsters. Lucy immediately takes to her bed in a hypochondriacal evasion of punishment, and David accepts the blame from Miles Darton and Aunt Ruth for leading Lucy into the cave.

After enduring Aunt Ruth's pressing questions and recriminations for a day, refusing to admit that entering the cave was Lucy's idea, David runs off. Darton suggests that Aunt Ruth notify the police, but her response is "Not for my boy. Wherever he is, he stays, if it comes to that" (*ML*, 72). Darton, who still rankles from David's supposed indifference to Lucy's safety, suggests that his shipyards could teach David

" . . . what he doesn't know, and what wilful boys must be taught."
   "Yes, sir. What is that, sir?"
   "His place in life, and the thing to do in it." (*ML*, 72)

Aunt Ruth does not take this response at all well and begins to upbraid Darton because her husband and her son were lost on ships of the Darton line. Her ire up, Aunt Ruth baldly states that the *Ebeneezer* sank because she was overloaded. Darton refuses to accept this and asks his master shipwright, Killick, for his opinion. Killick tries to evade the question, first referring to a report he had submitted before the *Ebeneezer* sailed and then trying to couch his response in less direct terms, but his assessment is the same:

"Sir, there were a dozen opinions about the *Ebeneezer* that day, when she was outside and under way. Her freeboard was a matter of inches. She would have been awash, but it was a calm day. I heard someone say, 'That ship will never reach port.'"
   "Who said such a damnable thing?"
   "The man who stowed her." (*ML*, 74–75)

Darton left abruptly, but this was not the end of the matter. Darton fired Killick for insubordination.

Meanwhile, David has decided to make his way to London, and he encounters a sailor named Bonser who is London-bound on a river boat. Bonser allows David to accompany him. Darton also travels to London to see Cree, his London agent. Although Killick's "disloyalty" had "forced" Darton to sack him, Darton realizes that his shipyard is suffering from Killick's absence and wonders where Killick has gone. He is also ill at ease because Killick's earlier statement that Darton was falling astern of the times was echoed by others whose opinion Darton respected more, including Cree. Darton then pays a social call to Lady Geraldine and suffers as he finds himself in the middle of her at-home. She arranges that Darton engage himself in conversation with a Mr. Lovett. Darton becomes appalled when he realizes that he "had allowed himself to be attached" to "the notorious working man and the offensive outrage who wrote for newspapers of the deepest and bloodiest red" (*ML*, 121). Despite the anachronism "red," which might lead a reader to assume a later date for this story, Tomlinson provides a more reliable clue that the story occurs in 1843. Although Lady Geraldine "had tried, and failed dismally, to get Mr. Carlyle to call on her, she presented his last work, *Past and Present*, to those who would read it, and to some who would not, because she had enjoyed it herself" (*ML*, 122–23). Darton, who finds himself uncomfortable in his exposure to pre-Victorian liberalism, takes his leave as soon as he can.

Aunt Ruth has also arrived in London, seeking David, but when she goes to her sister's old home in Islington, she finds that not even the name of the family is remembered. She finds shelter and comfort with Mary Summers, who teaches at the appropriately named "Ragged School" for laborers' children and who attends meetings that combine Unitarianism with semi-militant socialism. The plot of the novel begins to assume Dickensian characteristics when, at one meeting, Cree and Aunt Ruth are both present. Elsewhere during this meeting, David and Bonser have a close encounter with agents of the police. They escape, and neither David nor the reader knows exactly why the police take such an active interest in Bonser. Further questions arise when Bonser proceeds directly to the meeting to call Cree outside, apparently to warn him. The reader's curiosity is satisfied the next morning when Darton returns to Lady Geraldine's to find the household in an uproar. At first Darton thinks that something serious has happened to Lady Geraldine's daughter Dinah, but he finds that she has eloped. "'Good God!' said Mr. Darton, partly relieved" (*ML*, 179). He is not so calm, however, when he learns that his London agent, Cree, has absconded with Dinah, and that Cree has "been shipping in weapons for the rebellious lower orders" (*ML*,

179), which explains Cree's involvement with Bonser. Dinah has left a note to tell Lady Geraldine that Dinah and Cree are headed for America, but this upsets Lady Geraldine more than the elopement and arouses Darton's anger.

> Mr. Darton felt a deeper rage that America should gain Dinah than that Cree would find asylum there. America was welcome to a traitor—let America have him; but it was wrong that a gently-nurtured English girl should be lost amid forests, Indians, bears, and backwoodsmen. Was the good old world he had been proud of breaking up? (*ML*, 182)

Although David has worked with Bonser unaware of the criminal nature of Bonser's activity, his fate becomes tied to Bonser's, Dinah's, and Cree's.

The former captain of the *Star of Hope* "broke his leg, falling down the saloon companion, drunk again" (*ML*, 184), but the ship has a new captain, none other than Darton's former employee Killick. Bonser is the first mate, and David has accompanied him in the capacity of cabin boy, polishing brass and doing his best to avoid reprimand from Bonser or Killick. Cree and Dinah are passengers on the ship, and the cargo, for the most part, consists of the huddled masses bound for the dream of America.

> They were Scandinavians, Bohemians, and Germans, mostly. There were people from all over Europe in that crowd, and they could not make each other out, except the hardships they had been through. That was the same in all languages, from Irish to Greek. Those people were running away from stint and grudge, but hadn't got far yet, and looked it. They were escaping from famine, landlords, prison, princes, margraves, hospodars, bosses, bailiffs, potentates, lieges, stadtholders, gubernators, protectors, electors, debts, judges, and archdukes, but the sea and its weather were there, and short commons still had them. (*ML*, 203)

The ship, which recalls that in which Conrad's Yanko traveled to England in "Amy Foster," has a rough crossing, and David is locked below with the immigrant cargo when the seas become stormy. The stench of sickness and of the dead is overpowering, but David survives the storm and has an opportunity to speak briefly with Dinah about memories of Branton before the ship finally reaches America.

Despite his Aunt Ruth's wishes, David becomes a sailor. After this voyage to New York, he travels around the Horn to San Francisco. Meanwhile, Aunt Ruth, who still lives with Mary Summers, receives a letter from David, posted from New York, and suddenly realizes that "that letter was written by a man, or by a body very like a man" (*ML*, 241). Subsequently Captain Killick visits Ruth, bringing news of David from the voyage of the *Star of Hope* and stating that "when I left him he was beginning to overtake me in navigation" (*ML*, 249). David eventually returns by steamer, and his aunt realizes that the boy she has remembered is no more. David, working with Mr. Denny, has become something of an engineer and works in a shipyard. To his aunt's relief, although he has earned a certificate warranting him to command a ship, he was unwilling to accept a command dodging about the coast and could not expect an appointment to the new ships. He is content to work on the designs of new engines. He meets Lucy in his office, although little seems to come of the encounter, and he learns that Captain Killick has been given the chance of choosing between the sea and David's Aunt Ruth. The Crimean War breaks out in 1854, and David finds himself bound for the Black Sea on the *Serapis*. Even minor characters, such as Sir Digby Lovecott, gather at the pier to see the *Serapis* off, and there is some promise that David has not seen the last of Lucy.

Tomlinson continued to experience some difficulties with time in this novel. Although it is set in the era of pre-Victorian liberalism, the reader cannot pinpoint the time precisely until the novel is one-third under way, and only when the Crimean War breaks out can the reader tell how much time has passed from David's departure from Branton until his return as a young man. Some aspects of the plot are coincidental, as when Cree, Dinah, Killick, Bonser, and David find themselves together on the *Star of Hope*. Yet these problems do not distract from the story, for the narrative flows smoothly and Tomlinson indicates the passage of time with more transitional phrases than he did in his previous efforts. His characters are also much better than his earlier ones. Aunt Ruth and Darton, for example, are much more realistic than most of Tomlinson's earlier characters because they become involved in a wider range of emotions and act from motives that are consistent with their situations in life and their personalities.

While Tomlinson relies on coincidence to bring together such figures as Aunt Ruth, Cree, and Dinah, he does not rely on coincidence to explain or effect their actions. Also, changes in fortune and circumstance receive foreshadowing in this novel more than in earlier efforts. Killick, for example, is introduced as a former ship's captain before he loses his place in Darton's shipyard, which makes his subsequent command of the *Star of Hope* less a surprise. This novel also reveals a new dimension in Tomlinson's handling of factual or historical events. Instead of recording merely the actions and adventures of individuals within the framework of specific events, Tomlinson shows the interplay of different methods of thinking individuals grappling with a period of social and economic change. In *Morning Light* Tomlinson not only portrays a traditional shipowner in conflict with the men who sail his ships, but he also has provided samples of pre-Victorian liberalism in different shadings by bringing together Lady Geraldine's social interest with the more active involvement of Lovett, Cree, and Mary Summers, showing how their degrees of action contributed to the evolution of progress in education, social reform, and political thought as well as in the means of powering ships. Instead of pitting such opposites against each other as Dowland and Doughty of *All Hands!*, Tomlinson has admitted more subtle degrees of difference and has thus created a more authentic picture of the time. The plot remains one of historical adventure, but the range of characters indicates that Tomlinson has moved closer to Forster's realization that, in the novel, character is more important than plot.

IV The Trumpet Shall Sound

Tomlinson's final novel, *The Trumpet Shall Sound* (1957), has solved most of the problems the novelist encountered in his earlier efforts. The intrusion of coincidence does not disappear entirely, but it occurs less often because Tomlinson has limited his story to the affairs of one family. Time is less problematic because the novel occurs during the last few months of World War II; the shorter duration of actual time passing corresponds to the feeling of time passing in the novel. The characters also seem more realistic, revealing the divergence of opinion and philosophy that is common to most families whose members are both independent and strong-willed. The novel also is more successful in advancing Tomlinson's views without sacrificing plot or character to flights of authorial rhetoric. According to one reviewer, the handling of the plot

allows Tomlinson to look squarely at the terror of total war, to ask the fundamental questions about it. His answers are anything but facile or even definite, but he suggests a great working out of the pattern which the Greeks knew as *hubris* ("wanton arrogance . . . insolent disregard of moral laws") which, so the Greeks thought, was bound to meet with retribution.[4]

Tomlinson depicts the terror of total war even before the events of the novel begin by describing England under blackout.

The final night could have fallen, and nothing of worth was below for daylight to make plain again, nothing of the age-long and confiding. All was dark: coasts, ports and havens, hills and valleys, railways, high roads and the streets of the cities. Our country, after nightfall, was as amorphous as when it was without a name in an early age of the earth, and man not yet come.[5]

He wastes no time attributing the changes in London and in England to the machinations of man:

A traveler, back again in his own place, seeking for what used to be there, could believe that the creative word, giving light, shape, and promise, would never come again to renew what man had ruined and abandoned. On such a night, with the sky brooding as an unmeasured spread of war's somber wings over the frustration of good, it was possible for even a sanguine man to sigh with the doubt that his fellows had broken faith with virtue, and must suffer the penalty of failure with their earth. (*Trumpet*, 5)

Tomlinson continues to set the scene of Armageddon by introducing two air-raid wardens, who discuss their lack of faith in the rumored "second front," describe narrow misses from German rockets, and refer to White Stacks, the home of the Gale family. Once he has created the atmosphere of the darkest hour before dawn, Tomlinson moves to the Gale family, whose actions are the focus of the novel.

Sir Anthony Gale is an important government figure at Whitehall, his wife (never named beyond "Lady Gale") is a woman of quiet strength, their daughter Lucy is a sympathizer of the Russian cause who once welcomed the war for its possible hastening of an economic revolt, and their son Stephen is an idealist whose imagination has been fired by the poets of World War I—Siegfried Sassoon, Wilfred Owen, Edmund Blunden. The family also includes "Dr. Nicholas Tregarthen, Uncle Nick in the home," Lady Gale's brother, a disillusioned man whose pursuits are scholarly and whose attitudes, including an enjoyment of Heinrich Heine, recall Tomlinson's preferences. In *Old Junk*, Tomlinson remarked,

I like Heine then, though. His mockery of the grave and great, in those sentences which are as brave as pennants in a breeze, is comfortable and sedative. One's own secret and awkward convictions, never expressed because not lawful and because it is hard to get words to bear them lightly, seem then to be heard aloud in the mild, easy, and confident diction of an immortal whose voice has the blitheness of one who has watched, amused and irreverent, the high gods in eager and secret debate on the best way to keep the gilt and trappings on the body of the evil they have created.[6]

Before the end of World War I, commenting on the German conviction that Shakespeare was a genius and therefore German, Tomlinson finds one reason for gratitude: "Thank God Heine was a Jew, though even so there are rumours that a London memorial to him is to be removed."[7] Uncle Nick also refuses to take any precautions to save his life during raids, an eccentricity the other members of the family deplore.

The family discusses various ramifications of the war, and Sir Anthony, with grand disregard for security, informs the others that England has invaded occupied France, the second front will become a reality, and the Germans will not endure much longer. Stephen receives the news with mixed emotions, for he has long been eager to enlist. Unfortunately, from his point of view, an injury, which he sustained performing rescue work during a German raid, has made him unfit for service. He talks with his Uncle Nick and resolves to present himself to the recruiting station before the war ends without him. At the recruiting office the medical officer recognizes Stephen and advises him not to return until he is sent for. The surgeon, who has more practical knowledge of war than Stephen, advises the young man "Don't be a fool," and Stephen, chagrined that Sir Anthony has an active part while he does not, goes to the Adam and Eve pub to console himself. He meets a sailor named McLuckey, who beguiles Stephen with the tale of his first voyage, which ended in shipwreck. McLuckey was one of four survivors. Uncle Nick appears at the pub, and he and the sailor discuss the roles of the generations in the present war. When Nick and the sailor conclude that their generation has "let the world down," Stephen responds, "the world's all right. You didn't let it down" (*Trumpet*, 71). Nick is amused, the sailor becomes droll, and Stephen remains embarrassed.

There has been a lull in the bombings, but the raids begin again. When the bombs seem to be close to White Stacks, most of the family's members go to the cellar to await the end of the raid but Nick, ever disdainful of death, refuses to accompany the others and remains upstairs, reading. Stephen, when the bombing becomes worse, goes upstairs to persuade Nick to protect himself, and Lady Gale follows Stephen to assist his persuasions. One bomb scores a direct hit on the house, and both Nick and Lady Gale are instantly killed. Stephen survives and awakens at Bewley Hospital, where he is in critical condition. Sir Anthony and Lucy visit Stephen and speak with the attending physician, an old friend of Uncle Nick named Dr. Pickles. Pickles reflects that he is too old for war. "He couldn't help doubting that two long wars in one lifetime was overdoing honor. Rather too much of it for the ordinary heart" (*Trumpet*, 90). Only after this pause for reflection does Dr. Pickles realize that Stephen is Nick's nephew and that Nick has been killed. Dr. Pickles recalls being with Nick in Flanders during the last war and grieves for his friend. Subsequently, in Tomlinson's only major lapse into coincidence in the novel, the sailor McLuckey winds up in the bed next to Stephen's.

At this point Tomlinson shifts from novelist to historian to describe the state of London after this particular raid. Perhaps the memories stirred by the destruction of White Stacks (Tomlinson's home was destroyed by a bomb in October, 1944)[8] led to others, such as the odd immunity of St. Paul's Cathedral which Tomlinson described in *The Wind Is Rising*.[9] He shifts to a young man home on leave, bicycling across London to join his wife and child, and the young man has an opportunity to view a new London.

> He turned into Cannon Street, and continued with his eyes to the road round the cathedral. There, as ever, its mass lifted in buoyant ascendancy, but he took the noble landmark as he did the sky and the moon, and as he would the sun on the morrow, without a thought. There St. Paul's was, so he knew his way, though that night it ruled in lonely majesty over a waste as silent as a kingdom lost in ages forgotten. Around it, to a dreamlike distance, fugitive moonlight changed isolated jags of ruin into specters, gaunt and pallid, all that remained standing of a labyrinth of ancient streets in which men once had been busy in traditional confidence of purpose. They had vanished, they and their streets, and their purpose. In the midst of that phantom solitude, the abiding cross surmounting the cathedral's mass was occasionally as bright as a beacon, though nobody was there to see it, and in desolation it was the sole promise of the continuity of good. (*Trumpet*, 104-105)

As a balance to civil ruins, Sir Anthony goes to the front to have a firsthand view of the fighting, and he sees more than he wishes.

As he returns, he wonders at the difference between the soldiers' attitudes and his own. Previously he had regarded a ship destroyed as a loss of tonnage—"he himself had only known it hitherto as an abstraction called Tonnage. The loss of tonnage, officially, was a grave matter" (*Trumpet*, 138). As he goes ashore, he "was accorded a formal salute, but had the fancy that their courtesy was not without a touch of jovial mockery" (*Trumpet*, 138). His brief touch with reality has changed him, and he notices that "Quite a few of his other fixed ideas, too, were working loose" (*Trumpet*, 139). Perhaps the most indicative change in Sir Anthony's attitude toward war is his independent discovery of the motto of surviving combat veterans: "If another visit to the battle front became necessary, let a deputy do it. Once was enough. Never again for him. Let another clever person go over to get his notions unstuck, and find a new set, if he could" (*Trumpet*, 139).

Sir Anthony resolves to be a better advisor, but unfortunately he does not carry his resolution out. When he returns to his office he appears to doze off, but as Lucy discovers when she tries to awaken him, he has died. Lucy, who has lost her mother, her father, and her uncle in a matter of days, becomes unhinged. She wanders into the country, where she is found and sheltered by Mr. and Mrs. Martin. Even in the quiet of the countryside, however, Lucy cannot evade evidence of war. The Martins have an almanac open to May, 1940, and Lucy learns that they lost their son at Dunkirk. During her stay, Lucy examines her attitudes and concludes that she has been a fool:

Her own dread did not begin with the war. She always knew the war was as sure to come as midnight to strike. Faith goes when the truth seems to be that God has left us to make what we like of cruelty and lies. She had hoped the war would come. Hoped for it, the fool she was, to bring the work of iniquity to nothing.

She was a fool. War just suits iniquity. (*Trumpet*, 165)

After Lucy has resolved her difficulties, she returns to London. Stephen has mended surprisingly well from his injuries, but Dr. Pickles, in his conversation with the matron, notes that the loss of families like the Gales and of estates like White Stacks is the end of a long tradition.

"The ruins where White Stacks used to be—have you been up there lately?—weeds have begun to cover it up—that wreckage is only a sign of a general going off. . . . The pith and marrow of those families is our tradition. They led in war, and this war ends them. Their day is over." (*Trumpet*, 188)

Much to his surprise, Dr. Pickles discovers that his words have brought deep grieving from the matron, and he tries to assure her, only to discover that the matron had been upset by other matters, including the strain of constant bombing and her sense of frustration. Pickles assures her, however, that "The bell tolls for Germany," and that the war cannot last much longer.

Stephen continues to talk with the sailor, who tells Stephen the story of a long voyage upriver to the Rio d'Oro Mining Company in a steamship. The captain had been told this voyage was impossible, but the captain persevered. The steamer struggled up passages scarcely wider than she, the men fought off wasps and the stench of jungle, and the ship arrived only to find that the company to which the men were bringing supplies had sold out. The descriptions of the upriver journey and the disappointment at journey's end recall Tomlinson's first major voyage in *The Sea and the Jungle*. Dr. Pickles reminisces about Nick, including the latter's cynical commentary on the Germans' stupidity in arousing Russia and on the pointlessness of having a second war when the wounds of the first remained unhealed. Pickles's reflections on Nick allow Tomlinson to include some pages of criticism against the folly of warring humanity. Pickles, talking with Lucy, notes that the sailor McLuckey has begun to take up with the Gales' maid Nellie, and one can hope that the omen is good. Lucy and Stephen return to the site of White Stacks, where they see the revival of spring around the ruins of their former home, and they also encounter two men who saunter onto the grounds. The men are discussing the suitability of the grounds for a suburban development, but Stephen and Lucy end the novel on an optimistic note: Stephen asks,

"What do you believe? Would you call this a beginning? It doesn't look like a beginning, does it?"
"I suppose it never does. But it must be, it must be. It is, for us. I don't know what I believe. It changes. Sometimes I'm quite sure, and the next day I'm nearly all dark again. But I'm always quite sure of one thing. It's what we've heard called the Holy Ghost. That comes. I can't tell you any more. It keeps me quiet." (*Trumpet*, 239)

Tomlinson's final novel continues a theme that he mentioned in his earlier *Mars His Idiot* and *Waiting for Daylight*.[10] The place of honor in modern warfare is not necessarily in the trenches, but in "the cradles, the hospital wards, the pubs. Everybody shares it" (*Trumpet*, 88). In the process of presenting his final picture of England at war, Tomlinson chose to tell his story from the home front rather than trying to create the atmosphere of modern battle. In his final novel—and he described it upon its publication as his last novel—he

combined his philosophical perceptions with a simplified plot structure, limited time period, and small number of characters to reach his
audience more effectively than in his earlier novels. Although the
appearance of the sailor McLuckey seems gratuitous, enabling Tomlinson to write one long tale of a shipwreck and another of an inland
voyage upriver in Africa, *The Trumpet Shall Sound* is the most
effective of his seven novels and provides the most pleasurable reading experience of Tomlinson's fiction, with the possible exception of
All Hands!

V   *Development as a Novelist*

Tomlinson was fond of remarking that he was not a novelist born,
but one who was merely a writer of novels, thereby seeming to imply
that he lacked a special gift for the task. As an essayist with an
established style, however, his main difficulty seemed to be adapting
his preferred method to the requirements of the novel form. Like
many novelists, he began by writing fiction based almost entirely on
his own experience, and he soon learned that fiction consists of more
than a record of life with minor changes in names and circumstance,
whether the subject is the adventures of an individual (*Gallions
Reach*) or a history (*All Our Yesterdays*). When the pendulum swung
to the opposite extreme and Tomlinson attempted to rely almost
entirely on imagination rather than on memory, the result was the
implausible *The Snows of Helicon*, whose characters and plot seem to
lose touch with reality. When he returned to a subject with which he
was familiar in *All Hands!* and based his plot on actual events involv-
ing a hazardous voyage, conflicting interest, and the merchant
marine, he was much more successful in combining his readable style
with his desire to reform perceived wrongs.

All Hands! marks a turning point in his novel-writing career, for it
revealed to Tomlinson the proper balance between memory and
autobiography on the one hand, and historical fiction on the other.
The late novels—*The Day Before, Morning Light*, and *The Trumpet
Shall Sound*—treat aspects of English history which were important
to Tomlinson's personal experiences. *The Day Before* recalls the days
of his early manhood before World War I, *Morning Light* describes
the shipping trade during the sailing days of Tomlinson's father, and
The Trumpet Shall Sound presents the final months of the war that
compelled Tomlinson to shift from pacifist to war propagandist. As
these seven novels appeared, particularly after *All Hands!*, one can

follow his development as a craftsman grappling with major problems of fiction—the plausibility of event, the development of character, the successful handling of time—eventually resolving these problems of genre with the preferences of the writer.

Tomlinson's development as a novelist in the thirty years separating *Gallions Reach* from *The Trumpet Shall Sound* occurred more slowly than one would expect for several reasons. First, as a familiar writer with a pleasing and readable style, Tomlinson had the advantage of being read and published on merits apart from his fiction. Second, as many early reviewers noted, his prose, and the personality which shone through it, compensated for the flaws in his novels. Third, Tomlinson continued to write several other works of travel, essays, and history during the years he was writing his novels, so that his career as a novelist was only a minor part of his total literary activity. Finally, Tomlinson's first novel appeared after he had earned his living by his pen for more than twenty years. The combined struggle of becoming read and developing a style had occurred long before Tomlinson turned to fiction. These factors made his "apprenticeship" less urgent than it would have been had Tomlinson decided to try his hand at the novel earlier, before he had established a literary reputation and had mastered the rudiments of a style best suited to the essay. Had Tomlinson begun with the novel rather than with the essay, he might have achieved mastery in the tradition of Henry James, Ford Madox Ford, and Dickens rather than in the tradition of Emerson, Thoreau, and Lamb.

CHAPTER 12

The Man of Letters

WHAT are we to make of Tomlinson's long and varied literary career? First, the sheer volume and variety of his writing entitles him to a place among prolific writers of the modern age. His thirty book-length works, including collections of essays, novels, travel books, literary criticism, antiwar tracts, and war propaganda, represent a multifaceted view of modern life. This can be of equal value to the student of letters and the student of history. Tomlinson's faithful presentation of his personal view of the world, in terms which communicate his subjective impressions without alienating an "objective" reader, are invaluable guides to the events and spirit of the modern age. Tomlinson, even in his novels, drew almost entirely from his personal experience, and his experience was both varied and extensive.

Second, Tomlinson's style—particularly in his essays—offers some insight into the methods an author can employ to convey a sense of personality in expository writing. The techniques he has used to communicate a likeable personality as well as a description or explanation of external events provide further opportunity to study the techniques that have served a recognized master of a form. The essays of Tomlinson, apart from his other writings, are elegant enough to make a place for him among the masters of a literary form.

Third, Tomlinson's evocation of experience in his travel writings and in his literary criticism demonstrate the role of the acute observer in literary production. Although his literary criticism, in particular, is alien to contemporary standards, it argues and demonstrates the need for reviewers and critics of books to consider pleasure as a valid criterion for evaluation of others' work.

Fourth, Tomlinson's approach to the history of shipping, the evils of modern progress, the horrors of warfare, and the need for resistance to such enemies of civilization as Hitler lend further insight into the rhetorical problems of polemical writing. Tomlinson's failure to end war with *Mars His Idiot* can be as instructive as his successful propaganda published in the *Atlantic Monthly*. His involvement in the problems of his age also demonstrates the effect on literature of a man who is an active participant in public life as well as an observer and recorder.

Fifth, Tomlinson's novels deserve a place among the minor classics of the twentieth century. His development as a novelist reveals the problems of striking a balance between autobiography and experience on the one hand, and fiction and imagination on the other. His seven novels reveal different problems of craftsmanship, but once Tomlinson was able to resolve the conflicts imposed by the novel form, he produced *All Hands!*, *The Day Before*, *Morning Light*, and *The Trumpet Shall Sound*. These four novels alone, which remain pleasant reading experiences years after their initial appearance, entitle Tomlinson to a place among respected authors of the time.

Aside from the merits of his various works, Tomlinson deserves more consideration as a phenomenon who could combine a full and adventurous life with a prolific and variegated literary career. The influence of his style and personality on a younger generation of authors, his role as a spokesman during the between-the-wars period, and his unflagging involvement in the literary milieu of his age make him noteworthy as a figure of literary history. The life and art of Tomlinson can increase our awareness of a valid, if past, literary tradition and can balance often stereotypic notions of the effect of "movements" on a literary climate.

In all his works Tomlinson achieved the effects of intimacy, immediacy, veracity, and engaging personality in his style. Widely recognized during his lifetime for the superior quality of his prose, he has much to teach contemporary writers regarding the effect that prose can have on an audience, the means by which one can write gracefully without artificially developing a style, and the art of telling a story. Tomlinson's achievement as a writer more than justifies his being regarded as a minor classic, a representative of his age.

Notes and References

Chapter One

1. Helen and Richard Altick, "Square-Rigger on a Modern Mission," *College English* 5 (November, 1943), 76.

2. Edward Weeks, "H.M. Tomlinson," *Atlantic Monthly* 192 (August, 1953), 82.

3. H.M. Tomlinson, *A Mingled Yarn: Autobiographical Sketches* (New York: Bobbs-Merrill Company, 1953), pp. 1–2.

4. Ibid., p. 2.

5. Ibid., p.6.

6. Ibid., p. 7.

7. H.M. Tomlinson, "The Alien Sea," *Holiday* 8 (October, 1950), 53.

8. H.M. Tomlinson, *Waiting for Daylight* (London: Cassell, 1922), p. 141.

9. Ibid.

10. Ibid., p. 144.

11. London *Times*, "Obituary: Mr. H.M. Tomlinson," February 6, 1958.

12. H.M. Tomlinson, "H.M. Tomlinson, *By Himself*," *Wilson Bulletin* 5 (September, 1930), 20.

13. H.M. Tomlinson, "Adventure in a Shop Window," *Holiday* 6 (August, 1949), 86.

14. Ibid.

15. Edward Weeks, "Authors and Aviators," *Atlantic Monthly* 172 (November, 1943), 59.

16. Tomlinson, *A Mingled Yarn*, p. 20.

17. Ibid., p. 22.

18. J.A. Gibson, "H.M. Tomlinson," [London] *Bookman* 62 (April–September, 1922), 7.

19. Alva A. Gay, "H.M. Tomlinson, Essayist and Traveller," in *Studies in Honor of John Wilcox*, eds. A. Dayle Wallace and Woodburn O. Ross (Detroit: Wayne State Univ. Press, 1958), p. 211.

20. Arthur Mizener, *The Saddest Story: A Biography of Ford Madox Ford* (New York: World Publishing Company, 1971), p. 107.

21. Ford Madox Ford, *It Was the Nightingale* (London: J.B. Lippincott, 1933), p. 323.

22. Douglas Goldring, *The Last Pre-Raphaelite: A Record of the Life and Writings of Ford Madox Ford* (London: MacDonald & Co. (Publishers) Ltd., 1948), p. 149; Frank MacShane, *The Life and Work of Ford Madox Ford* (New York: Horizon Press, 1965), p. 79.

23. H. M. Tomlinson, "Of Ships and Shoes and Sealing-Wax," *Scholastic* 24 (March 17, 1934), 5.

24. *Letters of Ford Madox Ford*, ed. Richard M. Ludwig (Princeton, N.J.: Princeton Univ. Press, 1965), p. 118.

25. Tomlinson, "Of Ships and Shoes and Sealing-Wax," p. 5.

26. Ibid.

27. Tomlinson, "*By Himself*," p. 20.

28. H. M. Tomlinson, "C. E. Montague," introduction to C. E. Montague, *A Writer's Notes on His Trade* (London: Chatto & Windus, 1930), p. xv.

29. Stanley Weintraub, *Journey to Heartbreak: The Crucible Years of Bernard Shaw 1914–1918* (New York: Weybright and Talley, 1971), p. 216n.

30. Tomlinson, "C. E. Montague," p. xvii.

31. Ibid.

32. Frank Swinnerton, *Background With Chorus: A Footnote to Changes in English Literary Fashion Between 1901 and 1917* (London: Hutchinson, 1956), p. 207.

33. H. M. Tomlinson, "Shaw At Armageddon," *Literary Digest* 54 (March 10, 1917), 623.

34. Weintraub, p. 219.

35. Tomlinson, "Shaw at Armageddon," p. 623.

36. Ibid., p. 624.

37. Gibson, p. 7.

38. Tomlinson, "C. E. Montague," p. xviii.

39. Ibid., p. xix.

40. Ibid., p. xx.

41. H. M. Tomlinson, "Adelphi Terrace," in *H.W.M.: A Selection from the Writings of H.W. Massingham*, ed. H.J. Massingham (New York: Harcourt, Brace, 1925), p. 121.

42. Alfred F. Havighurst, *Radical Journalist: H.W. Massingham (1860–1924)* (Cambridge: Cambridge Univ. Press, 1974), p. 275.

43. Tomlinson, "Adelphi Terrace," p. 122.

44. Havighurst, p. 276.

45. Tomlinson, "Adelphi Terrace," pp. 122–23.

46. H. M. Tomlinson, "Historic Ghosts of London," *Holiday* 23 (January, 1958), 16.

47. Ibid., p. 130.

48. Tomlinson, "Adelphi Terrace," p. 125.

49. Ibid.

50. Havighurst, p. 294.

51. Ibid., p. 299.

52. Tomlinson, "*By Himself*," p. 20.

53. *The Collected Letters of D.H. Lawrence*, ed. Harry T. Moore (New York: Viking Press, 1962), p. 829.

54. *The Letters of D.H. Lawrence*, ed. Aldous Huxley (New York: Viking

Press, 1932), p. 640.

55. *Phoenix: The Posthumous Papers of D.H. Lawrence*, ed. Edward D. McDonald (New York: Viking Press, 1936), p. 342. This review originally appeared in *T.P.'s and Cassell's Weekly*, January 1, 1927.

56. Ibid.

57. Ibid., p. 345.

58. Altick, p. 80.

59. John Gunther, "The Tomlinson Legend," *Bookman* 62 (February, 1926), 686.

60. Ibid.

Chapter Two

1. Robert Lynd, *Books and Authors* (New York: Putnam's, 1923), p. 253.

2. Ibid., p. 259.

3. Frederick P. Mayer, "H.M. Tomlinson: The Eternal Youth," *Virginia Quarterly Review* 4 (January, 1928), 74.

4. Gay, pp. 214–16.

5. H.M. Tomlinson, "Introduction" to Christopher Morley, *Safety Pins and Other Essays* (London: Jonathan Cape, 1925), p. 7.

6. Ibid., p. 8.

7. Ibid.

8. H.M. Tomlinson, "Judges of Books," *Century* 3 (February, 1926), 431.

9. Stuart Hodgson, *Portraits and Reflections* (New York: Dutton, 1929), p. 191.

10. Tomlinson, "Shaw at Armageddon," p. 623.

11. H.M. Tomlinson, *Old Junk* (London: Andrew Melrose Ltd., 1918), p. 110.

12. Ibid., p. 27.

13. Ibid., pp. 36–37.

14. Ibid., p. 50.

15. Ibid., p. 86.

16. Lynd, p. 254.

17. Tomlinson, *Old Junk*, p. 138.

18. Ibid., p. 187.

19. H.M. Tomlinson, *Out of Soundings* (New York: Harper, 1931), p. 143.

20. H.M. Tomlinson, *Gifts of Fortune, With Some Hints for Those About to Travel* (London: Heinemann, 1926), p. 20.

21. Tomlinson, *Old Junk*, p. 201.

22. Tomlinson, *Out of Soundings*, p. 135.

23. Tomlinson, *Old Junk*, p. 9.

24. Mayer, p. 73.
25. Tomlinson, *Out of Soundings*, p. 83.
26. Tomlinson, *Old Junk*, p. 5.
27. H.M. Tomlinson, "Ports of Call," *Yale Review* NS 26 (June, 1937), 715.
28. Tomlinson, *Out of Soundings*, p. 23.
29. Tomlinson, *Old Junk*, pp. 22–23.
30. Ibid., p. 25
31. Ibid.

Chapter Three

1. J.B. Priestley, "H.M. Tomlinson," *Saturday Review of Literature* 3 (January 1, 1927), 478.
2. H.M. Tomlinson, "Concerning the Highbrows," *Saturday Review of Literature* 2 (August 22, 1925), p. 58.
3. Tomlinson, "Judges of Books," p. 433.
4. Tomlinson, *Waiting for Daylight*, p. 186.
5. H.M. Tomlinson, "Introduction" to Edmund Blunden, *The Bonaventure: A Random Journal of an Atlantic Holiday* (New York: Putnam's, 1923), p. 5.
6. H.M. Tomlinson, "Robert Louis Stevenson" in *Great Names: Being an Anthology of English & American Literature from Chaucer to Francis Thompson*, ed. Walter J. Turner (New York: Dial Press, 1926), p. 273.
7. Tomlinson, *Waiting for Daylight*, pp. 122–23.
8. Tomlinson, "Judges of Books," p. 426.
9. Ibid.
10. Ibid., p. 427.
11. Ibid.
12. Ibid., p. 430.
13. Tomlinson, *Waiting for Daylight*, p. 187.
14. Ibid., p. 189.
15. Tomlinson, "Judges of Books," p. 430.
16. Ibid.
17. Ibid.
18. H.M. Tomlinson, *Between the Lines* (Cambridge: Harvard Univ. Press, 1930), p.38. Reprinted by permission.
19. Ibid., p. 41.
20. Tomlinson, "Judges of Books," p. 427.
21. Tomlinson, "Introduction," *The Bonaventure*, p. 10.
22. Tomlinson, *Waiting for Daylight*, pp. 123–24.
23. Ibid., p. 124.
24. H.M. Tomlinson, "Letter from London," *Saturday Review of Literature* 2 (December 5, 1925), 394.

25. Tomlinson, "Judges of Books," p. 428.
26. H.M. Tomlinson, "The Power of Books," *Atlantic* 180 (December, 1947), 115.
27. Ibid., p. 118.
28. Ibid.
29. Ibid., p. 119.
30. Ibid.
31. Ibid.
32. Tomlinson, *Between the Lines*, p. 50.
33. H.M. Tomlinson, "Two Americans and a Whale," *Harper's* 152 (April, 1926), p. 620.
34. Ibid.
35. Ibid.
36. Tomlinson, *Waiting for Daylight*, p. 152.
37. Ibid., pp. 152–53.
38. Ibid., p. 153.
39. Ibid., p. 154.
40. Tomlinson, "The Power of Books," p. 117.
41. H.M. Tomlinson, "Books at Sea," *Living Age* 320 (February 23, 1924), 377.
42. Ibid.
43. Tomlinson, *Gifts of Fortune:*, p. 108.
44. Tomlinson, "Two Americans and a Whale," p. 619.
45. Ibid., p. 621.
46. Tomlinson, *Between the Lines*, p. 20.
47. Ibid., p. 15.
48. Tomlinson, "Concerning the Highbrows," p. 58.
49. Ibid.
50. Tomlinson, *Between the Lines*, p. 17.
51. Tomlinson, *Waiting for Daylight*, p. 49.
52. Ibid., p. 51.
53. Ibid., p. 52.
54. Tomlinson, *Between the Lines*, p. 14.
55. Tomlinson, "The Power of Books," p. 117.
56. Tomlinson, "Judges of Books," p. 428.
57. Tomlinson, "C.E. Montague," p. xv.
58. Tomlinson, *Waiting for Daylight*, p. 159.
59. Tomlinson, *Between the Lines*, p. 24.
60. Tomlinson, "Books at Sea," p. 379.
61. Tomlinson, *Between the Lines*, p. 11.
62. Ibid.
63. Ibid., p. 12.
64. Ibid., p. 11.
65. Tomlinson, "Judges of Books," p. 428.
66. Tomlinson, *Between the Lines*, p. 22.

67. Tomlinson, "The Power of Books," p. 116.
68. H.M. Tomlinson, *South to Cadiz* (New York: Harper, 1934), p. 67.
69. Tomlinson, *Between the Lines*, p. 33.
70. Ibid., p. 46.
71. Tomlinson, "C.E. Montague," p. xiv.
72. Tomlinson, *South to Cadiz*, p. 171.
73. Ibid.
74. Tomlinson, "Introduction," *The Bonaventure*, p. 9.
75. Tomlinson, *Gifts of Fortune*, p. 86.
76. Ibid., p. 104.
77. Tomlinson, *Between the Lines*, p. 32.
78. Tomlinson, "Judges of Books," p. 434.
79. Tomlinson, *Between the Lines*, p. 44.
80. Tomlinson, "Two Americans and a Whale," p. 620.
81. Tomlinson, "Introduction," *The Bonaventure*, p. 9.
82. Tomlinson, "Judges of Books," p. 431.
83. Tomlinson, *Between the Lines*, p. 35.
84. Ibid., p. 16.
85. Tomlinson, "Books at Sea," p. 379.
86. Tomlinson, "The Power of Books," p. 119.
87. Tomlinson, *Gifts of Fortune*, p. 88.
88. Tomlinson, *Waiting for Daylight*, p. 202.
89. Tomlinson, *Gifts of Fortune*, p. 85.
90. Swinnerton, p. 127.
91. H.M. Tomlinson, "Joseph Conrad," *Saturday Review of Literature* 4 (October 15, 1927), 191.
92. Ibid., p. 192.
93. Ibid.
94. Tomlinson, "Robert Louis Stevenson," p. 272.
95. Ibid.
96. Tomlinson, "Two Americans and a Whale," p. 619.
97. Ibid.
98. Tomlinson, *Between the Lines*, p. 4.
99. Tomlinson, *Waiting for Daylight*, p. 46.
100. Ibid., p. 47.
101. Tomlinson, *Out of Soundings*, p. 13.
102. H.M. Tomlinson, "The England of Hardy," *New Republic* 25 (January 12, 1921), 190.
103. Ibid., p. 191.
104. Ibid.
105. Ibid., p. 192.
106. H.M. Tomlinson, *Thomas Hardy* (New York: Crosby Gaige, 1929), p. viii. Subsequent references to *TH* are to this edition.
107. Robert Gittings, *Thomas Hardy's Later Years* (Boston: Little, Brown & Co., 1978), p. 213.

108. H.M. Tomlinson, *Norman Douglas* (London: Chatto & Windus, 1931), pp. 4–5. Subsequent references to *ND* are to this edition.
109. H.M. Tomlinson, "The Man I Knew" in *Norman Douglas* (London: Hutchinson, 1952), p. 21.
110. Ibid., p. 22.
111. Ibid., pp. 22–23.
112. Ibid., p. 23.

Chapter Four

1. Mayer, pp. 73–74.
2. Priestley, p. 477.
3. Tomlinson, *Waiting for Daylight*, p. 31.
4. H.M. Tomlinson, *London River* (New York: Knopf, 1921), p. 211.
5. Tomlinson, *Gifts of Fortune*, p. 1.
6. Ibid., p. 2.
7. Ibid., pp. 24–25.
8. Ibid., p. 26.
9. Ibid.
10. Ibid., p. 27.
11. H.M. Tomlinson, ed., *An Anthology of Modern Travel Writing* (London: Nelson, 1936), p. 3.
12. Ibid., p. 7.
13. Tomlinson, *Out of Soundings*, p. 195.
14. Tomlinson, *Anthology*, p. 2.
15. Priestley, p. 478.
16. Ibid.
17. Tomlinson, *South to Cadiz*, p. 165.
18. Tomlinson, *Gifts*, p. 2.
19. Ibid., p. 5.
20. Tomlinson, *Out of Soundings*, p. 15.
21. Tomlinson, *South to Cadiz*, p. 3.
22. Ibid., p. 4.
23. Ibid.
24. Ibid., p. 5.
25. H.M. Tomlinson, *The Sea and the Jungle* (New York: Modern Library, Inc., 1928), p. 121.
26. Ibid., p. 123.
27. Tomlinson, *London River*, pp. 230–31.
28. Tomlinson, *The Sea and the Jungle*, p. 65.
29. Ibid., p. 11.
30. Tomlinson, *Gifts*, p. 20.
31. Tomlinson, *The Sea and the Jungle*, p. 36.
32. Tomlinson, *Gifts*, p. 41.

33. Ibid.
34. Ibid., p. 61.
35. H.M. Tomlinson, *The Turn of the Tide* (New York: Macmillan, 1947), p. 21.
36. Tomlinson, *Old Junk*, p. 2.
37. Ibid., p. 3.
38. Ibid., p. 5.
39. Ibid., p. 9.
40. Ibid., p. 14.
41. Ibid., p. 20.
42. Ibid., pp. 22–23.
43. Ibid., pp. 24–25.
44. Ibid., p. 28.
45. Ibid., pp. 31–32.
46. Gay, p. 216.
47. Christopher Morley, introduction to *The Sea and the Jungle*, p. viii.
48. Ibid., pp. viii–ix.
49. Ibid., p. ix.
50. V.S. Pritchett, introduction to *The Sea and the Jungle* (New York: Time, Inc., 1964), p. xv.
51. Tomlinson, *The Sea and the Jungle* (New York: Modern Library, Inc., 1928), p. 1. Subsequent references to *S&J* are to this edition.
52. Gunther, p. 688.
53. Mayer, p. 74.
54. Ibid., pp. 76–77.
55. Ibid., p. 77.
56. H.M. Tomlinson, *Tide Marks: Being Some Records of a Journey to the Beaches of the Moluccas and the Forest of Malaya in 1923* (New York: Harper, 1924), p. 3. Subsequent references to *Tide* are to this edition.
57. Gunther, p. 688.
58. Ibid.
59. H.M. Tomlinson, *South to Cadiz* (New York: Harper, 1934), p. 10. Subsequent references to *South* are to this edition.

Chapter Five

1. Tomlinson, *The Turn of the Tide*, p. 159.
2. Tomlinson, "The Alien Sea," p. 53.
3. H.M. Tomlinson, "Books of Escape," *Saturday Review of Literature* 11 (September 8, 1934), 89.
4. H.M. Tomlinson, "The Wharves of London," *Living Age* 305 (May 8, 1920), 360.
5. Ibid.
6. H.M. Tomlinson, "The Ship Herself," *Holiday* 20 (July, 1956), 54.
7. Tomlinson, "Adventure in a Shop Window," pp. 86, 88–89.

8. Tomlinson, "The Historic Ghosts of London," p. 14.

9. Ibid., p. 130.

10. Ibid., p. 132.

11. Tomlinson, *Out of Soundings*, p. 55.

12. Ibid., p. 59.

13. Ibid., p. 60.

14. Ibid., p. 61.

15. Weeks, "Authors and Aviators," p. 58–59.

16. Tomlinson, *Old Junk*, p. 162.

17. Ibid., pp. 162–63.

18. Tomlinson, *London River*, p. 250.

19. Ibid., p. 251.

20. Weeks, "Authors and Aviators," p. 59.

21. H.M. Tomlinson, "The British Merchant Seamen," *Living Age* 270 (September 2, 1911), 600–605.

22. David W. Bone, "Idle Tonnage," *Saturday Review of Literature* 4 (February 11, 1928), 587.

23. Ibid.

24. Ibid.

25. H.M. Tomlinson, *The Foreshore of England or Under the Red Ensign* (New York: Harper & Brothers, n.d.), p. 2. Subsequent references to *Foreshore* are to this edition.

26. Bone, p. 587.

27. H.M. Tomlinson, *Below London Bridge* (London: Cassell, 1934), p. 3. Subsequent references to *Below* are to this edition.

28. H.M. Tomlinson, *Malay Waters: The Story of Little Ships Coasting Out of Singapore and Penang in Peace and War* (London: Hodder and Stoughton, 1950), p. 11. Subsequent references to *Malay Waters* are to this edition.

Chapter Six

1. Altick, p. 76.

2. H.M. Tomlinson, *Côte D'Or* (London: Faber & Faber, 1929), p. 17.

3. Tomlinson, *The Turn of the Tide*, p. 76.

4. Ibid., p. 127.

5. Ibid., p. 128.

6. Ibid., p. 129.

7. H.M. Tomlinson, "If War Should Come . . . .," *Harper* 156 (December, 1927), 73.

8. Ibid.

9. Ibid., p. 77.

10. H.M. Tomlinson, "Men of Action," in *The American Spectator Yearbook*, ed. George Jean Nathan et al. (New York: Frederick A. Stokes, 1934), p. 136.

11. Ibid., p. 137.
12. Ibid., p. 138.
13. Tomlinson, *Malay Waters*, p. 73.
14. Tomlinson, "The Power of Books," p. 115.
15. Ibid., p. 116.
16. Tomlinson, "Men of Action," p. 136.
17. Tomlinson, *The Turn of the Tide*, p. 79.
18. Tomlinson, "The Power of Books," p. 116.
19. Tomlinson, *The Turn of the Tide*, p. 71.
20. Ibid., p. 72.
21. Ibid., pp. 72–73.
22. Tomlinson, "If War Should Come . . . .," p. 76.
23. Altick, p. 76.
24. Ibid., p. 79.
25. Tomlinson, "The Power of Books," p. 116.
26. Tomlinson, "Men of Action," p. 135.
27. Tomlinson, *Between the Lines*, pp. 36–37.
28. Tomlinson, *Thomas Hardy*, pp. xxvii–xxviii.
29. H. M. Tomlinson, "Outward Bound," *Atlantic* 188 (July, 1951), 72.
30. Tomlinson, *Thomas Hardy*, p. xxviii.
31. Tomlinson, *Old Junk*, pp. 77–78.
32. Ibid., pp. 78–79.
33. Tomlinson, *The Turn of the Tide*, pp. 140–41.
34. H. M. Tomlinson, "Nemesis," *Forum* 88 (September, 1932), p. 132.
35. Ibid.
36. Ibid.
37. Ibid.
38. Ibid., p. 133.
39. Ibid., p. 134.
40. Hodgson, pp. 188–89.
41. Ibid., p. 189.
42. Ibid., pp. 189–90.
43. Altick, p. 79.
44. Tomlinson, *Between the Lines*, p. 9.
45. Tomlinson, "Nemesis," p. 134.
46. Altick, p. 80.

Chapter Seven

1. Altick, p. 75.
2. Ibid., p. 76.
3. Tomlinson, *A Mingled Yarn*, p. 143.
4. Ibid.
5. Tomlinson, "If War Should Come. . . .," p. 71.

6. H.M. Tomlinson, "War Books," *Yale Review* NS 19 (March, 1930), 447.

7. Tomlinson, *Waiting for Daylight*, p. 88.

8. Ibid., p. 87.

9. Tomlinson, "If War Should Come. . . .," p. 71.

10. Tomlinson, *Out of Soundings*, pp. 66–67.

11. Ibid., p. 70.

12. Tomlinson, *Waiting for Daylight*, p. 195.

13. Ibid., p. 196.

14. Ibid., p. 90.

15. Ibid., p. 91.

16. Richard Aldington, "Introductory Note," in James Hanley, *The German Prisoner* (Muswell Hill: Privately printed by the author, 1950), unnumbered.

17. Tomlinson, *Malay Waters*, p. 72.

18. Tomlinson, *Waiting for Daylight*, p. 18.

19. H.M. Tomlinson, "That Next War," *Forum* 86 (December, 1931), 323.

20. Tomlinson, *Old Junk*, p. 215.

21. Tomlinson, "If War Should Come. . . .," p. 72.

22. Tomlinson, *Waiting for Daylight*, p. 11.

23. Ibid., p. 13.

24. Ashley Gibson, "Through Western Windows," [London] *Bookman* 62 (June, 1922), 134.

25. Tomlinson, *Waiting for Daylight*, p. 5.

26. H.M. Tomlinson, "England Through English Eyes," *Harper* 145 (July, 1922), 261.

27. Tomlinson, *Old Junk*, p. 200.

28. Ibid., p. 201.

29. Ibid., p. 198.

30. Tomlinson, *Thomas Hardy*, p. xxix.

31. Tomlinson, *Old Junk*, pp. 203–04.

32. Tomlinson, "If War Should Come. . . .," p. 74.

33. Tomlinson, "England Through English Eyes," p. 259.

34. Tomlinson, "If War Should Come. . . .," p. 72.

35. Tomlinson, "England Through English Eyes," p. 261.

36. Ibid., p. 262.

37. Ibid., p. 259.

38. Tomlinson,, "That Next War," p. 322.

39. Ibid., p. 324.

40. Ibid., p. 325.

41. Ibid., p. 327.

42. Tomlinson, "War Books," p. 458.

43. Tomlinson, "If War Should Come. . . .," p. 72.

44. Tomlinson, *Waiting for Daylight*, p. 163.

45. Ibid., p. 150.
46. Ibid., pp. 161–62.
47. Tomlinson, "England Through English Eyes," p. 263.
48. Tomlinson, "War Books," p. 451.
49. Tomlinson, "England Through English Eyes," p. 264.
50. Tomlinson, *Waiting for Daylight*, p. 212.
51. H.M. Tomlinson, *Mars His Idiot* (New York: Harper, 1935), p. 1. Subsequent references to *Mars* are to this edition.
52. William Harlan Hale, "Mr. Tomlinson on War and Youth," *Saturday Review of Literature* 13 (November 30, 1935), 6.
53. Ibid.
54. Altick, p. 77.

Chapter Eight

1. Altick, p. 75.
2. Tomlinson, "England Through English Eyes," p. 260.
3. Altick, p. 78.
4. Ibid., p. 80.
5. Tomlinson, "That Next War," p. 327.
6. Ibid.
7. H.M. Tomlinson, *The Wind Is Rising* (Boston: Little, Brown & Co., 1942), p. 44. Subsequent references to *Wind* are to this edition.
8. Ibid., p. 45.
9. Tomlinson, *A Mingled Yarn*, p. 16.
10. H.M. Tomlinson, *The Turn of the Tide*, p. 74. Subsequent references to *Turn* are to this edition.
11. Ibid., pp. 74–75.
12. H.M. Tomlinson, "Propaganda," *Yale Review* NS 30 (September, 1940), 68.
13. Ibid., pp. 68–69.
14. Ibid., p. 67.
15. Ibid., p. 66.
16. Ibid., p. 68.
17. Ibid., p. 74.
18. H.M. Tomlinson, "Frankenstein in England," *Atlantic Monthly* 174 (October, 1944), 57n.
19. Ibid., p. 59.
20. Ibid.
21. H.M. Tomlinson, "A Presiding Spirit," *Atlantic Monthly* 176 (July, 1945), 76.

Chapter Nine

1. Rebecca West, "A London Letter," *Bookman* 69 (July, 1929), 520.

2. Ibid.

3. Mayer, p. 72.

4. H. M. Tomlinson, "Problems of a Novelist," *Saturday Review of Literature* 10 (May 12, 1934), 685–86.

5. H. M. Tomlinson, *Gallions Reach* (London: Harper, 1927), p. 2. Subsequent references to *GR* are to this edition.

6. Gunther, p. 689.

7. Henry Seidel Canby, "Life and Adventure: *Gallions Reach*," *Saturday Review of Literature* 4 (September 3, 1927), 83.

8. Ibid.

9. Mayer, p. 79.

10. Ibid., pp. 80–81.

11. Canby, p. 83.

12. H. M. Tomlinson, *All Our Yesterdays* (London: Harper, 1930), p. 5. Subsequent references to *AY* are to this edition.

13. Tomlinson, *A Mingled Yarn*, p. 143.

14. Samuel Hynes, *The Edwardian Turn of Mind* (Princeton, N.J.: Princeton Univ. Press, 1968), p. 58n.

15. Tomlinson, *Mars His Idiot*, p. 226.

16. Tomlinson, *A Mingled Yarn*, p. 13.

17. Tomlinson, *Waiting for Daylight*, p. 116.

18. Tomlinson, *Old Junk*, p. 204. The identical phrase appears on page 356 of *AY*.

Chapter Ten

1. E. M. Forster, *Aspects of the Novel* (New York: Harcourt, Brace & World, 1927), p. 41.

2. Ibid., p. 42.

3. Arthur Colton, "Inconsequent Fate," *Saturday Review of Literature* 10 (August 12, 1933), 39.

4. Ibid.

5. Ibid.

6. Harold de Wolf Fuller, "About Books and Their Authors," *Literary Digest* 116 (August 19, 1933), 22.

7. Ibid.

8. H. M. Tomlinson, *The Snows of Helicon* (New York: Harper, 1933), p. 5. Subsequent references to *Snows* are to this edition.

9. "A Ship in a Major Atlantic Storm," *Christian Science Monitor Magazine* (May 26, 1937), 10.

10. H. M. Tomlinson, *All Hands!* (London: Heinemann, 1937), p. 7. Subsequent references to *AH* are to this edition.

11. Tomlinson, *The Sea and the Jungle*, p. 37.

12. H. M. Tomlinson, "Thomas Hardy Country," *Holiday* 4 (November, 1953), 54.

13. Tomlinson, *London River*, p. 243.

14. Tomlinson, *Tide Marks*, p. 37.

15. H.M. Tomlinson, "The Master of the 'Rockingham,'" *Atlantic Monthly* 182 (December, 1948), 62–64.

Chapter Eleven

1. H.M. Tomlinson, *The Day Before: A Romantic Chronicle* (New York: Putnam's, 1939), p. 4. Subsequent references to *DB* are to this edition.

2. Tomlinson, *A Mingled Yarn*, p. 25.

3. H.M. Tomlinson, *Morning Light: The Islanders in the Days of Oak and Hemp* (New York: Macmillan, 1947), p. 15. Subsequent references to *ML* are to this edition.

4. "The Last of Tomlinson," *Newsweek* 49 (April 8, 1957), 116.

5. H.M. Tomlinson, *The Trumpet Shall Sound* (New York: Random House, 1957), p. 3. Subsequent references to *Trumpet* are to this edition.

6. Tomlinson, *Old Junk*, p. 61.

7. Tomlinson, *Waiting for Daylight*, p. 61.

8. Tomlinson, "Frankenstein in England," p. 57n.

9. Tomlinson, *The Wind Is Rising*, p. 98.

10. Tomlinson, *Waiting for Daylight*, p. 18; Tomlinson, *Mars His Idiot*, pp. 33, 53, 166.

Selected Bibliography

I have listed primary sources in the order of their publication, contributions of HMT to other publications by author or editor's surname, and secondary sources by author's surname. In those cases where I had access only to later editions, the date of the original publication appears in brackets.

SELECTIONS

HOPKINS, KENNETH. *H.M. Tomlinson: A Selection from His Writings*. London: Hutchinson, 1953.

BIBLIOGRAPHIES

BOTTELL, H.S. "Modern English First Editions: H(enry) M(ajor) Tomlinson, 1873– ." *Publishers' Weekly* (January 18, 1930), pp. 338–39. Includes a list of HMT's first editions through *All Our Yesterdays* and includes entries for prefatory notes and introductions by HMT. Bottell also lists bibliographical sources.

SADER, MARION, ed. *Comprehensive Index to English-Language Little Magazines: 1890–1970*. Millwood, N.Y.: Kraus-Thomson Organization, Limited, 1976, pp. 4549–50. Lists one primary source and six review articles.

PRIMARY SOURCES

1. Books

The Sea and the Jungle. Introduction by Christopher Morley. New York: Modern Library, Inc., 1928. [1912]. Account of HMT's voyage on the *Capella* to the interior of the Brazils.

The Tramp in a Gale. London: F. Chalmers Dixon, 1912. Limited edition of an article published in the *English Review* 12 (September, 1912).

Old Junk. London: Andrew Melrose Ltd., 1918. Previously published essays dating between January, 1907, and April, 1918.

London River. New York: Knopf, 1921. Essays reflecting aspects of British maritime adventure and trade.

Waiting for Daylight. London: Cassell, 1922. Essays dating from July, 1915, to

April 8, 1921, discussing the War, aspects of English life, and literary figures.

Katherine Mansfield: An Appreciation. Montreal: Foster Brown Co., 1923. Reprinted from *The Nation and Athenaeum.* (January 20, 1923).

Tide Marks: Being Some Records of a Journey to the Beaches of the Moluccas and the Forest of Malaya in 1923. New York: Harper, 1924. HMT's account of a journey undertaken at the request of *Harper's.*

The Foreshore of England, or Under the Red Ensign. New York: Harper, 1927. [1926]. English title *Under the Red Ensign.* An account of British seamen.

Gifts of Fortune, With Some Hints for Those About to Travel. London: Heinemann, 1926. Essays on travel, including one previously published in *Waiting for Daylight.*

Gallions Reach. New York: Harper, 1927. Novel.

A Brown Owl. Garden City: Henry and Longwell, 1928. Limited edition of a story about a family pet.

Illusion: 1915. New York: Harper, 1928. Limited edition (for presentation only). Fiction.

Côte D'Or. London: Faber & Faber, 1929. Essay on Tomlinson's postwar impressions.

Thomas Hardy. New York: Crosby Gaige, 1924. Essay of appreciation occasioned by Hardy's death.

The War: 1914–1917. London: The Reader, 1929. A booklist compiled by Edmund Blunden, Cyril Falls, HMT, and R. Wright.

War Books: A Lecture Given at Manchester University, February 15, 1929. Cleveland: Rowfant Club, 1930. Limited edition.

All Our Yesterdays. New York: Harper, 1930. Novel. Includes *Illusion: 1915.*

Between the Lines. Cambridge: Harvard Univ. Press, 1930. Lecture on literature delivered at American universities during HMT's 1927 tour.

Norman Douglas. London: Chatto & Windus, 1931. Essay of appreciation.

Out of Soundings. New York: Harper, 1931. Essays on diverse subjects, including *A Brown Owl, War Books* under the title "A Footnote to the War Books," and *Thomas Hardy* under the title "One January Morning."

An Illustrated Catalogue of Rare Books on the East Indies and A Letter to a Friend. 1932. Limited edition.

Easter MCMXXXII. London: Fanfare Press, 1932. Limited edition.

The Snows of Helicon. New York: Harper, 1933. Novel.

Below London Bridge. London: Cassell, 1934. An essay on the London Port followed by 37 captioned photographs.

South to Cadiz. New York: Harper, 1934. Contains the title travel essay, an essay on HMT's early vision of the sea, and an essay on HMT's visit to Concord and Boston.

Mars His Idiot. New York: Harper, 1935. Anti-war essay.

The Master. New York: New School for Social Research, 1935.

All Hands!. London: Heinemann, 1937. Novel. Published in América as *Pipe All Hands*.

The Day Before: A Romantic Chronicle. New York: Putnam's, 1939. Novel.

The Wind Is Rising. Boston: Little, Brown & Co., 1942. [1941]. Essays on British resistance (1939–1941) published in *Atlantic Monthly*.

The Turn of the Tide. New York: Macmillan, 1947. [1945]. Essays on British during World War II and travel essay of 1935 voyage.

Morning Light: The Islanders in the Days of Oak and Hemp. New York: Macmillan, 1947. [1946]. Novel.

The Face of the Earth, With Some Hints for Those About to Travel. Indianapolis: Bobbs-Merrill Company, 1951. Essays on travel, including three from *Gifts of Fortune* and the entire *South to Cadiz* under the title "A Spanish Journey."

Malay Waters: The Story of Little Ships Coasting Out of Singapore and Penang in Peace and War. London: Hodder and Stoughton, 1950. A history of the Straits Steamship Company.

The Haunted Forest. London: Hodder and Stoughton, 1951. Children's story.

Trinity Congregational Church. Poplar [London]: 1952. Limited edition of a privately printed pamphlet.

Norman Douglas. London: Hutchinson, 1952. Revised edition of the 1931 *Norman Douglas*, adding introduction "The Man I Knew."

A Mingled Yarn: Autobiographical Sketches. Indianapolis: Bobbs-Merrill Company, 1953. Includes ten essays from *Out of Soundings* and three essays from *Gifts of Fortune*.

The Trumpet Shall Sound. New York: Random House, 1957. Novel.

2. *Articles*

"Fog." *Living Age* 262 (July 24, 1909), 227–30.

"British Merchant Seamen." *Living Age* 270 (September 2, 1911), 600–05.

"Pictures of War." *The English Review* 18 (November, 1914), 513–22.

"A War Note for Democrats." *The English Review* 19 (December, 1914), 70–77.

"Labour and the War." *The English Review* 20 (June, 1915), 348–55.

"Shaw at Armageddon." *Literary Digest* 54 (March 10, 1917), 623–24.

"Wharves of London." *Living Age* 305 (May 8, 1920), 355–61.

"In a Coffee Shop." *Living Age* 307 (November 27, 1920), 545–48. Later appeared in *London River*.

"England of Hardy." *New Republic* 25 (January 12, 1921), 190–92.

"England Through English Eyes." *Harper's* 145 (July, 1922), 259–64.

"Katherine Mansfield." *The Nation and Athenaeum* (January 20, 1923). Later published separately as *Katherine Mansfield: An Appreciation*.

"The Day's Run." *Outlook* 136 (January 9, 1924), 60–61.

"Barbarism." *Living Age* 320 (February 23, 1924), 75–78.

"Books at Sea." *Living Age* 320 (February 23, 1924), 377–79.

"Through the Eastern Gate." *Harper's* 148 (March, 1924), 447–57. Appeared
in *Tide Marks.*

"To the Isles of Kings." *Harper's* 148 (April, 1924), 561–71. Appeared in *Tide
Marks.*

"Rice and Volcanoes." *Harper's* 148 (May, 1924), 805–14. Appeared in *Tide
Marks.*

"A Singapore Day." *Harper's* 149 (June, 1924), 57–66. Appeared in *Tide
Marks.*

"Island Magic." *Harper's* 149 (July, 1924), 165–73. Appeared in *Tide Marks.*

"Oceanic Volcano." *Harper's* 149 (August, 1924), 386–92. Appeared in *Tide
Marks.*

"From a Log Book." *Living Age* 322 (September 20, 1924), 601–04.

"In the Forest of Malaya." *Harper's* 149 (October, 1924), 624–33. Appeared in
Tide Marks.

"Concerning the Highbrows." *Saturday Review of Literature* 2 (August 22,
1925), 57–58.

"Letter from London." *Saturday Review of Literature* 2 (December 5, 1925),
394.

"On Leaving Guide Books at Home." *Harper's* 152 (January, 1926), 187–89.
Excerpts, later revised, from "Hints for Those About to Travel" in *Gifts
of Fortune.*

"Judges of Books." *Century* 3 (February, 1926), 425–34.

"Two Americans and a Whale." *Harper's* 152 (April, 1926), 618–21.

"Hints for Those About to Travel." *Harper's* 153 (September, 1926), 509–14.
Later published in *Gifts of Fortune* and *The Face of the Earth.*

"Illusion: 1915." *Harper's* 155 (September, 1927), 495–501. Later published
separately as *Illusion: 1915* and as part of *All Our Yesterdays.*

"An Old Favorite." *Saturday Review of Literature* 4 (October 1, 1927), 153.
Review of *Tom Cringle's Log* by Michael Scott.

"Joseph Conrad." *Saturday Review of Literature* 4 (October 15, 1927), 191–
92.

"If War Should Come. . . ." *Harper's* 156 (December, 1927), 71–77.

"Hardy at Max Gate." *Saturday Review of Literature* 4 (February 11, 1928),
585–87. Later incorporated into *Thomas Hardy.*

"Côte D'Or." *Saturday Review of Literature* 5 (December 8, 1928), 462-63.
Later incorporated into *Côte D'Or.*

"Colossus of the Ways." *Saturday Review of Literature* 6 (December 14,
1929), 558–59. Opening pages of *All Our Yesterdays.*

"War Books." *Yale Review* NS 19 (March, 1930), 447–65. Later published as
"A Footnote to the War Books" in *Out of Soundings.*

"H. M. Tomlinson, *By Himself.*" *Wilson Bulletin* 5 (September, 1930), 20.

"That Next War." *Forum* 86 (December, 1931), 322–27.

"Nemesis." *Forum* 88 (September, 1932), 130–34.

"Granada." *Yale Review* NS 23 (December, 1933), 217–31. Later published in

South to Cadiz, revised.

"The Derelict." *Scholastic* 24 (March 17, 1934), 4–6. Previously published in *Old Junk*.

"Of Ships and Shoes and Sealing Wax." *Scholastic* 24 (March 17, 1934), 5. Autobiographical sketch.

"Problems of a Novelist." *Saturday Review of Literature* 10 (May 12, 1934), 685–86.

"Books of Escape." *Saturday Review of Literature* 11 (September 8, 1934), 89–90. Also appears in *South to Cadiz* under the title "Sea-Light."

"Morning in Seville." *Life and Letters* 11 (October, 1934), 88–90. Appears in *South to Cadiz* under the title "Seville."

"Mars His Idiot." *Harper's* 171 (August, 1935), 298–307. Appears in *Mars His Idiot*.

"Ports of Call." *Yale Review* NS 26 (June, 1937), 704–17.

"The Black Shade." *Atlantic Monthly* 165 (April, 1940), 506–12. Appears in *The Wind Is Rising*.

"Propaganda." *Yale Review* NS 30 (September, 1940), 63–74.

"The Cliffs of England Stand." *Atlantic Monthly* 166 (October, 1940), 397–403. Appears in *The Wind Is Rising* as "The Cliffs of England."

"England Under Fire." *Atlantic Monthly* 166 (December, 1940), 732–39. Appears in *The Wind Is Rising*.

"The Battle of London." *Atlantic Monthly* 167 (January, 1941), 12–19. Appears in *The Wind Is Rising*.

"The Wind Is Rising." *Atlantic Monthly* 167 (April, 1941), 493–99. Appears in *The Wind Is Rising*.

"Fire of London." *Atlantic Monthly* 167 (June, 1941), 742–50. Appears in *The Wind Is Rising* as "Vistas of War."

"A Year of It." *Atlantic Monthly* 168 (December, 1941), 731–38. Appears in *The Wind Is Rising*.

"Back to First Things." *Atlantic Monthly* 169 (June, 1942), 713–18. Appears in *The Turn of the Tide*.

"Wreckage at Sunrise." *Atlantic Monthly* 170 (December, 1942), 69–75. Appears in *The Turn of the Tide*.

"Salute to Adventurers." *Atlantic Monthly* 171 (May, 1943), 99–104. Appears in *The Turn of the Tide*.

"The Common Man." *Atlantic Monthly* 173 (January, 1944), 85–91. Appears in *The Turn of the Tide* as "The Ordinary Fellow."

"Fish for Britain." *Rotarian* 64 (February, 1944), 28–29.

"Night Watch." *Atlantic Monthly* 173 (May, 1944), 91–95. Appears in *The Turn of the Tide*.

"Courage." *Atlantic Monthly* 174 (August, 1944), 93–98. Appears in *The Turn of the Tide* as "New Horizon."

"Frankenstein in England." *Atlantic Monthly* 174 (October, 1944), 57–59.

"Presiding Spirit." *Atlantic Monthly* 176 (July, 1945), 76–77.

"The Power of Books." *Atlantic Monthly* 180 (December, 1947), 115–19.
"The Master of the 'Rockingham.'" *Atlantic Monthly* 182 (December, 1948), 62–64.
"Adventure in a Shop Window." *Holiday* 6 (August, 1949), 85–86, 88–89.
"Architect with Charm." *John O'London's Weekly* (September 16, 1949), p. 558.
"London as Melville Saw It." *John O'London's Weekly* (November 11, 1949), p. 669.
"The Alien Sea." *Holiday* 8 (October, 1950), 52–59, 77–78, 80–81.
"Outward Bound." *Atlantic Monthly* 188 (July, 1951), 70–73. Appears in *A Mingled Yarn*.
"Golden Honeymoon." *Holiday* 10 (September, 1951), 56–59, 86–87, 89. Appears in *A Mingled Yarn* as "After Fifty Years."
"Thomas Hardy Country." *Holiday* 14 (November, 1953), 54–55, 124, 126–29.
"Call of the Tropics." *Holiday* 16 (December, 1954), 75, 78, 80, 145, 147–50, 152.
"The Ship Herself." *Holiday* 20 (July, 1956), 54–55.
"Historic Ghosts of London." *Holiday* 23 (January, 1958), 14, 16, 19, 21, 130, 132.

3. *Books to which HMT contributed*

An Anthology of Modern Travel Writing. Ed., H.M. Tomlinson. London: Nelson, 1936. HMT contributed "Preface and Prospect" and the essay "The Upper Amazon," previously published in *Gifts of Fortune* as "Out of Touch."
Best Short Stories of the War: An Anthology. With "Introduction" by HMT. New York and London: Harper, 1931.
BLUNDEN, EDMUND. *The Bonaventure: A Random Journal of an Atlantic Holiday.* New York: Putnam's, 1923. With "Introduction" by HMT.
BONE, DAVID W. *Merchantmen at Arms: The British Merchants' Service in the War.* London: Chatto & Windus, 1929. "Introduction" by HMT.
BUTLER, SAMUEL. *Erewhon, or Over the Range.* New York: Cheshire House, 1931. "Introduction" by HMT.
A Conrad Memorial Library: The Collection of George T. Keating. Garden City: Doubleday, Doran, 1929. Includes "Almayer's Folly: A Prelude" by HMT.
CUBBIN, THOMAS. *The Wreck of the Serica.* 1950. Ed., HMT. Limited edition.
Great Sea Stories of All Nations. Ed., HMT. London: Harrap, 1930. Collected by Elizabeth D'Oyley. "A Foreword" by HMT.
HAMMERTON, SIR JOHN., Ed. *The Great War . . . "I Was There!": Undying Memories of 1914–1918, Volume 3: October 25, 1917 to November 11, 1918, and After.* London: Amalgamated Press, undated. Includes "We Correspondents Saw War But Were Forbidden to Tell the Truth" by HMT.

HOULT, NORAH. *Poor Women!* New York: Harper, 1929. Prefatory letter by HMT.

MACK, H. LIDDELL. *Holidays at Sea in Homeland Waters and Beyond.* Ed., Prescott Row. London: Homeland Association, 1926. Prefatory Letter by HMT.

MASSINGHAM, H.J., Ed. *H.W.M.: A Selection from the Writings of H.W. Massingham.* New York: Harcourt, Brace, 1925. Includes "Adelphi Terrace" by HMT.

MELVILLE, HERMAN. *Pierre or, The Ambiguities.* New York: Dutton, 1929. "Preface" by HMT.

MONTAGUE, C.E. *A Writer's Notes on His Trade.* London: Chatto & Windus, 1930. Includes "C.E. Montague" by HMT.

MORLEY, CHRISTOPHER. *Safety Pins and Other Essays.* London: Jonathan Cape, 1925. Includes "Introduction" by HMT.

NATHAN, GEORGE JEAN, et al., Ed. *The American Spectator Year Book.* New York: Frederick A. Stokes, 1934. Includes "Men of Action" by HMT.

RUSSELL, LEONARD, Ed. *The Saturday Book.* London: Hutchinson, 1944. Includes "On Being Out of Date," later published in *A Mingled Yarn.*

TURNER, WALTER J., Ed. *Great Names, Being an Anthology of English & American Literature from Chaucer to Francis Thompson.* New York: Dial Press, 1926. Includes "Robert Louis Stevenson" by HMT.

SECONDARY SOURCES

ALIG, WALLACE B. "H.M. Tomlinson: Geographer of the Soul." *Americas* 3 (November, 1951), 38–39. Review of *The Face of the Earth.*

ALTICK, HELEN and RICHARD ALTICK. "Square-Rigger on a Modern Mission." *College English* 5 (November, 1943), 75–80. Addresses HMT's shift from pacifist to propagandist and relates it to his resistance to modern notions of progress.

Anon. "Below London Bridge." *Life and Letters* 11 (January, 1935), 487–90. Review of *Below London Bridge.*

Anon. "Crowding Conrad." *Literary Digest* 84 (February 21, 1925), 29. Review of *Tide Marks.*

Anon. "H.M. Tomlinson: A Selection from His Writings, comp. Kenneth Hopkins." *Dublin Magazine* 29 (October–December, 1953), 67–68. Review of Hopkins's *Selection.*

Anon. "The Last of Tomlinson." *Newsweek* 49 (April 8, 1957), 116. Review of *The Trumpet Shall Sound.*

Anon. "Out of Soundings." *Life and Letters* 7 (July–December, 1931), 148–49. Review of *Out of Soundings.*

Anon. "South to Cadiz." *Life and Letters* 11 (January, 1935), 487–90. Review of *South to Cadiz.*

Anon. "Visit With the Author." *Newsweek* 49 (April 8, 1957), 116, 118.

Interview with HMT regarding *The Trumpet Shall Sound* and his literary career.

Anon. "The Way Things Were." *Time* 62 (July 13, 1953), 102, 104. Review of *A Mingled Yarn*.

Anon. "Where Ignorant Armies Clash." *Time* 39 (March 16, 1942), 96–98. Review of *The Wind Is Rising*.

Anon. (E.M.P.). "A Ship in a Major Atlantic Storm." *Christian Science Monitor Magazine* (May 26, 1937), p. 10. Review of *All Hands!*.

Anon. (H.T.S.). "The Sea and the Jungle." *Reviewer* 1 (March 1, 1921), 54–55. Review of *The Sea and the Jungle*.

Anon. (L.B.M.). "London River." *Frontier and Midland* 6 (May, 1926), 27–28. Review of *London River*.

BONE, CAPT. DAVID W. "Idle Tonnage." *Saturday Review of Literature* 4 (February 11, 1928), 587. Review of *The Foreshore of England, or Under the Red Ensign*.

CANBY, HENRY SEIDEL. "Life and Adventure." *Saturday Review of Literature* 4 (September 3, 1927), 83. Review of *Gallions Reach*.

COLTON, ARTHUR. "Inconsequent Fate." *Saturday Review of Literature* 10 (August 12, 1933), 39. Review of *The Snows of Helicon*.

FORD, FORD MADOX. *It Was the Nightingale*. Philadelphia: J.B. Lippincott, 1933, p. 323. Ford describes his acceptance of HMT's articles for the *English* and *Transatlantic* Reviews.

FREEMAN, JOHN. "Mr. H.M. Tomlinson." *London Mercury* 16 (August, 1927), 400–08. Discusses HMT as a prose stylist.

FULLER, HAROLD DE WOLF. "About Books and Their Authors." *Literary Digest* 116 (August 19, 1933), 22. Review of *The Snows of Helicon*.

GALANTIERE, LEWIS. "Contemporary Reminiscences." *Arts and Decoration* 28 (November, 1927), 66, 124. Discussion of HMT's penchant for travel and his prose style.

GAY, ALVA A. "H.M. Tomlinson, Essayist and Traveller." *Studies in Honor of John Wilcox by Members of the English Department, Wayne State University*. Eds., A. Dayle Wallace and Woodburn O. Ross. Detroit: Wayne State Univ. Press, 1958, pp. 209–17. Discussion of HMT's prose style.

GIBSON, J. ASHLEY. "H.M. Tomlinson." [London] *Bookman* 62 (April, 1922), 6–7. Discussion of HMT's life and travels.

———. "Through Western Windows." [London] *Bookman* 62 (June, 1922), 134. Review of *Waiting for Daylight*.

GITTINGS, ROBERT. *Thomas Hardy's Later Years*. Boston: Little, Brown & Co., 1978, p. 213. Discusses Hardy's widow's negative reaction to HMT's "Hardy at Max Gate."

GOLDRING, DOUGLAS. *The Last Pre-Raphaelite: A Record of the Life and Writings of Ford Madox Ford*. London: MacDonald & Co., Ltd., 1948, p. 149. Discusses Ford as a "discoverer" of HMT.

GRAVES, ROBERT and LIDDELL HART. *T.E. Lawrence to His Biographers.* Garden City: Doubleday, 1963, p. 144. T.E. Lawrence discusses preference for HMT, et al., to "Lewis and Joyce and Stein," in a letter to Graves dated 24.12.27.

GUNTHER, JOHN. "The Tomlinson Legend." *Bookman* 62 (February, 1926), 686–89. Discusses HMT's long-standing acquaintance with the London Docks and with traveling.

HALE, WILLIAM HARLAN. "Mr. Tomlinson on War and Youth." *Saturday Review of Literature* 13 (November 30, 1935), 6. Review of *Mars His Idiot.*

HAVIGHURST, ALFRED F. *Radical Journalist: H.W. Massingham (1860–1924).* Cambridge: Cambridge Univ. Press, 1974, pp. 155, 275–77, 294–99, 318–19, 322–23. Discusses HMT's relationship with Massingham and *Nation.*

HODGSON, STUART. *Portraits and Reflections.* New York: Dutton, 1929, pp. 185–91. Discusses HMT as a journalist.

HUXLEY, ALDOUS, Ed. *The Letters of D.H. Lawrence.* New York: Viking Press, 1932, p. 640. Includes letter from Lawrence dated 17 April 1925 accusing HMT of making attacks upon him.

LAWRENCE, A.W., Ed. *Letters to T.E. Lawrence.* London: Jonathan Cape, 1962, pp. 14–15. Includes letter to Lawrence from Edmund Blunden describing HMT's departure from the *Nation.*

LUDWIG, RICHARD M., Ed. *Letters of Ford Madox Ford.* Princeton, N.J.: Princeton Univ. Press, 1920, p. 118. Includes letter from Ford to Ezra Pound stating that he enjoyed HMT's prose and wondered what had become of him.

LYND, ROBERT. *Books and Authors.* New York: Putnam's, 1923, pp. 252–59. An appreciation of HMT as stylist. Book dedicated to HMT.

MACSHANE, FRANK. *The Life and Work of Ford Madox Ford.* New York: Horizon Press, 1965, p. 79. Attributes "discovery" of HMT to Ford.

MAYER, FREDERICK P. "H.M. Tomlinson: The Eternal Youth." *Virginia Quarterly Review* 4 (January, 1928), 72–82. Examines HMT's enthusiasm.

McCAFFERY, JOHN K.M. "The Uneasy Chair." *Publishers' Weekly* 160 (December 1, 1951), 2145. Review of *The Face of the Earth.*

McDONALD, EDWARD D., Ed. *Phoenix: The Posthumous Papers of D.H. Lawrence.* New York: Viking Press, 1936, pp. 342–45. Contains Lawrence's review *"Gifts of Fortune,* by H.M. Tomlinson."

MIZENER, ARTHUR. *The Saddest Story: A Biography of Ford Madox Ford.* New York: World Publishing Company, 1971, p. 107. Describes the probable circumstances of Ford's meeting with HMT.

MOORE, HARRY T. *D.H. Lawrence: His Life and Works.* New York: Twayne Publishers, 1951; rev. 1964, p. 245. Refers to Lawrence's review of HMT's *Gifts of Fortune.*

————. Ed. *The Collected Letters of D.H. Lawrence*. New York: Viking Press, 1962, p. 892. Includes D.H. Lawrence letter to John Middleton Murry dated 28 January 1925 disparaging HMT.

MORLEY, CHRISTOPHER. "Introduction." *The Sea and the Jungle* by H.M. Tomlinson. New York: Modern Library, Inc., 1928, pp. v–x. Appreciation of HMT's skill as a travel writer.

POPE, T. MICHAEL, Ed. *The Book of Fleet Street*. London: Cassell, 1930, pp. 149–50. Describes an adventure of HMT as a journalist at sea.

PRIESTLEY, J.B. "H.M. Tomlinson." *Saturday Review of Literature* 3 (January 1, 1927), 477–78. Describes HMT as a travel writer.

PRITCHETT, V.S. "Introduction." *The Sea and the Jungle*. New York: Time, Inc., 1964, pp. xiii–xviii. Describes HMT's initial involvement with this voyage.

RATCLIFFE, S.K. "The Ultimate Ordeal." *Saturday Review of Literature* 25 (March 21, 1942), 7. Review of *The Wind Is Rising*.

ROBERTS, R. ELLIS. "A Publicist with Keen Eyes." *Saturday Review of Literature* 30 (June 14, 1947), 10. Review of *The Turn of the Tide*.

SAGAR, KEITH. *The Art of D.H. Lawrence*. Cambridge: Cambridge Univ. Press, 1966, p. 170. Lists Lawrence's review of *Gifts of Fortune* as having appeared before Lawrence's death.

SEVERN, DEREK. "A Minor Master: H.M. Tomlinson." *London Magazine* NS 18 (February, 1979), 47–58. Assesses HMT's literary achievement.

SWINNERTON, FRANK. *Background With Chorus: A Footnote to Changes in English Literary Fashion Between 1901 and 1917*. London: Hutchinson, 1956, pp. 13, 126–27, 204–08. Describes HMT's reputation as a journalist and his war correspondence.

WEEKS, EDWARD. "Authors and Aviators." *Atlantic Monthly* 172 (November, 1943), 58–59. Describes HMT's showing Weeks the sights of London during World War II.

————. "H.M. Tomlinson." *Atlantic Monthly* 192 (August, 1953), 82. Provides a thumbnail biography of HMT.

WEINTRAUB, STANLEY. *Journey to Heartbreak: The Crucible Years of Bernard Shaw 1914–1918*. New York: Weybright and Talley, 1971, pp. 216–20. Describes HMT's reputation as a war correspondent and his encounter with GBS at Arras.

WEST, REBECCA. "A London Letter." *Bookman* 69 (July, 1929), 519–20. Discusses the identification of HMT with Conrad and argues against it on the basis of style.

Index

255